FORGE
OF
LIBERTY

FORGE OF

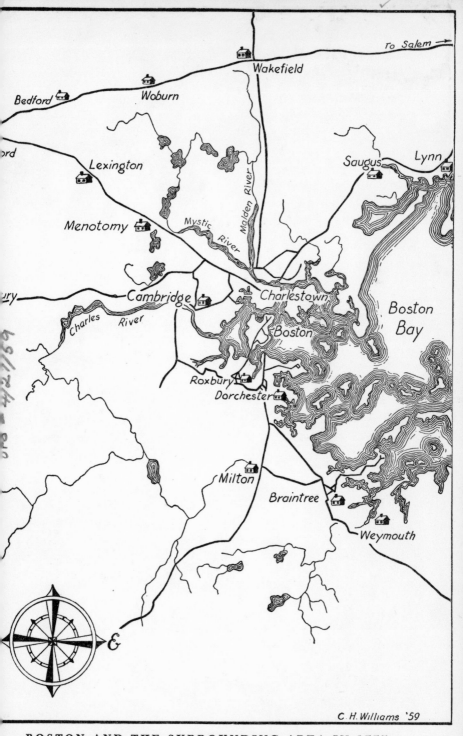

C.H.Williams '59

**BOSTON AND THE SURROUNDING AREA IN 1775.
MENOTOMY IS NOW ARLINGTON.**

LIBERTY

BY LEONARD FALKNER

The
Dramatic Opening
of the
American
Revolution

E. P. DUTTON & CO., INC., NEW YORK, 1959

Library of Congress Catalog Card Number: 59-5820

ACKNOWLEDGMENTS

AFTER FINISHING A PROJECT AS ABSORBING AS A BOOK ON THE opening of the American Revolution, one is likely to feel sentimental about it. The warmest memories are attached to the research. Walking the small roads into the past, the present has a way of dropping back out of sight and hearing. The other century, its vapors rising out of the brittle documents, the old letters and diaries, becomes the more vivid of the two.

It is a delight and a wonder to see how carefully time has preserved the details of those first crucial days of independence. Not in the history books, but in the on-the-spot reports, the letters and diaries and memoirs of the men who saw and made it happen: the minutemen, away from their home villages for the first time in their lives; the housewives in the paths of battle; the dedicated little band of Boston intellectuals who lighted the fires and kept them burning; the graying veterans of the French and Indian War hitched back into the traces of command; the professional British soldiers of the enemy garrison in Boston, and the vilified Americans who honestly sided with the king and were called Tories.

I should like to point out that the source for all the dialogue and conversation in this book is in every instance a contemporary account. Thus, the words the various characters speak are the very words they said or the words their contemporaries report them to have said. It is through them, the men and women who lived the story, whose adventures, moods, fears, prejudices and rugged convictions live so vividly in their remembrances, that I have tried to recreate those first dramatic days.

Without the friendly assistance of many people in widely scattered research places the book could not have been written.

5

10902

I am particularly grateful to the staffs of the Massachusetts Historical Society, the Boston Athenaeum and Public Library and Museum of Fine Arts, to the helpful ladies of the Cary Memorial Library in Lexington and the Concord Library and Antiquarian Society, and the attendants in the American History Room of the New York Public Library. A special vote of appreciation for their help and patience goes to Miss Geraldine Beard and Sylvester Vigilante at the New-York Historical Society.

I am indebted to the William L. Clements Library at Ann Arbor for making available the private papers of General Thomas Gage, to the Boston Museum of Fine Arts for permission to reproduce the portraits of Paul Revere, John and Samuel Adams, John Hancock, and Joseph Warren, and to the Independence National Historical Park Collection for the portrait of General Nathaniel Greene.

My thanks to Colonel R. V. C. Bradley of Newburyport, Mass., for permission to reproduce his painting of General Thomas Gage, to Charles Williams for his excellent maps, and to Edmund P. Bartnett for his sound editorial help.

Map of Boston and Charleston as they appeared in 1775

ILLUSTRATIONS

Following page 128

General Thomas Gage

Paul Revere

General Joseph Warren

John Hancock

Samuel Adams

John Adams

General William Howe

Engagement at the North Bridge in Concord

The Battle of Breed's Hill

The Battle of Lexington

A View of the South Part of Lexington

MAPS

End Papers

Map of Boston and the surrounding area in 1775

The tree of liberty must be refreshed from time to time with the blood of patriots and tyrants.

THOMAS JEFFERSON

BOOK ONE

ONE

IT WAS TUESDAY NIGHT, APRIL 18, 1775. A BRISK EAST WIND RIPPLED the new grass over the graves of the founders on Boston's Copp's Hill, shook the thin foliage of the elms on the Common. In the North End, a rowboat with two men stroking the petticoat-muffled oars slid out of a willow-covered inlet and headed cautiously across the darkness of the Charles River, steering far to seaward of the riding lights of the British man-of-war *Somerset* astride the ferry lane to Charlestown. Paul Revere, a stocky figure in black riding boots, woolen surtout and tricorn hat, sat in the stern.

As they passed midstream, the moon came up and laid a wash of silver on the river. The men bent low in the boat and pulled farther to seaward of the suddenly-outlined black bulk of the *Somerset*.

In the belfry of Christ Church, topping the Boston skyline, two candle lanterns glinted briefly. In Charlestown, on the opposite shore, Colonel William Conant, a leading member of the Massachusetts resistance movement against English oppression, stood waiting in the marsh grass at the water's edge. Behind him, in a barn dark among the trees, Deacon John Larkin buckled the bridle on his family's favorite saddle horse, Brown Beauty.

Sixteen miles away, in Lexington, Sam Adams, the middle-aged guiding genius of the Revolution, sat before the hearth in the Reverend Jonas Clark's parsonage, his hands clasped over his paunch, legs stretched comfortably to the fire. The slate-blue, quizzical eyes stared brightly into the flames. He was letting his supper digest and listening with half an ear to the casual bickering of John Hancock, elegant in a brocaded silk dressing gown and silver-gray wig, and his fiancee, Dolly Quincy.

11

No long clay pipe for Sam, or second helping of hot rum. A
Spartan man, strict Puritan. Only one romance in his life: the
romance of revolution. Only one grand passion: his hatred of
England. Not even his dedicated wife, Elizabeth, could keep him
looking tidy for long. The button she had sewed on his sleeve
with the strongest thread she could find before he left Boston's
South End a fortnight before was gone again, worried off by his
restless, palsied fingers. His graying hair fell back carelessly behind his ears. His long brown coat had a lived-in look. The stains
of forgotten meals decorated his waistcoat. But he was at peace.
At last, matters were shaping his way.

In the village of Braintree, south of Boston, plump, earnest-
faced John Adams, Sam's scholarly second cousin, fellow revolutionary, finished bedding down his horse and latched the barn
door. Squinting nearsightedly, he held his candle lantern at arm's
reach in front of him and walked houseward in the spring darkness to Abigail and the children.

And in her three-story brick house on the corner of Winter
Street in midtown colonial Boston, Mrs. John Stedman put the
children to bed and anxiously lowered the supper pot a notch
closer to the fire. Surely, her husband would be back soon; it was
just getting dusk when she at last was able to give him the message.

Her front windows looked up cobblestoned Marlborough
Street to Old South Church and Province House, the royal governor's mansion. In her distress, she wondered what new persecu-
tions for her family and neighbors General Thomas Gage and his
arrogant British staff were plotting behind those drawn portiers.

Her Boston, a city of eighteen thousand, was under lock and
bars, an armed camp garrisoned by four thousand British soldiers.
No ship could bring food or merchandise into its harbor; legally,
not even a raft might be poled from shore.

There had been crises before, but none as foreboding as this
one. The merchants were going bankrupt, the poor were out of
work, scavenging for food. All because, as a culminating affront
to her oppressors in London, her defiant citizens had dumped 342
chests of hated English tea, worth eighteen thousand pounds in
hard money, into the harbor. And the Parliament in London had

sworn that Boston was going to pay for it, protested tax and all, or starve!

The tight-mouthed opponents who faced each other across the Atlantic that spring of 1775 had one quality in common: both were inflexibly stubborn. But, separated by three thousand miles of lonely ocean and the vagaries of the winds, they were in their thinking as far apart as Bunker Hill and Piccadilly Circus.

Britain's victory in the French and Indian War, twelve years before, had left her with a staggering debt. It was only reasonable, the Tory ruling party in England thought, that the colonies should help the empire get back to solvency. Hadn't she saved them from being taken over by France?

But her colonies, particularly Massachusetts, were having their own troubles. The short prosperity that had followed the war had run out. Every edict Britain designed to siphon revenue out of America meant more hardships to the colonies. Besides, they felt no humble gratitude to England. Without the help of their skilled frontiersmen, they argued, the hated lobsterbacks might never have defeated the French in America.

So as John Stedman of Winter Street had often pointed out bitterly to his wife, what right did Parliament have to confine America's trade to British ships and ports? What right to issue Writs of Assistance—search warrants—in this far-off country of people who had come here to get away from that very kind of high-handed interference?

If the English could search a colonial merchant's warehouse for smuggled molasses, what was to stop them from ransacking a man's house? Next thing, they'd be saddling a Church of England bishop on Massachusetts Bay for the devout Congregationalists to support!

Without any colonial representation in Parliament, what right had the British government to impose "internal taxes"?

If—and it was a telling point—the people of Boston preferred to drink tea from Holland, which Mrs. Stedman did (it was cheaper), why should they be forced to buy English tea and pay a tax on it besides, just to rescue the British East India Company from bankruptcy?

Why, now that England had sent over an army of regulars to

force compliance to its highhanded demands, should the people of Boston give them lodging and help support them?

With each week's issues of the patriot Boston newspapers through the long winter of 1774-1775 the thunderheads had piled closer. A dispatch fresh in from Lodon to the Boston *Gazette:* Parliament had promised King George that every resource of the empire would be used to "crush the rebellion in Massachusetts."

By the latest packet: The Newfoundland waters, home of the cod, had been closed to colonial fishing. Twenty thousand fishermen would be deprived of a livelihood; four hundred ships, two thousand fishing sloops along the coast made idle.

A dispatch to the *Massachusetts Spy:* Still more reenforcements were on the way, and three of Britain's best generals: Howe, Clinton and Burgoyne! A dark rumor spread: Now that winter was gone, General Gage was preparing to unleash his army on the entire province.

In the villages and on the farms of Massachusetts and her neighboring colonies, men oiled and polished their muskets. They stored arms and ammunition in barns and meetinghouses. They spent their evenings making cartridges of brown paper wrapped around a charge of black powder and a hand-molded lead ball.

Minutemen, they called themselves. Organized in the late winter months under their local militia commanders, they drilled on the village greens, made ready to drop their plows or axes instantly in response to the church bell or drumbeat that would announce the British had finally decided to take the field against the colony.

From her kitchen window, this Tuesday night, Mrs. Stedman could see British grenadiers and light infantrymen in battle gear hurrying singly and in small groups down Winter Street toward the nearby Common and the Charles River shore.

Late that afternoon, Mrs. Stedman had put down her mending to answer the door. It was a gray day. A wash of intermittent rain had polished the cobblestones, darkened the roofs of the brick and wooden houses tight against the street. A sergeant of grenadiers was at the door asking for Private Gibson, the husband of the Irish-born housemaid she had recently hired. "I must find him," he said, desperation in his voice. He added, indiscreetly, "If you see him, tell him he's to report at the foot of the Common before ten o'clock equipped for an expedition."

An expedition! Before the sergeant was out of sight, Mrs. Stedman, gray shawl billowing behind her, was running up Marlborough Street looking for her husband. She found him near the office of Dr. Benjamin Church.

John Stedman listened to his excited wife. So this was what the lowering of the rowboats Saturday from the men-of-war in the harbor had meant! He watched her walk back down the street. Glancing around to satisfy himself they had not attracted attention, he strolled up the steps of a brick house and lifted the knocker beside Dr. Church's nameplate.

Dr. Church, debonair, portly, was a member of both the Massachusetts Provincial Congress and the Committee of Safety, the important group of eleven colonists ruling the province since resistance to the blockade had confined British operations to Boston. He was a prominent surgeon, a scholar and member of the Boston gentry. He had completed his medical education in London and had brought an English wife back with him. A clever essayist and facile poet, a persuasive orator, he belonged to the top echelon of the undercover movement against British rule.

He listened somberly to John Stedman's story. Dr. Joseph Warren, he said, must have this news immediately. Since Church did not have a messenger available at the moment, would Mr. Stedman take it to him?

The brown two-story house of the young widower, Dr. Warren, on lower Hanover Street, was secret headquarters for the informers keeping tabs on the British army of occupation. Dr. Warren, tall, blond, handsome, was one of the intellectual firebrands of the patriot cause. His warm nature and alert competence had made him, at thirty-five, the most popular physician in Boston. But this morning he had turned over the last of his patients to student assistants. The business of rebellion was to be his fulltime career from now on.

John Stedman found the severely furnished back sitting room a busy place. Almost immediately, he sensed the subdued tension in the air. Men were coming in every few minutes, talking with the doctor in low voices, sometimes consulting briefly with each other, and hurrying away again. There were a few in fine broad-cloth coats and bright silk waistcoats and more in the rough, worn clothes of mechanics. The doctor greeted Stedman with his quick, easy smile. His face went suddenly grave at the news Stedman gave him.

"Very interesting," he said. "That is very, very interesting." He looked around the room, seemingly lost in thought. "Do not talk to anyone else about this."

Stedman withdrew to the fireplace to warm himself. He exchanged nods with Dr. Samuel Cooper, the fiery young pastor of the nearby Brattle Street Congregational Church. He recognized one of the printers from the shop of Benjamin Edes and John Gill, publishers of the patriot Boston *Gazette,* and a middle-aged storekeeper from the Long Wharf.

A jolly, ruddy-faced man who looked as if he might have a gentle hangover and had slept oftener than not in his seedy farm clothes came in. Stedman knew him as one of the strange characters of the town, a thirty-year-old tanner from the North End named William Dawes.

Paul Revere, the well-known express rider with the square, wind-hardened face and dark eyes, the blunt talented hands, had been in briefly and had already left. By now, Stedman decided, he was probably back at the Green Dragon, just up the street, collecting the latest reports from his fellow scouts among the town's craftsmen and mechanics, or at the ancient Salutation Inn on the waterfront, the favorite meeting place of the ship and dock workers. He was almost any place these days except at his workbench in the silver shop on North Square.

A strange man, Revere; one of the best silver craftsmen in the colonies, engraver, jeweler, pioneer dental technician, but ready at any time to drop his tools and step into the saddle to ride the lonely roads to New York, Philadelphia, Worcester, Salem; sixty-five miles a day through good or dirty weather, carrying secret dispatches from the Committee of Correspondents or the Massachusetts Provincial Congress to other colonial leaders as the crisis darkened in Boston.

Back on her doorstep, Mrs. Stedman saw the British grenadier,

Gibson, and his wife come up the street. She gave Gibson the sergeant's message, and saw his face pale.

"Oh, Gibson! What are you going to do?" she asked.

Mrs. Stedman could see the strange glint in Gibson's blue eyes, the frightened twist of his young mouth.

"Ah, Madame," the young grenadier answered, "I know as little as you do. I only know that I must go."

Meanwhile other alarms had already funneled into Dr. Warren's sitting room. Old South Church, slanting across the street from Mrs. Stedman's house, had been stripped of its pews and pulpit and turned into a riding arena for General Gage's officers. Their stables were on Milk Street, skirting the church on the south.

One of the grooms from the royal governor's mansion across from the church had found a friend among the citizens, John Ballard, a man who worked in a stable down the street and who heartily agreed with him about "these damned cowardly rebels."

It was good for an Englishman's soul to see a native like John Ballard glare into his mug of still ale and sound off against his dull-witted, mulish countrymen whose unwillingness to cooperate with His Majesty's government was keeping homesick Britons cooped up in this smell-hole of a town.

The British groom had a bit of interesting gossip for his friend Ballard (he confided knowingly over his mug) as they sat down together that Tuesday afternoon. He had heard a group of officers talking as they watched their horses being shod in the forenoon for some quite mysterious expedition. One of them had said, "There will be hell to pay tomorrow!"

About time, John Ballard agreed, and took his time finishing his ale. He strolled away down Milk Street, turned into Dalton, and walked faster. A fellow member of the Sons of Liberty (the loosely organized fellowship of Boston rebels) fell into step beside him.

Near Dr. Warren's house, they met Paul Revere, and John Ballard told his story.

Revere showed more concern than surprise. "Don't tell another soul," he warned. "You are the third person we have heard from."

One of the these three was Colonel Josiah Waters, a Boston member of the patriot Whig party and officer of the colonial militia. Colonel Waters was visited that afternoon by a gunsmith of British birth, named Jasper, who lived in Hatter's Square. The gunsmith was on the rebel side, but kept it to himself. He worked for the British, and a British sergeant major was quartered with his family.

The sergeant major had suddenly returned to the Jasper house to pick up his equipment and had implied that something important was shaping up.

Paul Revere's warning of secrecy hadn't been passed along to Colonel Waters. After he delivered his message to Dr. Warren, he hunted up a friend, a leather dresser named Ebenezer Dorr who had the round face and shaggy look of a country bumpkin.

Ebenezer put on a floppy farm hat, a long brown coat, tied an old red handkerchief around his neck and mounted his horse, an ancient wagon nag. Saddlebags flopping behind him, he rode toward Boston Neck, the narrow strip of land that connected the city with the mainland.

Colonel Waters walked behind at a discreet distance until he saw his friend satisfy the sentries at the gate that he was an innocent farmer homeward bound.

But Ebenezer Dorr got only as far as the next village, Roxbury, with his alarm. He was picked up by a British patrol.

TWO

GENERAL GAGE'S PLAN FOR THE 19TH OF APRIL WAS THE MOST closely guarded secret in Boston, and the most loosely kept.

Gage, middle-aged, slow-moving, earnestly hopeful of bringing the colonists to an understanding with England without violence, had been doggedly enforcing the blockade for almost a year, ever since he had been sent from London to make Boston pay for the destroyed tea.

He should have had a better understanding of the American rebels than Lord North or the rest of the Tory ministry in Whitehall. He had fought with them under Braddock in the Pennsylvania wilderness and at Ticonderoga. He had lived in New York as Commander-in-Chief of the British Army in America after the French and Indian War. He had married an American girl—his wife, Margaret, was the daughter of well-to-do Peter Kemble of New Jersey.

But Gage underestimated the American temper.

Under cover of a Saturday night's darkness late in February, he had sent a detachment in transports to destroy some brass cannon and gun carriages the patriots had collected in Salem, twenty miles to the north.

Early that winter, Paul Revere had brought together thirty trusted fellow craftsmen to take turns patrolling the Boston streets at night and report any unusual British activity. They called themselves the Committee of Mechanics and met secretly in an upstairs room at the Green Dragon.

When one of them reported on that Saturday night that a British detachment was stealthily embarking at a wharf opposite Castle Island, Revere and five of his fellow mechanics rowed out to shadow them. They were picked up by a patrol and ignobly locked in the fort for the weekend.

When the British troops disembarked the next afternoon at Marblehead, a few miles from Salem, the people were in church. The minister's sermon ended in midsentence. The parishioners rushed out. Several mounted and galloped off to alarm Salem.

The cache of arms was on the other side of the little North River that ran through the town of Salem. When the troops arrived, the drawbridge had been pulled up. General Gage had picked one of his most personable and levelheaded young officers, Colonel Leslie, to command the expedition. Arriving with his command at the bridgehead, Leslie drew his sword and demanded that the townspeople lower the draw "In the name of your king!"

The massing crowd answered with an angry rumble of "No's!"

One of the crowd yelled, "It is our bridge! Not the king of England's!"

Several boats were tied to the shore. The troops, spoiling for a scrap after months of dull confinement in Boston, moved to board them. But the crowd blocked their way until the boats could be untied and shoved into the stream.

The church bells of Salem were ringing; a young drummer was sounding a staccato tattoo on the green. The winter wind carried the alarm across the fields and hills. Express riders spurred out the country roads, reining at each farmhouse to shout *"The regulars are out!"*

Farmers and villagers grabbed their long muskets and powder horns, mounted and rode to Salem. They swarmed around the crowd at the bridge, soon outnumbering the hundred and fifty redcoats almost ten to one. But they were no mob.

Moving quietly among them, was thirty-year-old Timothy Pickering, rebel pamphleteer and colonel of the Essex County Militia. He had been drilling these men for months, teaching them to wheel by line, oblique march, to fire in ranks without shooting each other. He had them in hand.

British Colonel Leslie looked at the lean, angry faces, the bristle of muskets hemming him in, and sensibly accepted a face-saving compromise proposed by the Congregational minister of Salem, the Reverend Mr. Barnard.

The bridge was obligingly lowered. He marched his troops exactly thirty rods onto the other side, about faced and marched them back.

The rebel stores were saved. The troops went back to Marblehead and their ships, flanked and followed by the tight-faced colonists, guns in the crooks of their arms; taunted from windows and doorways: "Go home, lobsterbacks!"

But General Gage, snug with his big family in the plush furnishings of the royal governor's mansion, was not seriously impressed. He did not think "the damned rebels" would actually fire on their king's troops. He still believed, as he had recently written to his superior in Whitehall, the Earl of Dartmouth: "If a respectable force is seen in the field, the most obnoxious of the leaders seized, and a pardon proclaimed for all the others, government will come off victorious."

One of his officers wrote home: "As to . . . their taking arms to resist the force of England, it is mere bullying, and will go no further than words; whenever it comes to blows, he that can run the fastest will think himself best off; believe me, any two regiments here ought to be decimated if they did not beat, in the field, the whole force of the Massachusetts province; for though they are numerous, they are but a mere mob, without order or discipline, and very awkward at handling their arms."

Now, with spring at hand, General Gage at last had his "respectable force," four thousand trained regulars. He had his paid informers among the rebels. One of them was a member of the Massachusetts Provincial Congress and the Committee of Safety. From him Gage had learned the location and quantities of almost all the war supplies and provisions accumulated by the colonists.

Four brass cannons and two mortars, the high-placed informer reported, were hidden in the cellar or barn of a Mr. Barrett, across the bridge on the other side of Concord; also a quantity of powder, bullets, guns and bayonets. There were several iron cannon before the town house, with a guard of three or four militia men on watch over them at night. Two tons of gunpowder, equivalent to two hundred large barrels, were hidden at the house of a Mr. Whitney, near the entrance to the village. A hundred barrels of flour, a considerable quantity of lard and

dried peas were stored in the malthouse of a man named Ebenezer Hubbard, near the church.

There were two routes, his informer advised, from Boston to
Concord. The first was by way of Charleston, Cambridge and
Lexington. The distance was about nineteen miles. The second
was by way of Roxbury, Watertown and Weston; about twenty-
two miles.

At Worcester, forty-eight miles away, the informer reported
munitions in the house of a merchant named Salisbury and a Mr.
Bigelow. There were fifteen tons of powder in hiding places not
yet determined. Before the church there were thirteen small cannons, badly mounted.

General Gage started laying his plans early in 1775 for a major
action in the spring to crush the signs of rebellion once and for
all. He took no one on his staff into his confidence. Only his
American wife knew what he had in mind.

The big three-story governor's mansion, with its cupola and
gold weather vane, its great oak trees and lawns sloping away to
Marlborough Street, was no ivory tower for the father of six noisy
sons and five daughters. It took an understanding wife to keep
them out of the General's way nights so he could work undis-
turbed.

On January 8 Gage issued a brief order: "If any officers of the
different regiments are capable of taking sketches of a country,
they will send their names to the deputy adjutant general."

The response was surprising, since there were no engineers
among his force at the time and map-making was not part of
general officer training. But colonial Boston was a drab place for
the young men whose good English families had bought them
commissions in His Majesty's Army. They could not leave town
except on assigned marches. The Bostonians who were "friends
of government," the Tory families, were too worried about the
darkening future to be interested in entertaining. About all that
was left to do was play cards at the British Coffee House on King
Street or get into an occasional scrap with the Town Watch; or
drink. One of them noted in his diary that you could get well
potted on a copper or two. New England rum cost only a shilling,
ninepence a gallon. The general's order sounded intriguing.

Of the many who responded, Gage picked young Ensign Henry
De Bernière of the 10th Regiment and Captain Brown of the
52nd.

Late in February, before his paid informer sent in his detailed
reports from rebel quarters, Gage called the two officers to
Province House and gave them their secret orders. They were to
go to Worcester, spy out what arms were stored there and map the
highways to and around it.

"Mark out the roads and distances from town to town," he
ordered, "as also the situation and nature of the country; all
passes must be particularly laid down, noticing the length and
breadth of them, the entrances going in and going out of them,
and whether to be avoided or taking other routes.

"You will notice the situation of the towns and villages, their
churches and churchyards, whether they are advantageous spots
to take post in, and capable of being made defensible."

De Bernière and Brown dressed in the "brown cloeths" of provincial civilians, big red handkerchiefs around their necks, floppy
hats, and took the ferry to Charlestown, accompanied by Captain
Brown's servant, John.

The two young British officers found Cambridge, just outside
Boston, "a pretty town, with a college built of brick."

They walked through Watertown, which was, De Bernière
noted in his diary, "a pretty large town for America, but would
be looked on as a village in England."

The road beyond, rutted, crusted with ice, wandered between
low, tree-crested hills. Log bridges spanned the frozen streams.
Stone fences reached up the rock-studded, snow-covered slopes.

They stopped at a country tavern for their midday dinner. The
Negro woman who waited on them was friendly at first. Then De
Bernière noticed that, after bringing in their roast, she remained
in the kitchen doorway, staring at them. She appeared particularly interested in Captain Brown who was looking at the map
they had been sketching. When she brought their second mug of
ale, De Bernière said: "This is a fine country." She backed away
from the table, hands on her hips, eyes narrowed. "So it is," she
said. "And we have got brave fellows to defend it. If you go up
any higher, you will find it so."

They paid and got on their way as soon as they could. The captain's servant, John, had eaten in the kitchen. He was frightened. The woman was a freed slave, he said. She had told him that she knew Brown was a British officer in disguise. She had lived in Boston and had seen him often enough to recognize him. She was certain De Bernière was an officer too, and that John was a regular.

John said, setting a faster pace, that the woman told him she knew what they were up to; they were spies, mapping the country. She had recognized the river and the road through Charlestown sketched on the paper in front of Brown.

She said it was fortunate for them that the innkeeper, a staunch Whig, was not at home. She had muttered darkly to herself, bending over the fire, something not completely audible about tarring and feathering.

"She told me to warn you not to go any deeper into the country," John said. "If we did, we should meet with very bad usage."

They sat down on a stone fence and held a council of war. General Gage's suggestion that they pose as surveyors did not sound practical any more. Perhaps they had better go back to Boston while they still had a chance. These provincials were plainly in a blacker frame of mind than the general realized. De Bernière remembered, with a new understanding, the hard, suspicious stares of some of the natives they had passed on the road.

These farmers and village tradespeople who were defying His Majesty's government called themselves Whigs. The "friends of government," the conservative people of property, most of them Episcopalians here in New England, were called Tories. Back home in England, De Bernière and Brown remembered, there were Whigs and Tories, too, and they got along well enough together. But it was different here. If they went back now, De Bernière and Brown realized, they would be in for a rough ribbing, particularly from the officers whose applications for this special mission had been rejected. So they agreed that "it was absolutely necessary to push on to Worcester and run all risks rather than go back until we were forced."

A few miles along the road they were overtaken by two men

with a team and wagon. The driver, a big, weather-browned man, greeted them cheerfully. He insisted on giving them a lift. The clipped accent of his companion convinced the two young officers that he was a British deserter. They knew there were many of them scattered over the colony. The provincials welcomed them heartily for the help they could give in drilling the militia.

When such a deserter was captured by the British he was shot publicly on Boston Common. But it hadn't discouraged the more daring.

The driver and his companion did not appear to have any particular destination. When, under casual questioning, Captain Brown said they were going to Worcester to visit friends, the driver said that was where they, too, were bound.

De Bernière and Brown felt a net closing around them. With John, they were three to two. But at any moment, they knew, they might meet other natives.

A house came into view, close to the road. A sign with a golden ball painted on it swung from the porch eaves. A tavern.

Brown gave his companions a quick look and hopped off. They were stopping here for a drink, he announced, and waved good-bye to the two on the wagon seat.

The tavernkeeper was a friendly little man. They could tell he was studying them silently as he talked about the weather and poked up the fire. When he said they could have anything they wanted to drink, including tea, they knew they were on Tory ground.

Since the blockade of Boston, a year ago, "tea" had become an ugly word in the colonies. Only Tories drank it, even secretly. Avaricious merchants and occasional housewives who let their appetites betray them had been publicly denounced for having it in their possession. They had been compelled to recant before their neighbors in gaudy, humiliating ceremonies on the town commons. The self-imposed embargo was religiously enforced.

The tavernkeeper gave them the names of other innkeepers on their way and in Worcester who would be friendly. Next morning, he packed lunch for them—a cold tongue and a bottle of cherry brandy—and waved them on their way.

They managed to hike the rest of the way to Worcester without getting into trouble. They arrived on a Saturday night and had to spend the next day in their room at the tavern. The Sabbath was strictly kept in Puritan Massachusetts and attendance at church was compulsory. Anyone found on the streets was picked up by the town watch and questioned.

After dark, they explored the town, sketching the streets, examining the bridges that might be destroyed by the patriots to impede an invading army, marking the places where their Tory tavernkeeper host and his friends told them the arms and supplies were stored.

By now, the word that three mysterious strangers were in the neighborhood was quietly spreading ahead of them. The morning they left Worcester a provincial horseman overtook them. He rode behind them for a long while, staring silently, then galloped past down the road which led to the town of Marlboro.

Marlboro was on their list, but there were other places they wanted to look into first. They turned off onto a side road and did not get to the town until the next day.

That night, they watched the local militia drill outside the windows of their inn in Shrewsbury. De Bernière thought the drummer and fifer could stand more practice.

He was interested in the fact that these men, despite their grim enthusiasm, had nothing in the way of uniforms. They wore their everyday clothes—leather or homespun breeches, dark stockings, drab checkered shirts, weather-stained tricorn hats. He wondered how they expected to fight battles in such nondescript, colorless outfits. Combatants had to have bright uniforms, like the British scarlet and white, to fight a war. Otherwise, how could they expect to see each other after the first volley or two covered the battlefield with a dark blanket of smoke?

Before they moved on to Marlboro they wrapped up their maps and notes and sent them off with Brown's servant, John, to Boston.

It snowed all day. By evening, as they neared the town, the snow was ankle deep in the road. The freezing wind chewed at their faces. A native rider came toward them. This one dourly asked questions. Where were they coming from? "Weston."

Did they live there? "No."

Where were they bound? "Marlboro, to visit a friend."

Who was the friend? Captain Brown gave him the name of a prominent citizen of the town, a Mr. Barnes, who they knew to be secretly in sympathy with the British.

Were they armed? the rider asked. "No."

He wheeled his horse and loped off toward the village.

The snow was coming down harder as they trudged into Marlboro. Even so, every doorway they passed stood open, the occupants staring silently at them.

A baker, his flour-white arms crossed over his apron, called out to Brown, in the lead, "Where are you going, Master?"

"To visit Mr. Barnes," Brown answered.

Mr. Barnes, in his big white house in the center of the town, was not happy to see them. He told them the horseman who had met them the day before had alarmed the townsfolk. They had been expected since yesterday.

Mr. Barnes was a worried man. He said he was as afraid for his wife and young children as he was for himself. Mobs had burned the houses of other "friends of government" in the province. There had been several tarrings and featherings of good citizens whose only crime was that they didn't go along with this "anarchy and rebellion."

While he was setting out food for them in the kitchen, the town doctor knocked on the front door. It was the first time in two years that he had been to the house. Now he announced casually that he had dropped in for supper.

"But I have guests, and there is not enough roast to go around as it is," Mr. Barnes protested lamely. "Please be good enough to come at another time."

The doctor pushed past him. He walked up to Mr. Barnes's young daughter, sitting primly with her homemade doll beside the fireplace.

"Who are these people in your father's house?" he asked.

The girl shook her head.

"I asked Papa, and he said it was none of my concern."

The doctor stalked out.

Mr. Barnes returned anxiously to the kitchen. "He will be

back soon, with the rest of them," he warned the young officers.
"You are not safe here."

There was no time to eat. De Bernière stuffed a loaf of bread
under his wet coat. Mr. Barnes led them out the back door, across
the snow-swept fields. He pointed to a back road.

"This will take you to Sudbury on the road to Boston." He
waved impatiently. "Good luck to you."

The wind came cold, stinging from the northeast. The snow
whipped at their faces, drifted over the narrow wagon ruts. It
was all they could manage to keep from losing the road in the
dark. They huddled after a while in the lea of a clump of trees
and divided their loaf of bread, washing it down by chewing
snow.

But the storm was a blessing, they discovered later. The next
time they saw Mr. Barnes, weeks afterward in the safety of Boston,
he told them a crowd of villagers had surrounded his house only
a few minutes after they left. Their leader, the town doctor, had
warned Mr. Barnes they were going to tear down his house if they
found that his visitors were what they suspected: British spies
reconnoitering the country.

When they discovered the two strangers were gone, they saddled horses and fanned out over the roads searching for them.
In the dark and beating snow, the hotheaded colonists failed to
track them down.

As the two officers got near Sudbury that night a man stepped
out of his door and stared at them. "What do you think is going
to become of you now?" he said dourly.

Soon afterward, four horsemen rode toward them from the
village. This, De Bernière and Brown thought, was the end for
them. But, mysteriously, the horsemen divided silently and let
them walk past.

They pushed on and finally came to the friendly tavern where
they had stopped the first night out from Boston. The tavernkeeper broke open a bottle of Madeira and mulled it for them.
He filled a warming pan with red coals and slid it between the
cold covers of their beds. Next morning, he directed them to a
road that would take them back to Boston without going through
Watertown.

Crossing Boston Neck, the two officers saw General Gage and several of his aides-de-camp inspecting the fortifications at the gate. They approached and saluted. The general stared incredulously at the pair of weather-soiled rustics who had the audacity to intrude on him. It took a while to convince him they were his officers. Then he brusquely ordered them to report to him later in the day at Province House.

A few weeks later, De Bernière and Brown were again back in disguise, off this time to map the roads to Concord and investigate the arms and supplies stockpiled there. With the help of the native Tories, they found there were fourteen cannons—ten iron and four brass, and two artillery pieces in the town. They discovered there were a magazine of powder and cartridges, vast stores of flour, dried fish, salt and rice.

A young woman in the village had politely shown them the way to the house of a Mr. Bliss, a Tory, who went late at night with them to point out the storage spots. Mr. Bliss was frightened, they learned as they sat with him afterward around his fireplace. He said he would like to move his family to the safety of Boston, but he knew too much. He had been warned by the village hotheads that, if he tried to leave, he would be killed.

While they were at breakfast, the girl who had directed them to his house ran in the back door. Her eyes were dilated with terror. She had been seen talking with the two strangers. "They told me if I didn't get out of town right off," she said between sobs, "I'd be tarred and feathered."

De Bernière and Brown returned to Boston from this mission in an understandably apprehensive frame of mind.

THREE

THE WAR SUPPLIES IN CONCORD AND WORCESTER HAD BEEN BROUGHT there mostly from town arsenals that had been established under British supervision long before the Boston blockade, for the provincial militia to use in case the French or Indians got troublesome again. They were inadequate for long resistance against any enemy. But the patriots in Boston and the interior were doing their best to correct that.

Farmers who brought provisions into Boston to sell to the British garrison loaded their wagons with manure for the trip back home. Hidden under the manure were British muskets that their friends in the city had contrived to collect from the regulars by means fair or otherwise. There were sailcloth bags of powder and lead balls, even small brass cannon lifted from their mountings at night or removed from supply depots while the sentry's back was turned. The farmers' wives, on the wagon seat beside them, bulged comfortably in their full skirts, the panniers stuffed with bundles of cartridges.

By early March it was no longer unusual to hear screams on the Common and see a British soldier, stripped to the waist, his hands lashed to a post, receiving five hundred lashes for selling his "Brown Bess" to a colonist.

With exasperating frequency, British officers were reporting to headquarters that citizens had gotten soldiers drunk and relieved them of their arms and ammunition. Hardly a morning passed, they complained, that a regular or two didn't report, with a hangover and a great show of injured innocence, and without his musket.

On March 9th, a provincial, Thomas Ditson, Jr., of Billerica, had just completed a deal with a redcoat to buy his musket for

four dollars and was negotiating for another, a rusty one, for a
dollar and a half, when he was seized by a patrol and hauled off to
the guardhouse. Colonel Nesbit and a group of officers of the
47th Regiment had him stripped to his breeches and tarred and
feathered. They decided then it would be a nice touch to tar
and feather his breeches, too. They tied him in a chair on the
back of a wagon and paraded him through the city streets. A
fifer and drummer went along, playing "Yankee Doodle."

It failed to discourage the provincials. A few nights later several of them slipped into the back window of a gun house while
the sentry's attention was diverted by roll call. They hauled out
two brass cannons and took them into the schoolhouse next door,
where they hid them under the logs in the woodbox. When a
squad of soldiers came to the school the next morning, the school-
master, a cripple, calmly kept his lame foot propped on the
woodbox throughout the search.

The next night the cannon were removed to a neighbor's barnyard. A Roxbury farmer stopped by and loaded his wagon with
manure—and the cannon.

Occasionally a farmer overdid it. On March 18th the guards at
the Neck stopped a countryman. They thought the wheels of his
wagon creaked suspiciously. They prodded the load of manure
with their bayonets, and yelled for shovels. Under the innocent-
looking covering they found bags filled with nineteen thousand
ball cartridges.

A group of young officers had the driver pulled down and
gave him a mauling with the flats of their swords. Then they let
him go. Instead of climbing back onto his wagon, he limped
back across the Neck and up Marlborough Street to Gage's
headquarters.

Lieutenant Frederick Mackenzie, of the Royal Welch Fusiliers,
saw the bruised, disheveled figure come up the steps of Province
House and shoulder his way past the sentries. "He had the in-
solence to demand redelivery of them [the cartridges]," Mackenzie said. "He said they were for his own use!"

General Gage's closely guarded plans for a surprise move
against the colonists were transparent from the start to the ob-

servant Mackenzie. While the roads were still ruts in the snow, Gage started sending detachments fully armed and accoutered on short marches into the country. He reasoned it would accustom the natives to seeing troops on the roads and so they would think nothing of it when he sent out his expedition.

Mackenzie, adjutant of his regiment, was a middle-aged professional, level-headed, conscientious, briskly competent. On the third of February he marched with his fusiliers to Cambridge. The practice of sending detachments into the country, he noted in his journal that day, was becoming more frequent. It was, he admitted, "conductive to the health of the troops." But he suspected there was a more important motive behind it. It would "enable the general to send regiments to particular parts of the country without occasioning so much alarm as would otherwise take place."

It hadn't yet achieved that effect, he noticed. The people they passed on the way watched them from their barnyards and doorways with plainly hostile faces. Some of them came into the road and trailed the column. After a mile or two they were replaced, and then others replaced them, silent and watching.

On February 8th, his regiment again took the road, this time to Watertown. "The country people," Mackenzie observed, "are extremely jealous of these movements, as they apprehend they are intended to cover some design the general has formed."

An order from Gage on April 7th convinced him the general "has some object in view." The order called for each corps to have at all times, "one day's pork ready-cooked, which the men may carry out with them in their knapsacks or haversacks with bread in proportion."

Lieutenant John Barker of the King's Own Regiment wasn't deceived either. Barker, a young man in his early twenties, was cynical, cocksure, and by now bored with Boston. He was the son of a British admiral and had a poor opinion of earnest, plodding "Tommy," as he called General Gage.

On Saturday, April 1th, Gage issued a peremptory order: the grenadier and light infantry companies of the regiments—the first group were strapping heavy-duty warriors; the second light and nimble skirmishers—were to be taken off active duty "to learn some new evolutions."

"This, I suppose, is by way of a blind," Barker wrote in his journal. "I dare say they have something for them to do."

General Gage did have something for them to do. He had finally decided on the exact time for the crushing stroke he had been secretly preparing for all winter: the expedition into the Massachusetts interior to destroy "once and for all" the province's ability to resist Britain's edicts. And he had picked his target. It was the colony's main depot of war supplies and provisions.

The Provincial Congress had left Cambridge and was now holding its sessions in the big, weathered-brown Congregational meetinghouse just east of the Common in Concord. Gage's paid informer among the top delegates to the congress had just sent him word that most of the rebel supplies were stored in the town. He warned the general that the congress was planning to have them moved farther inland for safety. But the delegates had not yet gotten around to doing anything about it. If Gage expected to destroy them, he would have to act promptly.

There was still considerable dissension among the delegates, his secret agent reported. Some of them wanted a recess so they could consult their constituents on how far they should go in raising an army.

"A sudden blow struck now, or within a fortnight," the agent added, "would overset all their plans."

FOUR

COLONIAL BOSTON WAS ALREADY AN OLD CITY IN 1775. ONE HUNDRED and forty-five years old. The midtown streets were cobblestoned. Some of them were even lighted on winter nights with whale-oil lamps. In the crowded North and South Ends, the streets were hardly more than dirt paths, many so narrow that a man on foot had to step into a doorway to let a single-horse market cart pass.

It was a city of charming street names: Pie Alley and White Bread Alley, Cow Lane, Blind Alley, Moon Street and Milk Street, Snow Hill.

Winter Street ran into Summer, Water Street into Bath.

It was a city of penetrating smells; the dead-fish smell of the tidewater marshes that surrounded it, the blended smells of stables and pigpens, cow sheds, smokehouses, breweries, slaughter sheds, of outhouses in crowded back yards, of pitch and turpentine and drying hemp from the wharves and ropewalks.

Until the occupation, a year before, its eighteen thousand inhabitants, most of them in small wooden or brick houses tight against the streets, had managed to live in tolerable comfort. Now there were four thousand troops besides. Some of them were encamped in a hut village on Boston Common, others in a distillery and on Griffin's Wharf, scene of the Boston Tea Party, two years before, which had triggered all the trouble. The others, particularly the officers, were lodged in homes.

Parliament's Quartering Act compelled the citizens, Whigs as well as Tories, to take in soldiers if they had spare room. Fortunately for Paul Revere, his hundred-year-old three-story dormered house on North Street was bulging with offspring. There were two rooms on each floor, but there were seven children, one a baby born that spring, and his young second wife, Rachel, living in them.

In the houses of many of Revere's friends and neighbors supper
had become a chilly, silent meal, with an aloof enemy or two in
infantry or marine uniform helping himself to the best cuts of
the roast.

From his leaded front windows mornings, Revere had seen
companies of marines, under tough, discipline-minded Major
John Pitcairn, drilling in North Square. Revere was seldom at
home nights any more. If he wasn't riding express for the Committee of Safety, he was patrolling the streets around the barracks
or meeting in the secret room upstairs at the Green Dragon with
his Committee of Mechanics, the little band of trusted craftsmen
helping him keep an eye on the British.

Saturday was a pleasant day, unusually warm for that time of
year. Bedclothes dangled from open windows getting their first
spring airing.

General Gage's order detaching the grenadier and light
infantry companies from the eleven regiments and the marines
in the city "to learn some new evolutions," filtered into the spy
net before it was hours old.

For some time the rowboats of the troop transports and men-
of-war in the harbor had been on the decks being overhauled.
Now, at midnight, a member of the Committee of Mechanics
who had been patrolling the Charles River waterfront tapped
softly on Dr. Warren's door, then another patriot spy, and another. In the doctor's blinds-drawn sitting room they reported
that the boats were being launched and moored under the sterns
of the men-of-war. Dr. Warren dispatched one of them to find
Revere.

The Provincial Congress had the day before ended its meetings
in Concord, twenty-one miles inland. In a few days the two leading delegates were to set off for Philadelphia to attend the second
session of the Continental Congress opening there early in May.
Meanwhile, the two were staying on in Lexington, five miles this
side of Concord, since word had gone out that if they came back
into Boston Gage would have them seized and packed off to
England for trial and hanging on the charge of high treason.

They were Sam Adams and John Hancock.

Somehow, Dr. Warren guessed that Gage was planning to send

an expedition to Lexington or Concord. It could only have been
a guess, because even the officers closest to the British general
had not yet been let in on his plans.

Dr. Warren did not doubt that Gage had been told by Tory
sympathizers about the stockpile of rebel war supplies in Concord. It was very likely that Gage had also learned Adams and
Hancock were staying in Lexington.

When Revere came in out of the dark that Saturday night, Dr.
Warren asked him to ride at once to Lexington and warn Adams
and Hancock and then send word to Concord to get busy moving the supplies to other places.

They were old friends, as well as fellow conspirators, these two,
the talented, handsome, scholarly doctor and the husky craftsman with the hands of genius. If it hadn't been for Revere, Dr.
Warren would not have been nearly so good looking. He had
lost two teeth, one in front. Revere had fashioned two false ones
of ivory to wire in their place. They might wobble a bit when
he ate, but they restored the full charm to his quiet smile.

Revere had his own horse, stabled behind his house. But to
ride out of town had been impossible for some months. Residents
going through the fortified gate at the Neck had to obtain a pass
from military headquarters at Province House. The pass had to
show identification and the purpose of the journey. Revere was
well known as an important rebel.

He had a rowboat hidden on the North End shore. Stopping
briefly at his home to put on boots and spurs, he rowed across
the river mouth in the darkness, woke a friend in Charlestown
on the other shore, and borrowed a horse.

Dawn met him well along the way. It was a pleasant uneventful ride, no more than a jaunt for a man so easy in the saddle that
he could ride sixty-five miles a day, day after day. The smells of
spring were in the morning air. Trees were breaking into full
leaf overhead. The slopes of the low hills were patched with
fresh-plowed brown fields.

At Lexington Green he turned to the right and rode a quarter
mile to the parsonage of the fiery, rebel-minded village pastor,
Jonas Clark. A familiar coach, gaudy and oversized, trimmed in

gold, upholstered in crimson satin, stood in the driveway. Revere looped his reins around one of the high wheels.

So John Hancock's stout and aging Aunt Lydia had finally decided to leave Boston! He could imagine why. With the British troops camped virtually in her front yard on the Common and even simple food hard to come by, life had become much too difficult there.

Aunt Lydia was a Boston aristocrat, widow of the fabulously wealthy shipping merchant, Thomas Hancock. When he had died a few years ago his seventy-thousand-pound mercantile fortune, the largest in New England, had been inherited by his young nephew, John Hancock, along with the stone-and-brick mansion on Beacon Hill, the gilded coach, phaetons, chaises, colored attendants—and Aunt Lydia.

Revere surmised there was another reason for Aunt Lydia's leaving Boston. Maybe she didn't like the way her pretty ward, Dolly Quincy, skipped to the nearest window every time a horseman galloped past, hoping it was Lord Percy, the handsome young British earl in immediate command of the troops.

Aunt Lydia had a romance on her hands beside which the difficulties with England were distinctly secondary. Dolly, the youngest, and prettiest, of the five pretty daughters of her widower brother, Edmund Quincy, had moved in with her aunt after her mother died. It was Aunt Lydia's dedicated mission to see her married to John and on the way to providing a Quincy heir to the Hancock fortune.

It looked simple. John, now thirty-eight, was one of the most eligible bachelors in the colonies, somewhat overbearing and stuffy, but a capable businessman and always a striking figure in his fine imported satins and lace. But there were complications. First there had been John's long and fruitless dallying with a Boston girl named Sally Jackson; then a mistress, Mrs. Dorcas Griffiths, buxom and handsome, who sold groceries and liquor in a shop on the Hancock wharf John now owned.

All that had ended. Sally Jackson had married Henderson Inches. After the British occupation, Mrs. Griffiths had taken up with one of the marines, Captain David Johnson. Now the prob-

lem was Dolly. She was probably the prettiest subject the busy
Boston portrait painter, John Copley, ever had: a reed-slim figure, tiny feet and hands, a little, tipped nose, big eyes. At twenty-
eight she should have been ready to settle down. But she was
capricious and spoiled. She had a nimble mind, a sharp tongue,
and, to Aunt Lydia's harassment, her romantic interests were
tinted with wanderlust.

It was a colorful group assembled in the brown frame parsonage. Jonas Clark was a fire-and-brimstone preacher, middle-
aged, broad of beam, with the creased face of an English bulldog
and the explosive temper of a chow. Bustling about, overly anxious to keep their important guests comfortable, were his wife
and older daughters.

Mrs. Clark was John Hancock's first cousin. The parsonage
had been built by their mutual grandfather, the Reverend John
Hancock. John's uncle and benefactor, Thomas Hancock, had
enlarged it for his parents after he became a merchant tycoon.
For years it had been John's favorite country retreat.

Aunt Lydia Hancock, this Sabbath morning, was in the biggest and softest chair, and overflowing it at that. Miss Dolly was
off by herself somewhere with her embroidery hoop. Being en-
gaged to John Hancock was dull. John had the gout and, although frail, a paunch. He was petulant and pompous. In Dolly's
opinion, Aunt Lydia had done a first-rate job of spoiling him.

At least one member of the Clark household was frankly
delighted by Dr. Warren's message. Sam Adams, more than anyone else in Massachusetts, even in all New England, had been
masterminding the rebellion against English oppression. He had
been waiting and hoping for some overt act by Gage's forces to
get the fighting started. This might be it.

Sam, whose pale blue eyes twinkled alike on enemy and friend,
had one bright-burning talent. He had been a failure at every
business he had turned his hand to. He had run his father's malthouse into bankruptcy. As tax collector for Boston, he had piled
up thousands of pounds in arrears. He had given up the practice
of law for want of clients. He had a Master's degree from Harvard, but he could not keep the simplest accounts straight.

But his abilities as an agitator and organizer of rebellion outshone everyone else's. It was triple-distilled genius. He had conceived the Committee of Correspondents, an organization first of representatives in every village and town of Massachusetts, then in every capital of the colonies, which kept the entire country alerted, through dispatches carried by hard-riding express messengers.

He had magnified into "The Boston Massacre" the killing of three members of a brawling mob by a tormented and abused British guard company outside the State House.

He had instigated, almost singlehandedly, the Boston Tea Party.

His enemies said his hatred of England stemmed from his father's loss of a large part of his fortune when Britain cracked down on the Land Bank, an honest project his father invested in, to issue continental currency. But Sam's obsession was more than a simple grudge. It was a dedicated and inspired mission. He was one of those few men who are born exactly at the right time for their particular qualities to shine the brightest.

Sam had a way with the plain people. He knew everybody in Boston, from barristers to chimney sweeps. At the noon hour he could usually be found, sitting on a stringpiece of one of the wharves, visiting with the shipwrights and calkers, the mast and sail and ropemakers. He listened and laughed easily. At the right moment, he could drive home a point with the simple directness of a sledge hammer.

Evenings he was at one of the workers' caucuses, at the old Salutation Inn on the water front or the Green Dragon in Union Street, again listening most of the while, but ready at the right moment with a sharp question or a telling answer.

He was equally at home with the doctors and lawyers, the Congregational clergymen and solid merchants at the top of the movement; the men who met under his leadership in the exclusive Long Room Club over the Edes and Gill print shop in downtown Boston. He had brought John Hancock and his shipping fortune into the conspiracy, and his own younger cousin, John Adams. He had inspired Dr. Warren.

By the time Revere brought Dr. Warren's first message that

Sunday, Sam Adams was no stranger in Lexington. He and Hancock had been living at the Clark parsonage and commuting daily in the Hancock chaise to Concord during the weeks of the Provincial Congress sessions. Now that the Congress had adjourned, they were waiting till it was time to start for Philadelphia.

Sam Adams spent the long spring evenings in Lexington at Buckman's Tavern, facing the Green, sitting around the big open fire in the taproom with the town patriots. Captain Parker in command of the local militia was there, with his gentle smile and hacking cough, and his cousin, Jonas; the Browns, Solomon and James; Ebenezer Monroe and his kinfolk, John and Robert; Jonathan and Caleb Harrington, and all the others, the farmers and shopkeepers, the blacksmith, wheelwright, harness maker, living around the Green and in the brown frame houses scattered along the stone-fenced roads that wandered away through the hills to Bedford, Concord and Boston.

Buckman's was the most popular of the half dozen inns in the village. Its closeness to the Green, where the minutemen drilled weekends, was a factor. But the main reason was that John Buckman was both a jovial host and served an excellent flip. A frothing tankard of flip was just the thing to drive the weariness and cold out of a man's bones after a hard day. It could also make little men feel big and big men gargantuan. It loosened tongues and simplified issues.

It was too heady a drink for the spartan Sam Adams, who could nurse a mug of warm milk through an entire evening. He had stimulus enough in the news from Revere that he brought to the village people gathered around him in the smoke-darkened taproom that night. Did the talented strategist persuade Captain Parker and his neighbors that they should make a stand on the Green if the British came marching through? *

Revere, for his part, rode back to Boston preoccupied with his own ideas for meeting the British threat. As he entered Charlestown, its cluster of wooden houses stretched long shadows down the streets sloping toward the river mouth. He could see the

* See Notes, page 241.

big, square-rigged man-of-war *Somerset* riding at anchor in mid-stream with her brood of rowboats close under her stern. Beyond, the church steeples of Boston glinted in the late sunlight: Christ's, the tallest, Old South's, Brattle Street's.

Revere stopped at the home of William Conant until darkness would make it safe to row back to Boston. With the group of Charlestown patriots that gathered that evening in Conant's living room he worked out a plan to alert the countryside, warn Adams and Hancock and the village of Concord, if the redcoats moved in force out of Boston.

They agreed, Revere wrote, "that if the British went out by water, we would shew two Lanthorns in the North [Christ] Church steeple; and if by land, one, as a signal; for we were apprehensive it would be difficult to cross the Charles River, or git over Boston Neck."

Revere would try to make it out of the city himself, but if a British guard prevented him someone from Charlestown would spread the alarm.

FIVE

Monday was overcast. a raw wind etched whitecaps on the bay. There was a smell of rain.

From talkative seamen coming ashore from the men-of-war came confirmation for the patriots that the rowboats had been overhauled and hurriedly launched for a mysterious purpose. Others, arriving after them, leaked word that orders had been sent to the ships to prepare a day's ration of cooked meat and bread.

Revere used the back door in coming and leaving home, taking no chances of being picked up by the marine sentries strolling outside his front windows.

William Dawes, the tall, thirty-year-old leatherworker with the puckish grin and amiable country drawl, was dressed in his usual disguise as a provincial bumpkin—old brown coat, floppy hat, red neckcloth, leather breeches—and hobnobbing with the British sentries at Boston Neck.

Unlike Revere, Dawes, one of Warren's most trusted agents, could come and go through the British lines almost at will. The sentries considered him a genial, somewhat drunken vagabond, with an earthy sense of humor.

Dawes had been one of the group that had raided the gun house that winter night and removed the cannon to the schoolhouse. One of the heavy brass barrels had gotten away from them as they lifted it out of the window. It fell on Dawes's arm and imbedded a sleeve button deep in his wrist. The wound turned ugly and Dawes went to Warren, the one doctor in Boston a patriot could trust. By the time the wrist healed, Warren and Dawes were close friends. Warren knew that if he ever

42

needed desperately to get a man past the British sentries, Dawes
was the one he could depend on.

Warren was staying close to home. When he had to go out, he
tucked two pistols under his coat. He knew an attempt to arrest
him and send him to the gallows for treason might come at any
moment, but: "These fellows say we won't fight. By heaven, I
hope I shall die up to my knees in blood!"

Of the intellectual leaders, the Boston Latin School and Harvard men of the Long Room Club, who through the years had
kept aglow and finally fanned into rebellion the opposition to
Tory dictation from Whitehall, he was the last left in Boston.

In Concord, now that the Sabbath was past, the church bell
had called out the townfolk and farmers at dawn. As the sky
lightened over the town house and church, the tavern, the Liberty Pole on its hilltop, the scattering of houses and country
shops, they gathered in the town square and got their orders
from the aged commander of the village militia, Colonel James
Barrett.

White-haired Colonel Barrett had fought as a captain of the
colonial forces in the French and Indian War. He had served
with Shirley at Oswego, Abercrombie at Ticonderoga, Amherst
at Crown Point. He had long ago resigned his commission.
When the Massachusetts militia was organized early in the year,
he had at first refused to return to service. But the townspeople's
petition prevailed.

"We don't want active service," they told him. "We want your
advice."

Now he was sending them off in little groups—lean, weathered-
faced farmers in plow boots and knee breeches, their women and
children—to attack the stockpiles of war supplies, carry them to
places of greater safety.

Soon high-wheeled oxcarts were trundling away down the long
roads to Groton and Sudbury, loaded with cannon and muskets,
kegs of gunpowder, bags of homemade cartridges, barrels of salt
fish and flour.

Plow horses pulled farm sleds, with the wide wooden runners
that could go where wagon wheels would mire down, across the

spring-softened fields. Piled on them were bags of lead balls, which were hauled to the nearest pond and rolled under the water.

Most of the supplies were in the barn on Colonel Barrett's farm, two miles outside the village. One of the younger Barretts plowed deep furrows along the edge of a field, trailed by his neighbors, in twos and threes, lugging cannon barrels. They laid the barrels in the furrows, and the next time around the plow turned a furrow of earth over them.

In her farmhouse attic, Mrs. Barrett pulled aside the featherbeds that had been stored away for the summer. Neighbor women and their children climbed the stairs, arms loaded with wooden bowls and trenchers, iron kettles. They were stacked in the corners and the featherbeds tucked over them.

Timothy Wheeler, the miller, cleared out his storeroom. The barrels of provincial flour were rolled in and Wheeler covered them with bags of grain bearing his own mark.

Henry Gardner, the Province Treasurer, and a companion lugged "a chest containing some money and other important articles" to an out-of-the-way room upstairs in the Jones Tavern, and locked the door.

The two provincial government committees, Safety and Supply, had stayed on in Concord after the Congress adjourned. They watched the villagers with grave approval from the sidelines. The stores were precious. While English law required every colonist to own a musket and ammunition—theoretically, every able man from sixteen to sixty was enrolled in the crown militia and could be called out if trouble threatened the king's government—families were large and there were many with only one ancient squirrel gun and powder horn over the mantel.

It was a busy day for the determined people of Concord, the Barretts and Buttricks, Butlers, Browns, the Chandlers, the Farrers, the Melvins and Minots, the Richardsons, the Walkers and Wheelers. By evening, most of the stores that hadn't been hauled out of town had been scattered where British snoopers would have a hard time finding them.

SIX

Tuesday forenoon a picked group of young officers were summoned to General Gage's private office in Province House. They were all men the general knew personally and felt he could trust with a secret. He knew their families back in England. They were on Mrs. Gage's guest list when she gave parties.

Among them were Captain Charles Cochrane of the King's Own Regiment, the 4th, whose wife was the daughter of Major Pitcairn of the Marines; Major Edward Mitchell of the 5th Regiment; Captain Charles Lumm of the 38th; Lieutenant William Grant of the Royal Artillery.

Gage had the door shut and, with studied deliberation, tidied the papers on his big walnut desk while the officers lined up in front of it. In the gray light coming through the velvet-portiered windows, he was a commanding figure; scarlet coat heavily trimmed in gold braid and blue piping, gray wig freshly curled and powdered.

The men who knew both said Boston's military governor looked like Sam Adams—a dressed-up Sam. He had the same long nose and thin mouth, slate-blue eyes. But the twinkle was missing. Gage was a ponderous man, slow and deliberate, basically kindly behind his military bluffness, anxiously hopeful still of settling the dispute with the colonies before it got out of hand.

"A respectable force in the field," he had written to Lord Dartmouth, would "come off victorious," and, he was sure, would put out the smoldering rebellion once and for all.

Complete secrecy, he now warned the officers lined up before him, was essential to the mission he was sending them on. They

45

were to choose their best mounts and ride across the Neck to
Cambridge. They would carry pistols and swords, but keep them
well concealed under their long blue coats. To all appearances,
they would be enjoying a carefree outing in the country.

They would drift casually in the direction of Medford and
Charlestown Neck on the Mystic and have dinner together at one
of the better taverns on the way. After dark, several of them
would conceal themselves alongside the road to Lexington. The
others would ride on and post themselves beside the road from
Lexington into Concord.

If they met with any interference, they were to say they were
out looking for deserters. Under no circumstances were they to
let anyone get past them into either village after dark.

So much he told them; no more.

"And now, off with you!"

The officers strolled, with exaggerated casualness, to their various quarters and collected their gear. They gathered in scattered
groups in the stables down Milk Street, watching their horses
being saddled, hooves inspected, loose shoes replaced by the
blacksmith.

Eyes bright with the prospect of an interesting adventure after
the drab months of confinement in Boston, they talked in muted
voices as they waited. A groom, walking by, heard one of them
say, "There will be hell to pay tomorrow!"

So they rode away, finally, trailing down Marlborough Street,
Newbury and Orange, trotting past the sentries at the Neck with
a swift snapping of salutes. Riding with them as attendants were
several noncoms, including a sergeant major whose transparent
anticipation had interested the gunsmith, Jasper, with whom he
was quartered in Hatter's Square.

Under the surface quiet of a drab Boston day spotted with
rain, the new alarm traveled circuitously to patriot headquarters
at Dr. Warren's before the group of officers were far on their way.

The gunsmith, Jasper, hunted up his friend, Josiah Waters,
and told him about the sergeant major coming home to get his
gear.

The British groom from the Milk Street   stables confided

what he had heard over a glass of ale to his hearty "Tory" ac-
quaintance, John Ballard.

Still another source, never identified, passed along the word
that something was shaping up, because Paul Revere told Ballard, "You are the third person we have heard from," and the
message that an expedition was to be sent out was still to come
from Mrs. Stedman.

In the afternoon, Gage called in three of his senior officers:
Lieutenant-Colonel Francis Smith of the 10th Regiment, Lieu-
tenant Colonel Bernard of the Royal Welch Fusiliers and Major
John Pitcairn of the Marines.

Again he had chosen with care. All three were men of long
service; levelheaded, steady, dependable. Smith was fat and slow-
moving, but as unperturbable as a parade horse. Bernard was
deliberate, ponderous. Pitcairn, although bluff and hearty, a man
who it was said could swear with a fine polish, was God-fearing,
capable, almost a father to his men. Not a fire-eater among them.

Gage clearly wanted no more trouble than was necessary.

Standing beside the general as he gave them his orders was
the able young Duke of Northumberland, tall, good-looking Lord
Percy, Dorothy Quincy's favorite breakfast companion.

Gage explained that the grenadier and light infantry companies which on Saturday had been detached ostensibly to learn
new evolutions were to be mustered on the Common at ten
o'clock for an expedition. There would be eleven companies of
grenadiers and ten of light infantry. Colonel Smith would be in
over-all command. Colonel Bernard would have charge of the
grenadiers and Major Pitcairn of the light infantry.

The longboats from the transports and men-of-war would be
waiting at the Magazine Guard on the shore of the Common to
carry the detachment of approximately seven hundred across the
Charles. At the time of embarkation the three officers would be
told their destination. Not before.

Assembly of the troops was to be done as inconspicuously and
as quietly as possible and not until after dark. No parading at
their barracks. They were to be sent in small groups to the Common by back streets and alleys.

No artillery pieces were to accompany them. The men would bring their haversacks and be provided with cooked rations before marching. No knapsacks. Gage was sternly emphatic on that point. He had a reason. His informer in the rebel high command had advised him that the provincials had been particularly warned by their leaders to spread the alarm if a detachment of any size moved out with artillery pieces or knapsacks.

He was confident, Gage assured the officers before him, that the provincials would not give them any trouble. "They are too cowardly a lot ever to take up arms against the king," he said. But just in case Colonel Smith should need help, a reserve detachment under Lord Percy would be ready to march out to him.

The three officers left and Gage was alone with Percy.

"I will tell you now the destination of the expedition," Gage said in a hushed voice. "It is Concord, to seize and destroy the arms the rebels have stocked there.

"Except for Mrs. Gage—from whom I could hardly keep such a secret if I tried—you are the only person I have told. I know I can trust you not to tell anyone until the time is ready."

By dusk Dr. Warren had the message brought to him by John Stedman from his wife in Winter Street, that the British grenadier, Gibson, had been ordered to report for an expedition. Warren was relieved when Billy Dawes came in and stretched out in the big chair by the sitting room window. It seemed, he thought, almost providential. Dawes, the bemused cutup, the apparent sot and ne'er-do-well, was the one man in the patriot organization who would stand a good chance to get out of the city if the British closed the Neck and threw a chain of sentries around the waterfront.

He took Dawes into his consulting room. The tall cordwainer was all alertness now. His sentry friends at the Neck would hardly have recognized him. He listened somberly to Warren's instructions: get out of the city somehow and ride to Lexington. Warn Adams and Hancock that a British expedition was about to march into the interior. Warn Concord to be on the alert. By now, Warren hoped, most of the stores that had not been sent to other towns were well hidden. But if any weren't, tell the villagers to get busy.

Dawes strolled away down Hanover Street. At his house on Anne Street, a few blocks from Revere's, his young wife, Mehitable, took the supper pot off the crane when she saw him come in. She noticed he appeared more preoccupied than usual. He ate fast, which wasn't like him. Most evenings he let his food get cold while he talked about where he had been during the day, whom he had talked with, what he had done.

They had been married seven years. She was twenty-four now and still pretty: big hazel eyes, slim, little. His silence worried her. She knew that a dark underswell of tension had been building up in the last few days. She asked him if there was news about the British plans. He didn't hear her.

He pushed back his plate and said he was going out again for a while. At the door he turned back and smiled at her.

"I may be late, but don't worry."

From the back window she watched him bring his horse out of the stable and ride away into the darkness. "Don't worry," he had told her. It was easier said than done.

At the fortified gate on Boston Neck, Dawes purposely dawdled a while as usual, swapping small talk with one of the sentries he knew. He sat idly on his horse watching as a chaise with an elderly couple in it came out of the darkness from the direction of Roxbury and stopped at the gate. While the sentry was inspecting the man's credentials, Dawes nudged his horse and moved casually away.

Another messenger was already riding to the Clark parsonage to warn Adams and Hancock.

The British officers dispatched by Gage in the forenoon had had a pleasant day in the country. They had dined at an excellent Tory inn in North Cambridge, had had a leisurely supper at another and had turned at last into the road that wandered westward through the Massachusetts hills from Charlestown to Concord.

The Provincial Congress' Committees of Safety and Supply, which usually met together, moving from town to town to help speed organization of the citizenry, had left Concord on Monday. Today they had met in Mr. Wetherby's Black Horse Inn in the village of Menotomy between Boston and Lexington.

They adjourned late in the afternoon. Three of the members stayed to pass the night. Richard Devens and Abraham Watson rode off in a chaise for their homes in Charlestown. Not far down the road they saw the group of British officers cantering toward them. As the British file opened to let them through, the wind flicked aside the blue greatcoat of one of them and Devens saw the glint of a pistol on his hip.

After riding a short distance, Devens and Watson turned around and drove past the officers again. One of the officers called to them, "Can you direct us to Clark's tavern?"

Clark's! Did they have the Lexington parsonage confused with an inn? Devens and Watson shook their heads in stupified silence, and rode on. Round a bend in the road, Devens laid the whip to his horse. They galloped into the Wetherby yard.

With the three members of the committees who were staying for the night, Elbridge Gerry, Azor Orne and Colonel Lee, they watched from an upstairs window as the officers rode past.

Elbridge Gerry hurriedly wrote a note to John Hancock that "eight or nine officers are out, suspected of some evil design." He gave it to a local dispatch rider, who traveled familiar bypaths, cut around the British detail and got to Lexington before them.

At the Clark parsonage, the message set off a flurry. Aunt Lydia was certain the British officers were coming to arrest and hang her nephew. Dolly, John's sprightly fiancée, who had been bickering with him on and off all day for want of something better to do, was suddenly herself again. John Hancock, with his flair for the dramatic, announced he would never be taken alive and started loading a gun to prove it. Sam Adams, blue eyes firm with anticipation, slipped away into the night to watch the road from Charlestown.

Meanwhile, a Lexington farmer, Solomon Brown, who had been to market in Charlestown, had also passed the officers—he counted nine—and had noticed the bulge of side arms under their blue coats. He urged his horse to full trot and drove to the home of William Monroe, orderly sergeant of the Lexington Militia.

Young Sergeant Monroe rounded up seven neighbors and, with guns primed and loaded, they threw a cordon around the Clark parsonage.

Brown and two other Lexington men, Elijah Sanderson and Jonathan Loring, saddled their work horses and set off to alarm Concord.

John Hancock sat down at the Reverend Clark's study table and composed a careful reply to Gerry:

"Lexington, April 18, 1775.
"Dear Sir:

"I am much obliged for your notice. It is said the officers are gone to Concord, and I will send word hither. I am full with you that we ought to be serious, and I hope your decision will be effectual. I intend doing myself the pleasure of being with you tomorrow. My respects to the committee.

"I am your real friend, JOHN HANCOCK."

SEVEN

IN BOSTON, THE BRITISH SUBALTERNS WHO WOULD COMMAND THE twenty-one companies of grenadiers and light infantry had hurried to their quarters to collect their gear.

Ensign Jeremy Lister, twenty-three, of the 10th Regiment of foot, was not among those assigned. He was the son of a landed family whose ancestral estate was Shipley Hall in Yorkshire. His commission had arrived there as a Christmas present when he was eighteen. The life of an ensign in His Majesty's Army hadn't been spiced with the bright adventure he had expected. Shortly after his induction, there had been a long and dreary ocean voyage to Canada, then a stretch of service on the Niagara frontier, sprinkled with a few brushes with Indians, and now the drab barracks routine of occupied Boston.

At last it appeared that something was to happen. There had been other night marches, but none involving as large a detachment as this one—seven to eight hundred men. None had had the build-up of suspense, of cryptic orders, dark rumors. The bored young officers of Gage's garrison sensed as expectantly as Dr. Warren that this was to be no ordinary expedition.

Ensign Lister was quartered with the Miller family in downtown Boston. It was a crowded household. A genteel Tory couple, Mr. and Mrs. Funnel, fugitives from the interior, had recently moved in. And, bunking with Lister, was Lieutenant Pettigrew of the grenadiers.

Lister sat on the bed watching with unmasked envy as Lieutenant Pettigrew strapped on his sword belt and buttoned his scarlet coat. Below the window he could hear an occasional muted beat of heavy footsteps on cobblestones as squads marched by on their way to the Common. A dog barked, followed by a strangled yelp as a bayonet silenced it.

When Pettigrew left, Lister tagged along. Entering the Common from Frog Lane they twisted through groups of citizens silently watching the activity under the distant red flare of torches on the river bank. A string of longboats, manned by seamen from the fleet, hugged the shore. A steady procession of squads was arriving, gathering into companies.

Captain Lawrence Parsons of the light infantry company of Lister's regiment was standing before one of the boats. When he saw Lieutenant Pettigrew, he came over. They were short one of their officers, he said, irritated. He had sent repeatedly for Lieutenant James Hamilton of the light infantry. The last messenger had finally brought back word that Hamilton was ill.

"He's no more ill than I am," Captain Parsons said. "He's afraid he might get hurt."

Ensign Lister saw his chance and took it fast. He begged to go in Hamilton's place, was accepted by Parsons, and hurried home to get his gear.

When he got back, Lieutenant Colonel Francis Smith, the broad-sterned commander of the expedition, stopped him as he was boarding one of the boats.

"Col. Smith wished me to return to Town again," Lister wrote later, "and not go into danger for others particularly Hamilton whose illness was supposed by everybody to be feign'd which twas clearly prov'd to be the case afterwards but wishing much to go, for the Honor of the Reg. thinking it would be rather a disgrace for the Comp. to march on an expedition, more especially it being the first, without its Compliment of Officers, therefore my offer was excepted."

Lieutenant William Sutherland of the 38th Regiment was another volunteer. He did not go as a replacement. He just went, boarding one of the boats in the darkness and joining Colonel Smith on the other side.

Lieutenant Sutherland was best known in the garrison as "The husband of the pritty Mrs. Sutherland." The blue-eyed young English beauty had been captivated originally by Sutherland's

effervescent daring and enthusiasm for adventure. She was going
to have to live with it now and try to like it.

Sutherland had got a smell that something was shaping up
when he saw his friend, Captain Charles Lumm of the same
regiment, ride off with the other picked officers that morning
on their secret mission for Gage into the country. He was accoutered and ready when the troops began to mass on the Common.

Lieutenant Frederick Mackenzie, the middle-aged adjutant of
the fusiliers, was with the company officers called to headquarters
for final briefing. He discovered, with silent misgivings, that the
high command expected to get the expedition embarked and on
the march without the rebels learning about it. The officers were
warned not to let the men make any noise. The barracks were to
be darkened and they were to slip out as stealthily as possible.
No formations. They were to keep to the back streets and rendez-
vous at the magazine guard on the remote shore of the Common.
If any were challenged, they were to answer, "Patrol."

Mackenzie had his two companies at the embarkation spot
well before ten. They were the first there. The boats were waiting in long rows at the wharf side, the seamen resting on their
oars. Mackenzie, finding no officer in over-all command, ordered
his men into the nearest boats and had them push off a few yards
into the river to make room for the others to load.

He could see it was going to be a long and probably confused
operation. Men were now arriving from all directions, singly, in
pairs, in groups of four or five; moving around in the darkness
hunting for the other members of their companies.

A procession of smoking flares came across the Common and
was distributed at wide intervals along the water's edge. Companies formed with aggravating slowness and marched to the
waiting boats, the men's faces darkly flushed in the wavering
torchlight. Mackenzie ran over in his mind the regiments that
were represented. With the marines, there were eleven companies
of grenadiers and ten of light infantry. Twenty-one in all. The
average strength of a company was thirty-two men. Including
the officers, he estimated, the detachment would total about

seven hundred. Nothing anywhere near that size had been sent into the country before.

He saw Colonel Smith arrive and take over command. Mackenzie stepped back into the darkness to watch. Now that he had brought his two companies to the waterside, his work was done. But he would have to be on call, to go out with Lord Percy's relief column if it were needed. He shrugged deeper into his coat. The wind had an edge to it. The big elms overhead were almost in full leaf. Spring had come unusually early. But the nights had a way of reminding that it was still only April.

The moon came up and sparkled on the bristle of polished bayonets and musket barrels. The boats were filled and moved toward the Phipps farm on the Cambridge shore. Mackenzie looked at his watch. It was going on eleven. After a long wait, the boats returned and slowly filled again. It was twelve o'clock before the last contingent was on its way.

General Gage had waited until a few minutes before ten to give Colonel Smith his final instructions, including the destination of the march. The order read:

"Boston, April 18, 1775.
"Lieu Coll Smith, 10th Regiment foot,
"Sir
  "Having received Intelligence, that a Quantity of Ammunition, Provisions, Artillery, Tents and small Arms, having been collected at Concord, for the Avowed Purpose of raising and supporting a Rebellion against His Majesty, you will March with the Corps of Grenadiers and light Infantry, put under your Command, with the utmost expedition and Secrecy to Concord, where you will seize and destroy all the Artillery, Ammunition, Provisions, Tents, Small Arms, and all Military Stores whatever. But you will take care that the Soldiers do not plunder the Inhabitants, or hurt private property.
  "You have a Draught [map] of Concord, on which is marked, the Houses, Barns, &c., which contain the above Military Stores. You will order a Trunion to be knocked off each Gun, but if its found impracticable on any, they must be spiked, and the Carriages distroyed. The Powder and flower, must be shook out of the Barrells into the River, the Tents burnt, Pork or Beef destroyed in the best way you can devise, And the Men may put

Balls or lead in their pockets, throwing them by degrees into Ponds, Ditches &c., but no Quantity together, so that they may be recovered afterwards.

"If you meet with any Brass Artillery, you will order their Muzzles to be beat in so as to render them useless.

"You will observe by the Draught that it will be necessary to secure the two Bridges as soon as possible, you will therefore order a party of the best Marchers, to go on with expedition for that purpose.

"A small party on Horseback is ordered out to stop all advice of your March getting to Concord before you, and a small number of Artillery go out in Chaises to wait for you on the Road, with Slege Hammers, Spikes &c.

"You will open your business, and return with the Troops, as soon as possible, which I must leave to your own Judgment and Discretion. I am,
> "Sir,
> > "Your most obedient
> > "humble Servant
> > "Tho Gage."

By "Artillery," Gen. Gage meant artillerymen. True to his rebel informer's warning, he was sending no artillery pieces to stir up a general alarm. The artillerymen would know how to operate on the rebel cannon so they could never be fired again. The trunnions were the two bars on the sides of a cannon barrel which supported it in the carriage. Without them, the cannon could not be mounted. Spiking consisted of driving an iron spike into the touchhole which carried the priming charge.

Until Colonel Smith unfolded the stiff parchment letter in the candlelight of the crystal chandelier over the general's desk that night, Gage had still told no one on his staff except Lord Percy the destination of the expedition.

Percy left Gage's office with Smith. On the steps of Province House they were joined by Major Pitcairn. The three walked up Marlborough Street and turned into Rawson's Lane. It was still an hour till moonrise and the only light on the cobblestones came from the patches of stars between the breaking clouds and here and there a candle-outlined window.

Percy left the other two at the Common and turned toward

the house he occupied at the foot of Winter Street. He decided
he had better get some sleep. He wasn't as confident as the general that this venture was going to come off without a hitch. He
might have to be on the march himself before dawn. Picking a
steeplechase winner back home had been a cinch compared with
foretelling what these uncouth troublemakers who called themselves patriots would do.

He was convinced the general should have struck out and
smashed this ridiculous uprising long ago. The general was much
too irresolute and easygoing for his own good, and the government's. It wasn't that he sympathized with the provincials. Percy
knew him too well to believe that. After all, Percy recalled, he
had himself been a member of the Whig party before he left
England a year ago, and he had been outspokenly opposed to the
uncompromising attitude of the king's ministry toward the Massachusetts Bay colony. But after a few months here in Boston he
had had a change of mind. He remembered the letter he had
written home:

"The people here are a set of sly, artful, hypocritical rascalls,
cruel and cowards. I must own I cannot but despise them completely."

Well, he thought, how could a sensible person think otherwise
after learning how respectable Tories were being treated in the
interior merely because they did not go along with the popular
point of view: forced to flee their homes with only the possessions
they could carry, and live on the charity of friends in Boston;
some of them even tarred and feathered by their hotheaded
neighbors. And the way the Boston toughs—Liberty Boys, they
had the gall to call themselves—strutted around and bullied the
decent people of the town!

He passed a group of citizens staring across the Common at the
torches on the river front, and suddenly he was all attention.

"The British troops have marched," he heard one of them say,
"but will miss their aim."

Percy strolled closer.

"What aim?" he asked. He was just another voice in the
darkness.

"Why, the cannon at Concord," the man answered.

Percy hurried back to Province House. General Gage was dumfounded.

"But how could they have found out?" he asked. "I have told nobody the object of this mission except my wife and you." He added, plaintively, "Nobody else!"

He grabbed Percy's arm and strode with him to the door.

"Get a messenger to the Neck as quickly as you can! Tell them to close the gates, let nobody pass! And have the guard doubled at the ferry to Charlestown!"

He stood in the doorway, shaking his head.

"How could they have found out—so soon?"

EIGHT

ACROSS THE CHARLES RIVER, AT THIS TIME, DR. WARREN'S EXPRESS
rider, Billy Dawes, was cantering into the center of Cambridge.
At Roxbury, just over Boston Neck, he had passed the word to
the captain of the militia that the British were coming out in
force. Now he stopped before a house in Cambridge and called
the news to the man who opened the door.

The road ahead wandered toward Menotomy through low
hills scattered with stone-fenced farms. It was slow going in the
pitch darkness under the overhanging trees. He rode with a slack
rein, leaving it to the horse's night sight to find the way.

Behind him, other horsemen, called out by the officers of the
minutemen in Roxbury and Cambridge, had saddled in a hurry
and were riding out to spread the alarm, riding the dark country
roads toward Watertown and Marlboro, Framingham, Westboro,
Milford, Brockton, Shrewsbury, Worcester.

Meanwhile, in Boston, one of Paul Revere's patrolling Committee of Mechanics had raced down Hanover Street and into
the back door at Dr. Warren's. He was out of breath and at first
it was hard for the doctor to understand what he was trying to
get out. Something about the Common, the magazine guard, the
regulars. Warren set a chair behind him and pushed him into it.
He told him to take a long, slow breath.

Now what was he trying to say?

"The regulars—" the man said, and took another deep breath.
"The regulars, hundreds of them, armed to the teeth. They're
gathering at the magazine guard down by the river front. The
boats from the warships are waiting to take them across. I got
near as I could, behind a tree down by the wharf. It's the grenadiers and light infantry, the companies that—"

The door opened and another patriot spy ran in. He told the same story. Another followed him.

Warren sent a messenger to the Green Dragon.

"Find Paul Revere! Tell him to come to me with the upmost haste!"

It was ten o'clock when Revere came into the doctor's sitting room. Warren told him the British were finally on the move. The nearest land across from where they were embarking, he pointed out, was the Phipps farm in Cambridge, on the salt-marshes of Lechmere's Point. A cartway led across the tideland to the road from Cambridge village to Menotomy and Lexington. It looked as though the British were going to Lexington to arrest Hancock and Sam Adams or to Concord to destroy the colonial stores. Possibly, he said, they were planning to do both. He had sent Dawes out earlier in the evening to try to get across the Neck. He had no way of knowing whether Dawes had made it. Now it was up to Revere to attempt to get word through to Lexington and Concord.

Revere hurried to the North End. He climbed the sloping streets to Christ Church. Its white steeple was the highest in Boston. After his Sunday trip to Lexington, he had arranged with Robert Newman, the twenty-three-year-old sexton of the Episco-pal Church, to hang the signal lanterns in the steeple if he were not there to do it; one lantern to alert Colonel William Conant, watching on the Charlestown shore, that the British were march-ing out across Boston Neck; two, that they were being ferried across the Charles.

Robert Newman lived with his mother in Sheafe Street, a block from the church. Several British officers were quartered in the house and were downstairs playing cards. Newman had been expecting all evening that he might be called. He knew that with the officers in the sitting room Revere would not dare come to the door. So he climbed out an upstairs back window and, with his young friend, John Pulling, one of the vestrymen at Christ Church, was waiting in the street when Revere arrived.

While Pulling stood guard outside, Newman unlocked the door to the church, took down two candle lanterns in the vestry, lighted them, and started the long climb up the wooden steps to the steeple window looking out over Copp's Hill and the mouth of the Charles to Charlestown, four hundred rods across the water. In midstream, her riding lights blinking in the darkness, the sixty-four-gun man-of-war *Somerset* rode at anchor, guarding the ferry lane from Boston to Charlestown.

Newman hung one lantern in the steeple opening, then the other. In less than a minute he took them down, for fear the signal would be seen by the watch on the *Somerset*.

Back downstairs, he unlocked the door, looked out and hurriedly locked it again. Pulling was gone. There were soldiers in the street.

Whether they were troops on their way to the Common or a patrol sent to investigate the lights in the steeple, Newman didn't know. He climbed out a side window and made his way across the dark churchyard and familiar alleys to the back yard of his home. As he climbed into his room, he could hear the officers downstairs talking and laughing.

Revere, meanwhile, had slipped quietly in at the back door of his house. North Square, out front, was now filled with soldiers, coming from their barracks and billets for the stealthy trip to the Common. The streets entering the square were barred to all civilians.

Revere put on his riding boots and surtout, the heavy, knee-length coat he hoped would keep the night chill away. Rachel knelt and buckled on his spurs while he told her where he was bound. They were a companionable couple, the stocky silversmith who had just turned forty and this second wife with the oval face and tilted nose, twelve years younger than he, whom he had married a year and a half ago.

As Rachel snuffed the candle, he went out the back door and started for the North Side wharf where he had kept the rowboat hidden all winter for just such trips as this. In his hurry, he realized, he had forgotten to take along cloth to muffle the oars.

Along the way he picked up two waiting members of his Committee of Mechanics, Joshua Bentley, a boatbuilder, and Thomas Richardson, to help him row across. It was going to be a longer trip than usual, and they might have to row for their lives, since the *Somerset* had been moved directly into the ferry lane.

Revere brought up the matter of muffling the oars. Bentley said he thought he could take care of that. He had a girl friend living down here at the corner of North Centre Street. Arriving under her window, he tossed up a stone. The sash came up. A whispering back and forth, a moment of waiting, and a woolen petticoat, still warm, fluttered down to them.

The oars wrapped, they pushed off. They kept well to seaward of the *Somerset,* expecting any moment to be hailed and fired upon.

"It was young flood," said Revere. "The ship was winding and the moon was rising."

His two companions ran the boat ashore near the Charlestown Battery. By now the night was bright with moonlight.

The Charlestown patriot, Colonel Conant, stood waiting at the water's edge. He had seen the signal lanterns in the church steeple while Revere was still far out in the river, he said.

Richard Devens, of the Committee of Safety, joined them at the head of the path. The roads were patrolled, he warned. He told Revere of passing the group of British officers on the way home from Menotomy. He was afraid the rider he had sent to warn Hancock and Adams had not gotten through to Lexington. He hoped Revere would have luck riding double with him.

Deacon John Larkin, a well-to-do farmer whose house and barns were nearby, said he had a good mount waiting.

"If any horse can get you through the British patrols, she can," he said. "She's my father's favorite."

He added, hesitantly, "Take good care of her, if you will," and was off into the shadows.

It was a good horse. A quick-stepping bay, high-strung, alert-eared, she shied away, snorting, as Revere took the reins from Larkin and reached for the stirrup. He was up in a quick, easy stride. A wave of the hand, and he was off.

It was eleven o'clock. Through the silent streets of the village, tucked away for the night, he rode at an easy canter. Lexington lay sixteen miles ahead, and Concord five miles beyond. He was too skilled a horseman to spur madly down the long, lonely roads, with a British ambush possible around every bend. He could feel the reserve of power in the muscles rippling under his thighs. It was something to husband for sudden emergencies.

On the outskirts of Charlestown, the road ran across a narrow neck of tidewater marshes, clay pits and scrub brush, rank with the smells of the sea. On his right, the Mystic River lay burnished with moonlight; on his left, the Charles. The road divided. He bore left, taking the short route that led through the Cambridge farmlands to Lexington. He passed the dark gibbet where the bones of the Negro slave, Mark, rattled in their rusty chains. Mark had been hanged twenty years ago for conspiring with three other slaves to murder his master, John Codman, a sea captain, by feeding him arsenic. His mummified remains had been left hanging here ever since as a warning to other slaves against doing in their masters.

Just beyond, the road cut narrowly through a patch of woods. As Revere approached he made out two shadowy figures on horseback under the trees. He pulled up when he saw by their cockades and the cut of their coats that they were British officers.

One of them spurred his horse toward Revere. The other moved into the road to block him if he tried to get past.

Now Revere found out what a good horse Deacon Larkin had lent him. The mare spun under his rein and spur and tore across the field. The heavy British charger, even with a running start, was no match for her. For three hundred yards, racing through the marsh grass and around the treacherous clay pits, Revere heard the hoofbeats fade away behind him. Then, no longer hearing them, he looked back. The British horse was bogged down in one of the pits.

Now he took the longer road to Lexington. He crossed the plank bridge into Mystic and awoke the captain of the minute-men, leaning down from his saddle to pound on the door.

"The regulars are coming out!" he announced, and rode on.

He crossed the Mystic again, into Menotomy, a long, straight street of houses, and awoke the militia commander there.

After that, he stopped at every house to shout his message.

It was going on one o'clock when he rode into the little Middlesex village of Lexington. The Monroe Tavern, a square, two-story, weathered brown building on his left, was dark. A mile down the road, on the village Green, stood the Lexington meetinghouse, its three long rows of windows glinting darkly in the moonlight. Beside it was the belfry, an unpainted one-story shack with an open cupola on top housing the bronze village bell.

Across the road, on the right, the first-floor windows of Buckman's Tavern were yellow with candlelight. Inside, taproom chairs scraped back and men rushed to the door and windows as the horseman galloped past.

A short ride down the road branching to the right of the Green brought Revere to the Clark parsonage, dark and silent under the trees. As he leaped off his horse and ran to the door, Orderly Sergeant William Monroe of the local militia stepped out of the shadows, musket poised. With his squad of minutemen he had been guarding the house since the alarm had been received early in the evening that British officers were on the road.

"Let me in!" Revere shouted.

"Not so loud!" Monroe commanded. "The family are all asleep and have left orders not to be disturbed by any noise."

Revere pushed past him and pounded on the door.

"Noise! You'll have noise enough before long! The regulars are out!"

An upstairs window creaked open and the Reverend Jonas Clark stuck out his white head. He did not immediately recognize Revere.

"I will not admit a stranger at this hour of the night," he called, "without knowing who you are and your purpose."

Another window slid open. John Hancock's head popped out, for once shiny, naked of a wig.

"Come in, Revere," he said. "We are not afraid of you."

Sam Adams was never strong on formality. In his flannel shift, his gray hair still rumpled from the pillow of the double bed he had been sharing with Hancock, he threw up the latch and grabbed Revere's hand. His eyes were sparkling.

"What's the news?"

Hancock came down the stairs, his silver-gray wig neatly in place now, and he was wrapped in a satin dressing gown, slippers to match. Aunt Lydia, a hastily-pulled-on robe billowing over her vast nightgown, grunted down in his wake, followed by Pastor Clark, his wife and the two olders girls, and last, Dorothy Quincy, tripping lightly, dainty and trim, eyes wide with anticipation.

Revere told them there were not only scattered British patrols on the road out of Boston; a full-sized detachment of regulars was on the march, undoubtedly bound for Lexington. He thought there were "over a thousand light troops!"

Sam Adams sank back into a chair, his expression smiling, assured. Word must be gotten to Captain Parker at once, he said, looking at Sergeant Monroe.

Pastor Clark said they had better get the team harnessed and pack off Aunt Lydia and Miss Dorothy in the chariot. Sam and John would, he supposed, be taking the chaise.

And leave Mrs. Clark and her twelve children behind? Aunt Lydia demanded.

Pastor Clark stared back at her, defiantly.

"Of course! It is their home. None of the other families in Lexington will be running away."

The others could do as they pleased, John Hancock declared. As for himself, he was staying. Not only staying. He was going to get dressed, buckle on his sword and load his gun. He was going out on the green and stand up with the men of Lexington. If the redcoats were coming to get him, they'd have to take him by force. His face was red with determination.

Aunt Lydia protested shrilly. His fiancée, Dorothy, told him primly he was being "absurd, sir!"

Paul Revere had never felt great warmth toward Hancock. He was too showy about his wealth. There was too much of the grand manner about him: his elaborate wardrobe, his fine house and carriages, his absorbing interest in food, in the ritual of eating.

He was the only one among the gentlemen of the Long Room Club, the intellectual leaders of the rebellion in Boston, who would make an artisan like Revere feel his place.

The first chance Revere had, he interrupted.

Dr. Warren, he said, had sent out another messenger, William Dawes. Had they heard anything from him?

They hadn't.

It was strange, Revere thought. Dawes had a longer route to ride, but he had left Boston considerably earlier in the night. One of the patrols must have picked him up.

It was a half hour after Revere's arrival that Dawes rode into the yard. He hadn't met any patrols on the way. It had been slow going at first, before the moon came up. Another reason for his belated arrival was that he was more loquacious than Revere. It took him longer to deliver his message each time he stopped.

Mrs. Clark set out a joint of cold meat, bread and a pitcher of ale before the kitchen fireplace for Revere and Dawes. While they ate, the argument went on in the sitting room. By now, Hancock was dressed. He had strapped on his sword, was polishing his musket with a piece of flannel and goose grease.

"I will never," he said, "turn my back on those troops."

Dolly Quincy thought her fiancé was being falsely heroic and, in a small, amused voice, said so. Sam Adams stood quietly by, letting rotund Jonas Clark carry most of the argument with Hancock.

Sergeant Monroe had left. Suddenly, the church bell on the Green began to ring. It was a rapid peal, angry and loud in the stillness of the colonial night.

Revere and Dawes walked out together, mounted their horses and started for Concord. As they trotted past the Green a group of villagers was gathering beside the meetinghouse, muskets in the crook of their arms. Revere recognized the tall lanky figure of the French-and-Indian-War veteran, Captain Parker. Another group stood around the doorway of the Buckman Tavern, across the road. In their drab knee breeches, some of homespun, some of leather, and heavy work shoes, they looked anything but military.

The bronze bell in the little belfry was swinging as rapidly as the man at the end of the rope could yank it, sending its staccato peals out across the hills and farmlands, awakening the darkness with its frightening message: "The British are out!"

NINE

As REVERE AND DAWES TURNED INTO THE ROAD TO CONCORD, A YOUNG horseman caught up with them. He was Dr. Samuel Prescott, twenty-three, of Concord, and he had been courting Miss Milliken in Lexington until this late hour. It was soon apparent to Revere that he was "a high son of Liberty." Also, his horse was fresh and looked fast. Revere thought that might be important.

By now, Revere surmised, the British patrol had probably spread out along the road to stop any riders attempting to carry the alarm to Concord. Every wooded spot along the way was a possible ambush. With luck, they might be able to make a run for it and one of them might get through. Meanwhile, here was a house to be alerted.

Dr. Prescott said he knew the family. He knew everyone along here. They would recognize him and credit his word more readily than they might a stranger's in the night.

Revere waited in the road while the young doctor and Dawes rode to the door. They trotted on, and again Prescott rode into a farmyard and shouted the alarm. This time Revere rode with him.

When they were nearly halfway to Concord, Prescott and Dawes stopped at a house and Revere rode slowly ahead. The road ran between high stone fences and scattered trees. He had gone about a hundred rods when he saw, just ahead under a big tree at the roadside, the dark figures of two horsemen. He turned and shouted to Dawes and Prescott: "Come up! Here are a couple of them!"

They drew together and, riding at a walk, watched the two officers come toward them. Revere sat, seemingly relaxed in his saddle, waiting the moment to give the signal and spur past them. Just then, two other mounted officers, whom Revere and his companions had not seen, dashed through an opening in the fence at their side, cocked pistols in their hands. One of them yelled, "God damn you, stop!"

The four troopers herded the express riders up the road a few yards and through an open rail gate into a pasture. Dr. Prescott was in the lead, Revere and Dawes tight behind him. Two of the officers rode in front of them, two in their rear.

As they cleared the gate, Prescott ducked low over his horse and yelled, "Have on!" He dug in his spurs. One of the officers slashed at him with his sword, cutting the bridle rein, and charged after him. At the same time Revere and Dawes made their break.

Prescott put his horse over a stone fence and raced away down a cowpath. His fresh mount soon outdistanced the pursuing officer.

Dawes galloped across the field toward the house and outbuildings of the Hartwell farm, two officers close behind him. As he neared the Hartwell barn, he slapped his leather breeches and yelled, "Helloo, boys! I've got two of them!"

It was a good act. His pursuers pulled up, thinking they were riding into a rebel trap. But Dawes's horse swerved suddenly before a stone fence, and he tumbled into the brush.

He picked himself up and limped away. It wasn't until he was well along on the lonely walk back to Boston that he discovered he had lost his watch. He went back and hunted through the brush in the dark until he found it.

Revere, meanwhile, had "observed a wood at a small distance, & made for that."

But as he reached it six British troopers rushed out and surrounded him. One of them ordered him to dismount.

"What's your name?" he demanded.

"Paul Revere."

"Where are you coming from?"

"Boston."

"Are you riding express?"

Revere said, bluntly, "Yes."

"What time did you leave Boston?"

"Soon after ten."

He added, in the same easy voice, "Your troops have catched aground in passing over the river. There will be five hundred Americans here in a short time, for I have alarmed the country all the way up."

The officer thought that over, scowling down at Revere. He waved him forward with his sword and the procession started back across the field. The officers who had captured the three in the road joined them. One of them, Major Edward Mitchell, of the 5th regiment, took over the questioning.

"He clapped a pistol to my head," said Revere, "called me by name, and told me he was going to ask me some questions, and if I did not give him true answers, he would blow my brains out."

In a clump of trees behind the stone fence, four provincials who had been taken in earlier by the patrol sat on their horses. The reins were held by a British sergeant sitting on a stump with a pistol in his other hand. One of the four was Elijah Sanderson, a twenty-four-year-old Lexington cabinetmaker. He could hear Mitchell's questions and his prisoner's blunt, unruffled answers. So this was Paul Revere, the express rider who had come to Lexington from Boston on Sunday to warn Adams and Hancock! He liked the way the man sat his horse, the obvious defiance and lack of fear in the dark, scowling face, the quiet assurance in his voice.

When Mitchell paused, Sanderson saw Revere scan the circle of officers around him.

"Gentlemen, you have missed your aim," Revere told them.

"What of our aim?" Mitchell asked. "We are out looking for deserters."

Revere answered, "I know better. I came out of Boston after your troops landed at Lechmere's Point."

He added: "If I had not known that other people had been sent out to give information to the country, I would have ventured one shot from you before I would have suffered you to have stopped me."

In the stillness that followed, the distant pealing of the Lexington bell rose and faded with the gusting wind.

Jonathan Loring, one of Sanderson's companions under guard in the clump of trees, called out: "The bell's aringing! The town's alarmed!" His voice rose. "And you are all dead men!"

Major Mitchell ran his hands over Revere, searching for arms. Finding none, he told him to get back onto his horse. The young British officer snapped orders. The sergeant mounted his horse and brought out the four countrymen. Surrounded by the British patrol, the prisoners rode slowly back up the road toward Lexington.

The village had spent an anxious night. In appearance it was just another of the many crossroads settlements scattered over eastern Massachusetts. The road from Boston came in from the east between low-sloping hills scored with stone walls and occasional rail fences into pasture lots and small cultivated fields.

There was good reason for the predominance of stone walls: field rock was the most abundant material at hand and it had to be cleared off before the land could be plowed for crops.

From the Monroe Tavern the farmhouses and barns, mostly unpainted like the tavern, an occasional group neatly whitewashed, drew gradually closer together, interspaced with village shops; the wagon and harness maker's, the pump maker's, the mill.

At the triangular Green, the road forked, the left branch going off to Concord, the right to Woburn and Bedford. Pastor Clark's meetinghouse stood at the fork, facing Boston. Around the Green, between rail-fenced cow pastures and farmhouses, were more village shops: Nathan Mulliken's watch and clock shop among them, Daniel Harrington's blacksmith shop.

Buckman's Tavern, across the Bedford Road from the meetinghouse, was no better or worse than other country inns of the time, except for John Buckman's robust flip. The hearty innkeeper made a fine ritual of preparing it. He measured two-thirds of a quart of beer into a pot over the fire. Into a stone pitcher he broke four eggs, added a heaping spoon of sugar and a ladle of cream, and beat it furiously; then slowly stirred in a gill of New England rum.

When the beer began to bubble, he poured it into another

pitcher, and from that slowly into the one containing the eggs and rum mixture; very slowly, so the eggs would not curdle. Now, standing straddle-legged before the fire, he poured the foaming liquid back and forth from one pitcher to the other; four times, sometimes six, until he was satisfied it was perfectly blended; then into the fat pewter tankard waiting before his guest.

The price was three cents a tankard.

Downstairs, besides the taproom, there was a parlor, for meetings, and the kitchen. The bar was an L-shaped counter in a corner of the taproom behind which John Buckman kept his kegs of dark home-brewed beer and West Indies molasses, his jugs of rum, crocks of eggs and sugar, his racks of stone mugs and pewter tankards. Above it hung a fence of vertical wooden bars —the "bar"—which was let down and locked at closing time.

The family living quarters were on the second floor. The third floor was a large, bleak, whitewashed room filled with narrow rope and straw-tick beds rented out to transients.

By dusk of April 18th, while Revere was still in Boston, apprehension was sending its dark tendrils through the group of villagers around the fireplace and oak tables in the taproom.

Young Sergeant Monroe, his face purposeful and grim, had come in with Solomon Brown. Soon, in response to a messenger sent by Monroe, John Parker, the captain of the local militia, joined them.

Brown, whose farm was just up the Boston Road, told his story again. He had driven to market in Charlestown that morning. On his way home this evening, he had passed a mounted patrol of British officers, riding this way!

In recent months the sight of British officers and their servants on a day's outing along the roads from Boston had become fairly common. But before this they had always turned back by dusk. This group was miles from their lines and still riding westward!

Captain Parker agreed with Monroe that the British detail might be coming to Lexington to arrest the two patriot bigwigs, Adams and Hancock, staying at the parsonage.

Amos Muzzey, his high forehead glistening with sweat, boots muddy, came in, his musket cradled in his arm.

He had been standing in his barnyard up the road when the

group of officers rode past. The wind had whipped aside the blue greatcoats of several of them and revealed the short swords and pistol holsters at their sides. He had grabbed his flintlock and cut across the fields to find out what was up.

Parker ordered Sergeant Monroe to take a squad of militiamen to the Clark parsonage, place themselves around it and let no one in.

The guard left, Muzzey among them. Those of the squad who hadn't their muskets with them ran across the street to the meetinghouse and helped themselves from the village arsenal in the gallery.

Minutes after they left, Elijah Sanderson, the young cabinetmaker, who lived three-quarters of a mile up the Boston Road, entered the taproom. He, too, had seen the group of British horsemen and had been alarmed at their being abroad this late and riding away from Boston.

As he was taking off his cartridge box and setting his musket in the corner, another villager ran in.

The officers, he shouted, were coming down the road!

The group in the taproom rushed to the windows looking out on the Boston Road. In the fading light they saw the patrol pull up at the fork. For a breathless moment the men at the windows waited. Then the officer in the lead raked his horse and they took the turn toward Concord.

The villagers went back to their chairs. Solomon Brown, who had been the first to sight the patrol, settled down to his tankard of flip. Jonathan Loring came in, spurs clanking on the plank floor. Sanderson's younger brother joined them. His voice high-pitched with excitement, he said he had followed the patrol down the road, dodging along behind the fences so they wouldn't spot him.

With the British horsemen gone on their way, the tension in the Buckman taproom lightened. Puzzlement took its place.

Why would the patrol want to go to Concord at this hour? Surely Gage would send more men than that to seize or destroy the colonial arms stored there.

Sanderson suggested that perhaps the officers had ridden toward Concord as a ruse, and would double back after dark to seize or assassinate Adams and Hancock.

An old man sitting by the fire said querulously that someone ought to trail them, find out what they were up to. Sanderson said he'd be glad to go if he had a horse.

Thaddeus Harrington answered, "Mine is outside, saddled and ready. Take him."

Jonathan Loring said he'd go along. So did Solomon Brown. Sanderson told his brother to take home his musket and cartridge box, and the three rode off in the darkness toward Concord.

With moonrise still hours away, the sky overcast, it was hard to see the road under the trees more than a horse's length ahead. They rode close together, ducking every now and then as an overhanging branch brushed their heads.

They were nearly halfway to Concord when two horsemen stepped out of the woods on either side, both yelling, "Halt!" They rode up brandishing pistols and grabbed the bridle reins of the three country horses.

"If any of you moves," one said, "we'll blow your brains out!"

While one officer covered them, the other let down the bars into a pasture. The three were led in. Several other officers surrounded them and searched them. One, who appeared to be in charge, questioned them while a sergeant took over their reins.

What were they doing out at this time of the night? Where had they come from? Where were they going?

Solomon Brown did most of the answering. They had been visiting friends in Lexington. They were going home.

The officer—Major Mitchell—did not appear to believe them. Whether they lived in Concord or not, he said, they weren't going home tonight. They weren't going anywhere.

The two who had captured them went back to the road. Mitchell and the other officers rode away into the darkness. A sergeant led the three mounted countrymen under the trees and settled himself on a stump.

Time dragged its feet. Occasionally several of the officers rode back out of the darkness, stared silently at the three men and rode off again. The wind came up, cold and damp. The clouds broke and patches of stars blinked through.

The moon rose. One of the officers took out his watch and stared at it. It was forty-eight minutes after ten, he said.

After a while the officers on the road captured another prize, a one-armed peddler named Allen, and his horse, and brought him in for the sergeant to guard.

Midnight passed. One o'clock. None of the countrymen possessed such a luxury as a watch. They didn't need one. The stars were their timepiece as well as the sun.

Now, distantly, they heard hoofbeats on the road. At first it was the dull drumming of several cantering horses. A silence, and then only one rider, coming steadily nearer.

The rider stopped. They heard a voice calling, but couldn't make out the words. A long silence this time. Then a shout:

"God damn you! Stop!"

They saw the British officers bring their three new prisoners through the gate and heard young Prescott yell, "Have on!" The way the tight cluster of horsemen burst apart reminded Sanderson of an explosion. The fugitives and their pursuers streaked off across the pasture.

Loring yelled, "Go it, boys!" The sergeant angrily waved his pistol at him. But Loring had noticed that none of the officers had fired at their escaping prisoners. It gave him sudden courage.

"Go ahead and shoot," he said scornfully.

The officers drifted back. Sanderson saw that a group of them had Revere in tow. The four under the trees grinned at each other when they heard Revere say there were five hundred Americans on the march.

Now Sanderson and his companions were led back onto the road. The sergeant mounted his horse, a stocky little animal. Major Mitchell ordered him to take Revere's reins and ride beside him.

"Blow his brains out if he tries to get away," Mitchell said.

They moved at a walk toward Lexington. Gradually, the sound of the village bell grew stronger. Now, far across the dark fields, they could hear the faint cry of another bell. It was Lincoln's, on the road to Concord. Somewhere, nearby, a musket went off. The officers, now hurrying their captives along, talked together in low voices.

Major Mitchell called a halt. He ordered the four countrymen to dismount. An officer went quickly from one horse to another, slashing the saddle girths and bridle reins.

The cavalcade rode off with Revere, leaving Sanderson, Brown and Loring, and the peddler, Allen, standing in the road, their saddles scattered around them.

As the patrol and its one remaining prisoner started down the grade into the village, an alarm volley sounded from the Green, drowning out for a moment the pealing of the bell. Mitchell pulled up and spoke to Revere, anxiety apparent in his voice.

"How far is it to Cambridge?"

"A fast hour's ride," Revere told him.

"Is there any other road than this?"

Revere shook his head.

Mitchell looked at the little horse the sergeant was riding. "Is your mount tired?"

"It is that, sir. Very tired."

Mitchell told Revere to dismount.

"Take his," he said, "and let's be off."

Revere stood in the road and watched the patrol gallop away down the road, the sergeant's horse running after them, the empty stirrups flapping at its sides. He looked around in the waning moonlight. He was on unfamiliar ground, but if he stayed in the road he might be picked up again. The meetinghouse bell would serve as a beacon. He climbed over the stone wall into a field and followed a fence that twisted northward. When he came to a burying ground, he knew he was near the Clark parsonage.

Coming across the back yard, he saw a light in the root cellar doorway. He looked in. Mrs. Clark was holding a candle over the potato bin and Dolly Quincy, on her knees, her sleeves pushed back above her elbows, was making a hollow in the potatoes and dropping a watch and a handful of jewelry and coins into it.

Aunt Lydia was in the kitchen. She didn't see him at once. Her broad back was turned and she had a silver porringer in one fat hand and a church ewer in the other. He recognized the porringer as one he had made for Hancock a few years back as a birthday gift for Elizabeth, the eldest of the Clark children.

Aunt Lydia was looking frantically around the room and repeating "Oh, dear!" in a half whisper. With sudden decision, she went to the big soap crock under the window and pushed the two pieces deep into it.

She said, "Oh!" when she saw Revere, and added, "Oh, it's you! Have they come yet? Don't tell Mr. Hancock if they have," she urged, an edge of hysteria in her voice. "He's bound to go out and shoot at them. He'll surely be killed. Maybe you can make him come to his senses. If Mr. Adams would only talk to him. But he just sits there and smiles.

"I do believe," she continued, "Dolly is even more annoyed with John tonight than usual. The dear girl. If it weren't for me that betrothal would never last. I sometimes think she actually dislikes him. I can't say that I blame her much tonight, the way he's been acting: polishing at that silly musket of his, and his sword; thinking to sacrifice himself with those poorly-armed people out there on the Green. What chance will they have against the king's regulars?"

Sam Adams came in the kitchen door, unwinding his long muffler. Revere told him of his capture by the patrol. He said he guessed the British officers had been thoroughly alarmed by the signal guns and the clamor of the village bell, and wanted to get back to Boston while they still had a chance.

Adams nodded. Either that, he said, or they thought it was high time to alert the detachment. He had been down to the Green again and had heard the patrol ride past at full gallop.

He said Captain Parker had called out the minutemen at one o'clock in response to Revere's alarm. They had paraded on the Green. Parker had sent several off on their horses to look for the British force. When one of them returned and said he had ridden a good distance and had found no sign of the British troops, Parker and his officers had held a council of war.

They had decided the British maneuver was probably nothing more than a ruse. It was going on half past three then, and the men, standing in a double line on the Green, were stomping their feet and slapping themselves to fight off the cold. Parker told them they were dismissed, but warned that they should not go beyond the range of the drum and should be ready to hurry back if he sounded the call to arms.

Those who lived around the Green, Adams said, had gone back home. The others—a very sizable number—were waiting the night out around the meetinghouse and at Buckman's. More were coming in every few minutes in response to the bell and the alarm guns. Just now, on his way back from the Green, he had passed a minute company from Woburn, coming at a dogtrot.

Adams unbuttoned his long brown coat and looked at his watch. Didn't Revere think it was strange, he said, that at this late hour none of the other mounted scouts Parker had sent out had come back? What might be keeping them?

"Have you mentioned that to Captain Parker?" Revere asked.

Adams looked at him with his wry smile.

"I wouldn't think of interfering in a local matter," he said. He rebuttoned his coat and wound the muffler back around his neck. "I think we had better be moving along."

He and Revere walked into the sitting room. Aunt Lydia had come in ahead of them. Dolly Quincy and Mrs. Clark were in a corner talking with Hancock's young clerk, John Lowell. Hancock was standing by the fireplace, faultlessly dressed in the uniform he had acquired as captain in the Boston militia. The Reverend Jonas Clark, his round face flushed from the exertion of futile argument, looked helplessly at Adams.

"Mr. Hancock still insists—"

Adams put a fatherly hand on Hancock's shoulder.

"The province has elected you and me to represent it in the Continental Congress," he said. "This is not our business. We belong to the cabinet."

He looked at young Lowell.

"It's time we were off. Have the chaise hitched up."

Adams asked Revere to go with them.

"If the British arrive, it will not be long now," he said. "You can do no good here."

They were going to the home of an old family friend of the Clarks, Mrs. Thomas Jones, widow of the Woburn minister, he explained. It was about four miles up the road.

Aunt Lydia and Dolly had decided to stay with the Clarks a while longer. By now, Dolly would have risked almost any danger to be free of John Hancock and his posturings for a while.

There was a last-minute clash of temperaments. Dolly announced she was going back to Boston tomorrow to be with her father. Hancock indignantly disapproved.

"No, Madam," he said. "You shall not return as long as there is a British bayonet left in Boston."

Dolly stamped her foot.

"Recollect, Mr. Hancock, I am not under your control yet. I shall go to my father if I wish."

As the chaise, carrying Hancock, Adams and Revere, and the clerk, Lowell, drove away up the road, young Dr. Prescott, the only one of the three express riders who had successfully escaped from the British patrol, was cantering into Concord. After getting clear of the British trooper, he had knotted the slashed reins and cut across the fields into Lincoln, the village between Lexington and Concord. He had awakened the captain of the militia and ridden on.

In Concord, he pulled up at the town house and told the militiaman on all-night guard duty that the British were on the march. Then he continued up the road to the next village, Acton, four miles away.

Behind him, now, he could hear the rounded peals of the great bronze bell in the Concord meetinghouse, where, less than a week ago, the Provincial Congress had been in session. He rode to the home of the thirty-year-old Acton gunsmith, Isaac Davis, captain of the militia there. Captain Davis had been awakened by the Concord bell. He was standing in his doorway when Prescott rode up.

A neighbor came on the run while Prescott was dismounting. Davis sent him to ring the Acton bell. The next arrival he sent to the barn to saddle one of his horses and carry the message to Chelmsford.

In a short while twenty members of the Acton minute company were gathered in the Davis kitchen. None of them, including their captain, had ever seen a redcoat, since they had no reason to travel as far as Boston. But they had heard plenty about them from their pastor and the militant elders of the village. They visualized the British regulars as evil monsters sent by their bullying overlords in London to take away the colonists' coveted liberties, force them to accept unfair and ruinous taxes, meddle with their stern religious convictions.

Captain Davis' wife, Hannah, set out breakfast for the men at one end of the long pine table. At the other end, her gunsmith husband and those who hadn't brought along enough ammunition rolled powder and balls into brown paper cartridges. Dr. Prescott, sitting by the fire with his coffee, discovered he was suddenly very weary. Now that the village bells and other riders were spreading the alarm, he decided to go home.

The four countrymen left standing in the road when the patrol rode off with Revere picked up their saddles and went looking for their horses. Brown and Loring and the one-armed peddler, Allen, found theirs grazing by the roadside. The peddler led his back up the road to retrieve his pack under the trees. Brown and Loring started for Lexington, leading their horses and carrying their saddles.

Sanderson decided his horse had run home. He wanted to get back to the Green and tell Parker that the patrol had taken Revere with them. If he took a short cut across the fields, he thought, he might be able to get to the village ahead of the British officers.

He dropped his saddle and gear behind a stone wall and started off, running across the pastures and plowed fields. But when he got to the Green he learned that the patrol had passed some time before, riding at a hard gallop. Those who had seen them said they doubted there was a prisoner riding with them. They were strung out in single file and, so far as it was possible to tell in the night, were all in British uniforms.

There were groups of minutemen standing in front of the meetinghouse, swinging their arms to keep warm. Others were walking around on the parade on the north side of the building. Still others were coming down the roads from the direction of Bedford and Boston.

The taproom at the tavern was crowded. John Buckman was the busiest he had ever been. Sanderson found an extra chair in the parlor and brought it to the fire. He had Buckman fix him a hot rum. After a while he saw Solomon Brown come in, and Jonathan Loring. Captain Parker was in and out, the young drummer, William Diamond, tagging at his heels.

The talk was loud around him. Most of the villagers, he gathered, believed that it was all a false alarm and Parker should let them go home. Who was this Boston fellow, Revere, anyway? Did he really know the British were marching this way? It would soon be daylight and time to get to work in their fields and shops. Others argued just as strongly that they had to wait. Only one of Parker's scouts had come back so far, they pointed out. Another might arrive at any minute and confirm the Revere fellow's alarm.

Sanderson tried to keep his eyes on the men who were talking. But the air was heavy with smoke and the pungent smells of simmering beer and rum, and he had had a hard day. The voices kept fading away, the faces blurring. He was soon hard asleep.

He was awakened at dawn by a sudden scuffling of boots on the plank floor and the staccato beating of young Diamond's drum outside on the Green.

TEN

It was after midnight when the last boatload of British regulars waded ashore across the Charles River from Boston Common.

Lieutenant John Barker, the carping young subaltern of the fashionable 4th Regiment, the King's Own, had been in the first group across. The tide was in and the boats grounded far off shore. The troops in their spick-and-span scarlet and white uniforms had to jump overboard and wade through the cold surf and muck. Every time Barker moved, the sea water in his boots oozed between his toes. He looked at the men huddled in the marsh grass around him. The order had been to travel light, so they had had to leave their greatcoats behind. The chattering of their teeth sounded like a weird chorus of castanets.

The men were all assembled, and still the order to march did not come. All Barker knew was that they were going on an expedition. He had no idea what its destination might be. He saw the boats pull away again. After a long wait in the moonlit swamp, the boats returned, loaded with provisions.

Most of the troops had filled their haversacks with bread and cold meat before leaving their barracks. The new provisions were dutifully passed around, and the men, having no place to store them, tossed them away.

It was two o'clock by Barker's watch when the column finally got under way. They had to wade across a wide ford, and the water came up to their waists. They reassembled on the West Cambridge Road.

Smartly caparisoned from the hips up, drenched and muddy from there down, each stood in his own widening puddle of brine. They were a grotesque spectacle, Barker realized, but he was too cold and miserable by now to see any humor in it.

For the first three miles of the march through the moonlit countryside it appeared that General Gage had achieved his aim of secrecy by sending the detachment across the river into thinly settled farmland instead of over either of the established routes out of the city.

The road wound between low, tree-topped hills, past long stone fences twisting up the slopes, over log-bridged creeks. Occasionally a horse grazing in a pasture lifted its head to watch the army tramp past, a cow stared, solemnly chewing her cud, the dark windows of a farmhouse glinted in the cold moonlight.

Now they were approaching the village of Menotomy, a long street of houses half-way to Lexington.

Lieutenant William Sutherland, of the 38th, who had waited until he got across the river before presenting himself as a volunteer so he couldn't be turned down, was in the van with the light infantry. Eager for excitement, he had persuaded Major Pitcairn to assign him to scout duty in advance of the column. He was walking with a local Tory who had come along as guide.

Lieutenant Adair of the marines was a few strides ahead of them. He yelled, "Here come two fellows riding express to alarm the country!"

The provincials, mounted on shaggy farm horses, galloped out of a side road. As they wheeled their mounts, Sutherland and the guide sprinted up to them and grabbed the bridles. Sutherland ordered them to dismount. He backed them against a tree with his sword and held them there until Major Pitcairn came up with the infantry.

In the center of Menotomy, Pitcairn sent a patrol to search the Black Horse Tavern. The Tory guide had told him that the Provincial Committee of Safety had met there the day before and some of the members might be spending the night. The patrol reported back that three beds upstairs had been recently slept in, were in fact still warm. But they had found nobody on the premises except the innkeeper, Mr. Wetherby, and his wife.*

Now they were in open country again. One of the scouts was mounted and had ridden some distance ahead. He came back on

* See Notes, page 242.

the gallop. He told Sutherland and his companions that alarm guns were being fired up the road. Sutherland, too, could now hear the shots in the distance. It was between three and four o'clock, "a very unusual time for firing," he thought.

A rumble of hoofbeats, faint and far away at first, swelled in volume, and down the road toward them in full gallop came a group of horsemen. It was Major Mitchell and the patrol that had captured and released Paul Revere and the four countrymen beyond Lexington.

Mitchell pulled up before his friend, Sutherland. The entire country was alarmed, he said. They had had to gallop for their lives. He was sorry he had had to let his rebel prize, Revere, go, but it was either that or give up all hope of getting through to alert the detachment.

Farther along, another provincial dashed out of a side road. Sutherland and Adair called to him to halt, but he galloped away up the road. Surgeon's Mate Simms of the 43rd was on horseback and took out after him. They disappeared up the road. After a while, Simms came back, leading the horse and rider.

A sulky came from the direction of Lexington. Sutherland stopped the driver and found him "a very genteel man." He didn't appear surprised to see the troops in the road. He told Sutherland in a quiet, earnest voice that there were six hundred armed provincials assembled and waiting for them at Lexington. Sutherland waited with him until Pitcairn came up with the head of the column, and had him repeat his story. The man was relieved of his sulky and Lieutenant Adair climbed in and trotted ahead of the column.

Sutherland, still afoot, rejoined the advance scouts. He was passing a country crossroad and saw a provincial coming down it on the gallop. He stepped into the surprised rider's path and, grabbing the bridle rein, dragged him to a stop.

The tall young officer was having the best time he'd had in months. He turned his prisoner over to the infantry. The Tory guide told him he thought he had made a prize catch this time. He couldn't exactly place the man but he was sure he had seen him at sessions of the Provincial Congress.

By now Sutherland's legs were getting weary. He mounted one

of the captured horses. The first grayness of dawn was lightening
the sky behind the column. With Lieutenant Adair trailing him
in the sulky, he rode far ahead of the light infantry. They met a
man with a wagonload of wood. They asked him if he had come
from Lexington.

He said, "I came through there."

"Is everything quiet?" Sutherland asked.

The man thought that over, chewing his cud. He spat expertly
into the weeds at the roadside.

"I would hardly say so," he answered. "There are a good thousand men in arms waiting to fight you."

Sutherland left him with another member of the patrol and
rode to the crest of a hill. In the brightening dawn, he could see
a dark cluster of buildings far across the fields. That would be
the center of Lexington, he decided. There were men moving
down the roads leading to it. Most of them were afoot.

Coming back down the slope, he overtook a provincial armed
with a musket and bayonet. Sutherland said, "I mett him in the
Teeth." This time the adventurous young officer almost dared
too far. The provincial—he was a Lexington farmer named Benjamin Wellington—faced about with his gun at the ready as
Sutherland waved his pistol and rode at him. He showed no in-
clination to yield up his weapon. For a moment they confronted
each other. Then the sulky came up and Adair jumped out. He
held his gun on Wellington while Sutherland dismounted and
disarmed him.

Going back down the road with their prisoner, they discovered
that the head of the column had halted. Pitcairn's fast-moving
light infantry had gotten some distance ahead of Colonel Smith
and the grenadiers. After questioning the "genteel man" in the
sulky, Pitcairn had decided to wait for the rest of the detachment
to come up. He rode back and conferred with Smith.

The colonel was a fat man, deliberate and slow-moving. He sat
his heavy charger digesting the information Pitcairn brought
him. He had been hearing the alarm bells, he said. He had already sent back a messenger on a good horse to inform General
Gage there might be trouble ahead and he had better send out
the re-enforcements. Purely a precaution, he said. These rustics

were hardly capable of any serious interference. But since a sizable number of them appeared to be collecting in Lexington, it might be well for Pitcairn to send the infantry ahead to scare them away. In fact, he'd better detach six companies, Smith said, and press on to Concord.

Back with the head of the column, Pitcairn questioned briefly the armed farmer Sutherland and Adair had brought in. Wellington answered with candor that he had heard the alarm bell and had been on his way to join the militia on the Green. He didn't know how many were assembled since he hadn't yet been there. He was so straightforward that Pitcairn told him they had to keep his weapon but would release him if he gave his word he would go back home. Wellington promised stoutly and strolled off across the fields.

Major Pitcairn put the column into motion.

In the front rank as it swung into the outskirts of Lexington was Ensign Jeremy Lister, the young volunteer who had had a hard time back on the Common persuading Colonel Smith to let him go along. He was afoot and, like the men marching beside him, anything but soldierly smart since they had waded across the Cambridge ford.

The two and a half hour march in the chill April night hadn't dried the sea water out of his breeches. His boots were still sodden. The wind had risen and whipped, cold and penetrating, at his back.

In the first light of the dawn, the gray faces of the regulars reflected his own discomfort. By their sullen looks he surmised that the increasingly frequent firing of alarm guns around them was leaving its mark on their dispositions.

Now, so close by that some of the men flinched, a gun blasted; then several more. Lister saw Major Pitcairn gallop up and speak with Sutherland and the other mounted officers in the van.

The column halted. The order to load snapped down the line. With drill-ground precision, the infantrymen pulled paper cartridges out of their cartouche boxes, bit off the ends, filled the pan and closed it, dropped the rest of the black powder and the ball down their musket barrels, the cartridge paper after it, tapped it home with their ramrods. Guns shouldered, they resumed their march, on the double.

Distantly, Lister heard a drum rattle the call to arms.

Now they were in sight of the Green and the triple-rowed windows of the oblong weathered meetinghouse. The road forked around it. On the right of the meetinghouse and slightly behind it, Lister saw a double line of armed countrymen assembling, some sixty or seventy, with their flintlocks poised at the ready.

Except for the villager who had not ridden far enough, the men sent out by Captain Parker during the night to scout the road from Boston had been swallowed by Pitcairn's advance patrol. The major's method was simple. Two light infantrymen walked far ahead of the patrol. They stayed close to the fences beside the road. When a rider approached, they dodged out of sight and let him pass.

If, on coming in view of the patrol, the provincial tried to double back, they stepped into his path, muskets leveled.

So it wasn't until Thaddeus Bowman's high-strung horse outsmarted the advance scouts, a mile beyond Lexington, that a rider got back to the Green with the news that the British were actually on their way.

Bowman's mount spotted the scarlet uniform of one of the advance scouts on the roadside ahead of him before either of the soldiers saw him. The horse stopped and snorted, ears pointed. Bowman urged him on. The horse shied backward. Bowman dug him with his spurs. The horse still refused to go forward. It was a battle of wills, and Bowman's horse was holding his own.

Then Bowman caught a glint of musket steel as the scout edged closer. At the same time, far beyond in the pale predawn light, he saw the advancing column.

He spun his horse and gave him full rein.

Captain Parker was standing with a group of militiamen beside the meetinghouse. Bowman dismounted on the run and shouted that the regulars were "just up the rocks!" They would be here any minute!

Parker turned to the drummer boy, Diamond, told him to

sound the call to arms. As the drumbeat pierced the village stillness, Benjamin Wellington came running out of the adjoining
field. He was out of breath and it took a moment for Parker to
realize that he was telling him the same news as Bowman had.

Wellington was a devout churchman and it bothered him that
his neighbors might think he had broken his oath to the British
officer who had released him. He explained, although Parker had
more important things to think about now and wasn't listening,
that he actually was bound for home; he had merely stopped by
the Green on his way there.

The doors of Buckman's Tavern and the houses around the
Green had opened to the sound of Diamond's drum and the
minutemen of Lexington were coming on the run. Those who
lived farthest away fired their flintlocks to spread the alarm as
they ran.

Parker ordered Sergeant Monroe to form the men in two ranks
on the parade to the north and rear of the meetinghouse. The
British column, if it took the road to Concord, would pass the
south side of the building and its detached belfry tower.

As the men were falling in, twenty-three-year-old Sylvanus
Wood arrived from his home three miles up the road toward
Woburn. The Lexington bell and the alarm guns had awakened
him. He had grabbed his father's musket and powder horn and
started out. Seeing a light in his neighbor's house, he had gone in
and waited for young Robert Douglass to finish dressing and
come with him.

Captain Parker told them they could join the company on the
Green if they wanted to. Wood and Douglass got into line. Since
there wasn't as yet any sign of the British, Wood stepped out of
formation and walked from one end of the ranks to the other,
counting the men. He counted thirty-eight, but more were still
coming in.

The tavernkeeper, John Buckman, although a member of the
Lexington minute company, was not in the lineup. With the prospect of trouble ahead, he had to lock the "bar" and the cellar
door. He had been busy most of the night serving his neighbors.
The mugs and tankards had to be rinsed and hung away, the
pitchers and pans used to make the flip washed, the tables pushed

back into place. After the excitement was over outside, the men would probably be back for a last drink before the long walk home.*

By now the Hancock chaise was in the northern outskirts of the village on its way to the home of the widow Jones. Hancock, with a sudden flare of annoyance, remembered his trunk. It was filled with valuable secret papers, he said, grabbing at the reins in Sam Adams' hands. They pertained to the recent proceedings of the Provincial Congress and he intended to take them to Philadelphia with him. He had had the trunk especially made to fit onto the back of the chaise. He asked Lowell where it was.

Lowell said it was under one of the windows in the big third-floor room at Buckman's Tavern, where he was staying. He supposed he had better go back and get it.

He most certainly should, Hancock agreed sternly, and hide it in the barn-loft at the parsonage.

Paul Revere said he would go with Lowell and help him carry it. They got out and Adams turned the chaise into a cartway that led up the slope into a woods.

It was almost four-thirty.

Revere and Lowell cut across the fields and entered the Green from the north just as Sergeant Monroe was mustering the Lexington minutemen on the parade. They crossed the road and climbed to the upstairs room at the tavern. As Revere was helping Lowell lift the trunk from in front of the window, he looked out and saw the head of the British column up the Boston Road.

Lugging the heavy, metal-bound trunk between them, they hurried down the stairs and across the Green again. They had to pass through the lines of minutemen. Revere estimated there were between fifty and sixty by then. Captain Parker was addressing them. Revere heard him say, "Let the troops pass by, and don't molest them without they begin first."

* See Notes, page 242.

BOOK TWO

ELEVEN

A HALF MILE TO THE EAST OF THE GREEN THE ROAD SLOPED OUT OF
the hills onto a level plain. Neat stone walls stretched along
the sides, the houses and village shops set close behind them.

Lieutenant Sutherland rode ahead of the column with a foot
patrol of eight men and a sergeant. The musket shots were more
frequent now, coming from behind the distant stone walls and
woods on both sides. But since he heard no "Hissing of Balls,"
Sutherland decided they were merely to warn the village that
the regulars were arriving. He looked apprehensively at the fast-
marching infantrymen. With their muskets loaded, he realized,
the invisible rebel firing could put them in a dangerous mood.

As he arrived within gun range of the meetinghouse, Sutherland saw a provincial dart behind the stone wall near the road
fork on the right and level his musket. For a startled moment he
looked down the barrel. There was a white flare at the firelock,
a whisp of smoke. The gun had flashed in the pan!

Sutherland wheeled his horse and galloped back to the column,
shouting to Lieutenant Adair as he passed him that one of the
rebels had fired on him. He charged up to Pitcairn, riding with
a group of officers, and told him.

The head of the column, still moving on the double, was now
at the road fork. The infantrymen saw the double line of militia,
their muskets poised, facing them to the right and rear of the
meetinghouse. They broke into a run and charged onto the
Green.

Major Pitcairn came up at a hard gallop, surrounded by the
other officers—Major Mitchell, Captains Lumm and Cochrane,
Lieutenants Sutherland and Barker. As they cleared the road,

Sutherland thought he saw three gun flashes from the corner of
the house on the right, the Buckman Tavern. The cavalcade raced
around the left side of the meetinghouse and pulled up between
the charging regulars and the disintegrating ranks of the provincial militia.

Sutherland heard Major Pitcairn shout to his troops:

"Soldiers, don't fire! Keep your ranks!"

He added, with a swing of his sword: "Form and surround
them!"

The provincials were backing away. Some were running.
Others were climbing over the stone wall that ran along the
right of the Green.

"Then," said Sutherland, "some of the Villains who got over
the wall fired at us."

A few of the regulars leveled their flintlocks and discharged
them. In a moment there was a heavy blast of gunfire from the
front ranks of the column.

Lieutenant Barker's sense of discipline was outraged. The
men had fired against orders! He saw Pitcairn swing his sword
down in a desperate attempt to stop the firing. Barker's horse
shied away as Sutherland's, on his right flank, reared on his hind
legs and screamed with gun-fright. He marveled that Sutherland
managed to keep his seat.

The horse gallowed across the Green and up the Bedford road
with Sutherland sawing vainly at the reins. He rode a quarter
mile before he could bring the frightened animal under control.
As he galloped back he saw Colonel Smith arriving at the head
of the grenadiers. There was still fitful firing on the Green. The
infantry appeared completely out of hand.

Colonel Smith called to him: "Can you find a drummer?"

Sutherland found one. Smith told him to beat "To Arms!"

The firing died away.

A private named Johnson in Ensign Lister's company had been
wounded in the leg. Major Pitcairn's horse had two red bullet
streaks on its flanks.

Eight provincials lay dead on the Green.

A cloud of thick white smoke covered the six infantry companies, blotting out everything but the occasional head of an officer's rearing horse. There had been a scatter of shots from the meetinghouse. The twitching body of a provincial lay in the doorway. An officer called to Colonel Smith that he had seen musket flashes from the upstairs windows of the tavern across the road.

Smith saw a sergeant and a group of yelling regulars running toward the meetinghouse. Another squad was starting for the tavern. He shouted to his officers to head them and bring them back.

He had arrived on the scene late and did not know what had triggered the firing. But it could well have been some irresponsible person, he realized. He knew that fleeing provincials had taken refuge in the meetinghouse and the tavern; probably, too, in the other houses close to the Green. If the raging troops were allowed to go in after "these deluded people," they would bayonet every last one to death. He was not going to let that happen.

Major Pitcairn and his officers were riding among the infantrymen, swinging their swords and shouting them back into formation. Barker, riding beside him, could see the blazing anger in the major's eyes. Pitcairn was one of the few officers in General Gage's top command that the cynical young lieutenant genuinely respected. Knowing the marine commander's tough devotion to discipline, he felt sorry for him now, and furious at the infantrymen for having gotten out of hand. Pitcairn's marines, he knew, would never have done anything like this to him.

Twenty minutes after the troops had charged onto the Green, Pitcairn had them back on the road and falling in at the head of the column again. Colonel Smith rode up. The two officers sat their horses, staring at the sullen-faced soldiers. Sutherland saw Major Pitcairn shake his head. His face was still flushed, his eyes smoldering. Pitcairn said he deeply regretted "the too great warmth of the soldiers." Smith nodded sternly.

"I shall recommend a more steady conduct to them for the future," he said.

The sun was a red ball balanced on the eastern skyline. Great white clouds roamed leisurely overhead. The east wind was heavy with the smells of new leaves and freshly-turned fields. The grass on the roadsides glinted with dew. The meetinghouse blocked off the parade ground with its windrow of dead.

Colonel Smith signaled with his hand. The column started off for Concord.

Paul Revere and young Lowell, with Hancock's trunk between them, were walking across a field toward the back yard of the parsonage when the head of the British column arrived in front of the meetinghouse. Revere heard a shot and looked back. He saw the infantrymen running across the road, shouting. There was a scatter of shots, then what sounded like a volley.

A house beside the Green blocked their view of the militiamen on the parade. They hurried on with the trunk. When they had it safely hidden under the hay in the barn loft, they went into the house.

Aunt Lydia was leaning out of a front window, trying to see what was going on down the road. A spent bullet sang by her head and plopped against the barn.

She asked, "What was that?"

"A musket ball," Lowell told her.

Aunt Lydia decided it was high time to take Dolly and herself away from there. She told Lowell to have the carriage brought around.

"And don't forget," she said, "to tell the coachman to get Mr. Hancock's salmon out of the icehouse and put it under the seat. He'll be famished by the time we join him."

Revere walked to the stable with Lowell. He said he guessed it was time he got back to Cambridge. He would probably be needed. He was going to see about borrowing a horse. Lowell said he'd better rejoin Hancock and let him know that the trunk was safe.

Standing on a rock on the wooded hillside where he was waiting with Hancock, Sam Adams heard the sounds of gunfire.

"Oh, what a glorious morning is this!" he said.

John Hancock was surprised. In all the years that he had

known Sam, he had never before heard him comment on the weather.

Thomas Willard could not have found a better spot from which to see what happened that morning at Lexington if he had had the entire Green to pick from.

Willard was visiting in the home of Daniel Harrington, the village blacksmith and clerk of Parker's company of minutemen. The house stood on the north side of the Green, facing the rear of the meetinghouse. It was a large, two-story house. It had to be: Daniel and his wife, Anna, had seven children and the eighth was on the way.

Willard was looking out an upstairs window when the British troops arrived. There had been little sleep for any of the family that night. The rumors of a British patrol on the road had kept them all up later than usual. Then, some time after one o'clock, Daniel and his fifteen-year-old son, Levi, who shared with young Diamond the job of drummer for the company, had gotten out of bed in response to the alarm bell and had lined up with the other minutemen on the parade.

After two hours, they had come home, pulled off their boots by the fire and warmed the stiffness out of their hands before climbing back into bed.

At four-thirty, Diamond's drum, rattling the call to arms, awoke the family again. Daniel took his flintlock out of the chimney corner, sifted a fresh priming charge into the pan and hurried out with Levi.

Willard, standing at his upstairs window, watched the two run across the Green. The light was paling in the east. Traces of rose and pink stained the horizon. A sharp wind was sweeping the clouds up the sky. He could see the shadowy figures of neighbors scurrying to the parade: Robert Monroe, Mrs. Harrington's father, from his house across the way; Daniel's cousin, Jonathan Harrington, thirty-one, who lived in the farmhouse next door with his wife, Ruth, and eight-year-old son.

The company was falling into line, some sixty-odd villagers and farmers, Sergeant Monroe, at their head, shouting commands; Captain Parker a few paces to the side, waving with his long arms to the stragglers to hurry.

They were still coming in, from the Bedford road on the left, across the fields, over the stone fences, out of the Concord Road across the way, running with big, clumsy strides in their field shoes, their muskets swinging at their sides, bobbing on their shoulders.

The ones who belonged to the minute company stepped quickly into their places. The few others who did not filed off to the sides. Some who weren't armed ran into the meetinghouse to grab a musket and ammunition from the village arsenal in the gallery.

The light was brightening rapidly now. Sunrise was a half hour away.

Coming down the Boston road, a red swath between the brown and green fields, Willard saw the quick-stepping British regulars. He thought there were at least four hundred of them. They were marching four abreast. As the head of the column reached the fork in front of the meetinghouse they came in sight of the double line of provincials on the Green.

Willard saw an officer with the lead company wave his arm and shout something. Whether it was a sergeant or a commissioned officer he couldn't tell. The men broke into a run, around the meetinghouse and onto the Green. They ran to within eight or nine rods of the minutemen, who, on Captain Parker's order to "Disperse, men!" were falling back and breaking up.

Willard saw several officers on foot swing their arms at the militia and huzza. The regulars huzzaed after them. He saw an officer on horseback ride toward the militia and shout:

"Lay down your arms, damn you! Why don't you lay down your arms?"

Until now, Willard was sure he had not heard a shot. The minutemen were filing off in orderly fashion to the right and left.

Now a few scattered guns flared among the regulars. But nobody appeared to be hurt.

Mrs. Harrington's father, Robert Monroe, a French-and-Indian-War veteran who had been the standard-bearer of his company at the capture of Louisburg, was still in his place near the center of the line.

Jonas Parker, who had often said he never would run from a redcoat, was stubbornly standing his ground.

Isaac Muzzey stood near him.

Jonathan Harrington, from the house next door, was still at the left end of the disappearing line, a few rods from his home.

Now, suddenly, a slash of flame ripped from one end to the other of the foremost British platoon. A cloud of smoke hung for a moment above the row of muskets, blotting out the faces of the men who had fired.

The erect line of militiamen was gone. Some were running off to the sides. Some were on their knees, some writhing on the ground. A few were stretched out and still.

Willard saw that Robert Monroe was among those on the ground, and thought with a spasm of horror of Monroe's daughter with her brood of children downstairs.

Isaac Muzzey was doubled up where he had stood, and now slowly, like a man hunting a comfortable spot for his body, he stretched out and lay still.

Another of the Harrington clan, Caleb, had just come running out of the side door of the meetinghouse, where he had gone to replenish his supply of powder, when the British volleyed. He fell as if he had been pushed down.

Samuel Hadley and John Brown had already left the line. The bullets struck them as they were walking away, slowly bent them over onto their knees.

Asahel Porter was one of the scouts who had been sent out earlier by Captain Parker and who had been captured by the British. Willard saw him break out of the massed regulars and run toward the far end of the line of militia. He stumbled as the guns blazed, fell headlong, tried to get up and slowly sank back.

Willard saw Jonas Parker drop his musket and clutch his knee in sudden pain. Then, crouching on his good knee, Parker slowly set his hat on the ground and emptied the ammunition from his coat pockets into it. As he reached over and picked up his musket, one of the regulars, who were now running and firing in all directions, stabbed him down with his bayonet.

But the death of Jonathan Harrington from next door was the one that wrenched Willard the hardest.

Jonathan Harrington fell with the blast of guns. He got back onto his feet slowly and looked with an expression of blank surprise at the spurt of blood coming out of his chest. He turned and, still with the unbelieving look in his face, started walking toward his farmhouse, across the road from the parade.

His knees bent and he fell at the roadside. He raised himself on his hands and started to crawl across the road as his wife came screaming out of their doorway.

Harrington reached a hand out to her, pulled himself with painful slowness across a wagon rut, and collapsed as she knelt over him.

John Robbins was in the front rank of the minutemen. He saw the redcoats first when they were sixty or seventy yards away.

He stood his ground as they charged across the Green, huzzaing. The group of officers came at a gallop around the south side of the meetinghouse and pulled up in front of the militia. The officer in the lead yelled:

"Throw down your arms, ye villains, ye rebels!"

He waved his sword, said Robbins, and shouted:

"Fire! By God, fire!"

For an awful moment, Robbins stared at the row of black muzzles of the British flintlocks. Then a streak of red flame spit from them.

"Being wounded," he said, "I fell."

He believed "Captain Parker's men had not then fired a shot."

Thomas Fessender, a spectator, was in a pasture adjoining the meetinghouse. Leaning on the rail fence, he watched the British charge across the Green.

He saw a mounted officer gallop between the regulars and the militia and heard him yell, "Disperse, you rebels, immediately!"

"On which," Fessender said, "he brandished his sword over his head three times. Meanwhile, a second officer about two rods behind him fired a pistol. The other pointed his sword down towards the militia. The regulars fired a volley."

Elijah Sanderson, one of the three Lexington men who had

been captured and released earlier in the night by Major Mitchell's patrol, had fallen into line with the other minutemen. As the British column rounded the meetinghouse, he heard Captain Parker shout to the militia to disperse. He was hurrying off the parade when he heard, in the confusion of galloping horses and charging regulars, one of the British, "which I took to be an officer," yell, "Damn them! We will have them!"

"Immediately the regulars shouted aloud," he said, "run and fired on the Lexington Company."

Solomon Brown, who had been picked up with Sanderson by the Mitchell patrol, was near him in the line of minutemen and among those who got off the Green as the firing started. Brown jumped a stone wall into the adjoining cow pasture, knelt and leveled his musket. He fired into the midst of the foremost platoon.

Corporal John Monroe, in the militia line, thought for a moment that the regulars were firing nothing but powder.

But Ebenezer Monroe, next to him, said, "No. Ball."

Ebenezer had been hit in the arm. He added, with New England pungency, "I'll give them the guts of my gun!"

"We both took aim at the main body," Corporal Monroe said, "but the smoke prevented our seeing anything but the heads of some of their horses."

As the smoke lifted and the regulars broke out of line and charged with their bayonets, the Monroe cousins left on the run. Young Ebenezer stopped under a tree at the far end of the Green. Blood was dripping off his arm, and he decided he had better do something about it. He took off his coat and rolled back his sleeve. Although it was bleeding badly, he saw it was only a flesh wound. He guessed he'd live.

With his jackknife he tore two strips off the tail of his shirt and wrapped one of them around the wound. Holding an end of the other strip in his teeth, he wound it around the bandage and knotted it. He saw that the officers were driving the redcoats back into formation. He heard the British drumbeat, and for a moment it was so still he could hear himself panting. Then the officers spurred their horses again, shouted commands. The regulars were moving back to the road.

Six of his slain neighbors lay in a ragged line on the parade. In front of the Jonathan Harrington house he could see Jonathan's young wife, Ruth, sitting in the roadway with her dead husband's head in her lap, calling his name.

A wild fury burned in Ebenezer's eyes as he watched the scarlet and white column fall in and step off briskly up the Concord Road, the sunlight sparkling on their slanted bayonets. He shook his good fist at them.

"God-damned lobsterbacks!" he yelled.

Now the women and children were coming out of the houses and helping the wounded home and weeping over the dead. Daniel Harrington's wife and children knelt around the body of Mrs. Harrington's father, Robert Monroe.

Monroe had fallen near the center of the line. Close to him lay the bodies of Jonas Parker, his checkered shirt slashed open and blood-soaked from the bayonet, and Isaac Muzzy, and, off to the sides, Samuel Hadley and John Brown. Caleb Harrington was sprawled before the doorway of the meetinghouse. Asahel Porter, of Woburn, who had been captured by the British and shot when he tried to escape, lay a few yards in front of the others.

Some of the mourners hovered over one body, then ran weeping to another. In the closely-related little farm community, almost every one of the dead was linked by blood or marriage to others.

Robert Monroe had had two sons and two sons-in-law with him in the line. Isaac Muzzy's was one of the oldest families in Lexington. One of his ancestors, listed as "nibor Muzzy," had in 1711 deeded the Green to the village "for the common use of all." The two slain Harringtons were kin. Jonas Parker was an elder cousin of Captain John Parker.

Most of the minutemen had retreated across a swamp to the high ground north of the Green. The rest had fled up the Bedford Road. Soon, Captain Parker had them assembled again. They returned to the Green and carried the dead into the meetinghouse. Then they stepped back into formation on the parade.

Silent and hard-faced, they responded to the brisk tap of William Diamond's drum, shouldered their flintlocks and marched off toward Concord.

The meetinghouse bell was ringing again; a slow, measured toll now, the toll for the dead.

The Reverend Jonas Clark arrived from the parsonage with his wife and his twelve-year-old daughter, Elizabeth, carrying the baby, Sally. While the white-haired pastor and his wife tried to comfort the widows and children of the dead, Elizabeth tagged along behind them, her six-months-old sister on her hip. She watched the elders of the village nail wide pine planks into coffins and lay the dead in them while her father prayed over them.

When they were all ready, she followed the little procession to the back of the Green, where other old men and their young grandsons had dug a long common grave. The eight coffins were lowered and the ground stomped down and covered with last year's leaves so the British would not find the spot if they returned.

John Hancock and Sam Adams had arrived at the widow Jones's house, four miles from Lexington. Aunt Lydia and Dolly joined them there. Hancock and Adams hadn't had anything to eat since the night before. For once, even Adams admitted he was interested in food.

The fresh salmon was unwrapped and Mrs. Jones outdid herself preparing dinner for her distinguished guests.

They had sat down to the table and the Reverend William Marett, the new Woburn minister who was boarding with Mrs. Jones, had bowed his head to offer grace. The door flew open and a man from down the Lexington Road ran in, red-faced and out of breath.

"My wife, I fear, is by this time in eternity!" he shouted. He stared at Adams and Hancock. "And as to you, you had better look out for yourselves, for the enemy will soon be at your heels!"

The fine baked salmon was forgotten. Pastor Marett ran out the back door with Adams and Hancock and across the fields to the home of Amos Wyman on the road to Billerica. The coachman hurriedly hitched the horses back into Aunt Lydia's gilded carriage and drove it up a back lane into the woods.

Adams and Hancock found the Wyman home crowded with

the women and children of the neighborhood militia who had
gone off to pursue the British.

When Mrs. Wyman learned that her two new guests had had
to leave their dinner untouched, she took a wooden tray off the
shelf and fed them. It was all she had: a cut of boiled salt pork,
leftover potatoes and a loaf of black bread. But by now even
Hancock was hungry enough to eat it.

TWELVE

IN CONCORD, DR. PRESCOTT'S SHOUTED "THE BRITISH ARE ON THE march!" had started a swift chain reaction. Amos Melven, who was on all-night guard duty in front of the town house, fired his musket into the air as an alarm signal and ran to the meeting-house at the south-eastern end of the Common. He yanked on the heavy bell rope with a fury that soon brought rivulets of sweat running down his face.

The Reverend William Emerson, Concord's stormy young pastor, was a light sleeper. Although he lived almost a mile north of the Common, he was among the first on hand, his musket cradled in his arm. The cartouche box hanging from his husky shoulder was packed with ammunition. Between drafting his sermons and counseling his Congregational flock, he had found plenty of time to mold bullets and roll cartridges. Preaching to a gathering of the militia companies of Concord, Lincoln and Acton, a few weeks before, he had taken as his text: "And behold God Himself is with us for our captain, and His priests with sounding trumpets to cry alarm against you."

Reuben Brown, the harness maker, whose shop and house were up the Lexington Road from the meetinghouse, beat the minister to the Common by a few minutes. John Buttrick, major of the minutemen, joined them. Others came from all directions, across the freshly-plowed fields, leaping the stone walls up the ridge, out of the houses around the Common.

Reuben Brown had a fast horse. Major Buttrick told him to ride to Lexington and bring back more detailed information. Brown got within sight of the Lexington Green. He saw the minutemen lined up behind the meetinghouse and the British

regulars coming toward them on the run. He heard a scatter of
shots and then saw the long slash of flame and heard the roar of
many muskets. He had seen enough. He turned his horse and
galloped back to Concord.

Major Buttrick listened to his story and said, "Were the regulars firing ball?"

"I do not know," Brown answered, "but I think it probable."

Galloping in now on their farm horses and marching afoot,
first from Lincoln on the Lexington Road and then from Acton
to the west, came more minutemen and, behind them, the older
members of the militia and the half-grown boys—the alarm company men.

Amos Barrett, twenty-three-year-old nephew of the colonel in
over-all command, was one of the privates in the Concord minute
company. It was three o'clock when the alarm bell awakened
him. When he got into town his company was already assembled
on the Common. While they waited for the scout, Reuben Brown,
to come back, the company from Lincoln arrived. Then Captain
Isaac Davis and his men came down the road from Acton.

"Before sunrise," Amos Barrett said, "there was a hundred and
fifty of us and more."

They had Reuben Brown's report now that the British detachment had fired on the Lexington militia. But they did not know
that eight of their compatriots had been killed by the indignant
regulars.

The road from Lexington entered Concord along the crest of
a steep, flat-topped ridge that extended from Meriam's Corner,
a mile out, past the center of the town. Approaching the Common, the road dropped along the foot of the slope. The parish
meetinghouse, the taverns, the town house, the homes and shops
around the Common were on the level plain beside the ridge. On
the summit, high above the meetinghouse, stood the Liberty Pole,
the colonial pine-tree flag of liberty whipping at the top.

Major Buttrick had the drummer tap "To Arms." The older
men and boys climbed the ridge and posted themselves around
the Liberty Pole. The minutemen marched toward Lexington to
reconnoiter. As they approached Meriam's Corner they saw the
scarlet column coming up the road. They waited until the Brit-

ish were a hundred yards from them, then their commander, Captain David Brown, ordered them to about-face and march back into the village.

The British drums and fifes were playing "The White Cockade." Captain Brown called to his drummer and fifer to play the same tune.

"We had grand Museck," said Amos Barrett.

The returning minutemen and the alarm company that had gathered around the Liberty Pole moved back along the ridge to the high ground fronting the Common. Joseph Hosmer, the adjutant, formed them into squads, the minute companies on the right and the alarm companies on the left.

Pastor Emerson strode in front of them.

"Let us stand our ground!" he shouted. "If we die, let us die here!"

But the men listened to Colonel Eleazer Brooks of Lincoln, a man of more years and solid judgment. He pointed out that the militia had been organized purely "for defense" by the Provincial Congress and that they had no authority to ask for trouble by making a stand in the invaders' path. Besides, he said, they were greatly outnumbered. He concluded: "No! It will not do for us to begin the war!"

As the British, in two columns—the grenadiers along the road, the light infantry flanking them on the ridge—came into the town to the swinging rhythm of "The White Cockade," the colonists retreated up the road to the wooden bridge that crossed the little Concord River a mile north of the town. They marched over it and across the swampland and meadows to Punkatasset Hill, a mile farther north.

On the way, Mr. Emerson and his neighbor, Elisha Jones, dropped out of the ranks to go to their homes and see to their families. If trouble came, their houses would be along its path. Emerson's house adjoined the North Bridge. Jones's house was across the road.

Jones had another reason for wanting to watch his home. Fifty-five barrels of cured beef and seventeen thousand pounds of salt fish from the provincial stores were now stacked in his cellar and wagon shed.

A number of other militiamen had already been dropped off, members of the alarm company, to take post on the roads leading in from Acton, Bedford, Lincoln, Sudbury, Carlisle, Chelmsford, Natick, and direct the minutemen to the gathering spot on Punkatasset Hill as they arrived in response to the alarm bells.

The Concord bell had been silenced by the arrival of the red-coats. But Acton's had taken up the call and sent it along, and Bedford's and Sudbury's. Like a tonal bucket brigade, the alarm spread across the hills and fields: to Billerica, Danvers, Lynn, Lowell, Reading, Tewksbury, Dedham, Westford, Watertown. And the bells there passed it on, until Marblehead and Salem knew that the regulars were on the march, and Worcester and Portsmouth; all of Massachusetts.

In faraway Pomfret, Connecticut, plump, white-haired old General Israel Putnam left his plow standing in the furrow and ran to round up his men.

Express riders galloped down the roads from the swinging bells to tell the next village where the alarm originated. So that, as soon as Bedford knew the British were marching on Concord, a rider dashed off to pass the news to Carlisle. As the bell there went into action, a Carlisle rider set off for Chelmsford. From Chelmsford, one rode for Lowell.

On the village commons, the company captains mustered their men. The minister, a midweek bristle of beard on his face, stood before them, many a one of them with his powder horn or car-tridge box hanging at his side, his musket on the grass in front of him, and offered a quick prayer.

Then they were off, the wives and children trailing along be-side them for a while, gradually dropping back to stand in lonely little groups in the dust of the road watching the column till it disappeared around the next bend.

The five-mile road the British had to travel from Lexington to Concord wound in easy curves through deep patches of woods and between long stone fences. Near the Hartwell farmhouse, two miles on their way, Major Mitchell pointed out to his friend, Lieutenant Sutherland, the spot beside a pasture gate where his patrol had seized the four countrymen and "Paul Revierre."

It was unfortunate that the two express riders with Revere had gotten away, Mitchell said. By now, he surmised, another country mob was probably waiting for them in Concord. Well, the regulars would give them a dose of the same medicine they had fed Lexington. These peasant louts could not face up to the king's army.

A shot sounded from the hillside on the right and a spent bullet sang over the advancing column. Another musket spoke from a pasture farther along. Occasionally a horseman was outlined briefly against the morning sky on one of the ridges. Faces stared at them out of the windows of the farmhouses close to the road.

Mostly they were hostile faces, but silently hostile. These people, too, had not yet heard of the massacre at Lexington, the death of men who were more than names to them, to some relatives, to all of them people whose first names they knew as well as their own, whom they had sat at supper with in each others' houses, who had helped them tend a sick cow or horse, shared their fall cider with them.

Now and then a doorway opened and a smiling family watched the long line march past. These were the people known as Tories, the ones "who did not go along with the rebel tommyrot" about British tyranny and oppression.

Colonel Smith, sitting his charge in the middle of the column, saw the preponderance of hostile faces, the horsemen stopping for a moment on the ridge tops and galloping off. He was glad he had sent word back to General Gage before dawn for reenforcements. It looked as if there might be still more bloody work ahead.

But now they were in Concord, and the little band of rustics that had marched out to meet them had meekly retired out of sight. Smith set up headquarters in the Wright Tavern, next to the meetinghouse. Major Pitcairn and the young officers had Amos Wright bring tables and chairs onto the grass beside the road. It was going on seven-thirty and the sun had a warm touch where the wind didn't bite.

Smith ordered his grenadiers to search out and destroy the supplies in the village. He sent a company of light infantry un-

der Captain Mundy Pole to secure the South Bridge, and a larger
detachment under Captain Lawrence Parsons to hold the North
Bridge and destroy the stores at Colonel Barrett's farm, two miles
beyond. Ensign De Bernière, who had spied out the stores for
General Gage a month before, went with Parsons.

Colonel Smith ordered himself a stiff drink. No need to rush
things. It was too bad that the infantry had gotten out of hand,
back there in Lexington, and killed men. But it had probably
taught these provincial scoundrels a lesson that they wouldn't
soon forget.

Innkeeper Wright set a brandy and water in front of Major
Pitcairn and saw him stir it with his finger. He heard Pitcairn
say, "I hope I shall stir the damned Yankee blood so before
night."

The grenadiers were having fair sport ferreting out the provincial supplies. They found two good-sized cannons, twenty-
four-pounders, concealed in the Jones Tavern, around the corner from Wright's. The artillerymen knocked off the trunnions
and drove spikes into the touchholes.

One squad climbed the ridge, cut down the Liberty Pole and
burned it.

Another found several barrels filled with trenchers and wooden
spoons, stacked them on the Common and built a bonfire of them.

Another searching party accidentally set fire to Reuben
Brown's harness shop, and hurriedly put it out.

They hauled five hundred pounds of lead balls out of a shed
and threw them into the millpond beside the Common.

If they had wanted the church silver, they would have had a
hard time finding it. While the officers were having their morning
nip on the lawn at Wright's, one of the women of the village ran
back and forth between the tavern and the meetinghouse next
door, carried the silver under her apron through the back door of
the tavern and submerged it in the soft soap barrel.

Elderly Thomas Barrett, one of the leading citizens and deacon
of the parish, was brought to the tavern and questioned by Colonel Smith's aides. General Gage's high-placed informer had sent
him word from the Provincial Congress meeting in Concord less
than a week ago that there were "Ten Iron Cannon Before the

Town House and two within it. . . . The ammunition for said
Guns within the house.

"Three Guns, 24 Pounders, lodged in the Prison yard with a
Quantity of Cartridges and Provisions.

"A Quantity of Provisions and Ammunition in other Places,
the Principal Deposits are the Houses of Messr Hubbard, near
the Meeting, Butler, Jones the Tailors, near Hubbards, two men
of the name of Bond, and particularly at M Whitneys who lives
on the Right Hand near the Entrance of the Town, at a House
plaistered white, a small yard in Front and a railed Fence. A
large Quantity of Powder and Ball is reported to be deposited in
his store adjoining the House."

The officers wanted to know from Deacon Barrett what had
become of most of those implements of rebellion since then.

From De Bernière they had learned that the deacon's son had
a gun factory back of the Barrett house. Even there the grenadiers
had found no guns.

The deacon stood before them, dignified and defiant, telling
them nothing. One of the officers told him finally he was a rebel
and they guessed they'd shoot him.

Deacon Barrett was unperturbed.

"You may save yourself the trouble," he said, "for I shall soon
die of myself."

They gave up.

"Well, old daddy, you may go in peace."

The search squads had better luck at Ebenezer Hubbard's. In
his storehouse they found sixty barrels of flour that the villagers
hadn't gotten around to carting to a safer place. The grenadiers
knocked down one side of the shed and rolled the barrels across
the road into the millpond. Some of the flour spilled out on the
road. It looked as if there had been a snowfall.

Most of the provincial flour was stored in Timothy Wheeler's
barn. There were also some bags of his own. These he had
stacked in front, with his name printed on them. When the
search party arrived, he let them in willingly.

"Every gill of this is my own," he said blandly, and waved his
hand at the bags concealing the provincial supply. "I am a miller,

sir. Yonder stands my mill. This is my wheat. This is my rye. This is mine."

The officer in charge nodded.

"Well," he said, "we do not injure private property," and politely took his squad away.

Henry Gardner, the provincial treasurer, had hidden "a chest containing some money and other important articles" in a room at the Jones Tavern. As the soldiers came up the stairs, a young Concord woman named Hannah Barns faced them with her back against the door.

"This is my apartment," she said, "and contains my property."

The officer bowed and went on.

Captain Pole, on his way to the South Bridge, was equally taken in by the devout but enterprising prevaricators of the Reverend William Emerson's flock.

Behind a locked door in the house of Amos Wood, the room was piled high with provincial property. When Captain Pole ordered his men to break the door down, Wood pleaded that the terrorized women of the household were hiding in there. Pole countermanded his order and on the way out gave Wood a handful of coins.

"Here is a guinea apiece," he said, "for the female attendants to compensate them for their trouble."

The widow Martha Moulton lived alone next door to the town house. She was seventy-one and not very spry any more. The families in the other houses around the Common had taken the few possessions they could carry and fled to friends or relatives in the country, or to the woods on Punkatasset Hill. Mrs. Moulton was too frail and timid to venture out of her house.

When the British arrived she closed her doors and peeked at them in fluttering terror from behind her drawn blinds. The tall grenadiers with their muskets and razor-edged bayonets looked like monsters out of another world to her. She saw them moving in squads around the Common, going into the shops and into Mr. Wheeler's mill.

When some of them entered her front yard and walked toward the door, she thought her heart would stop. She sat, frozen, in her chair by the fireplace when they knocked. Getting no answer, they pushed the door open and walked in. They were officers, and her eyes fastened with horror on the swords at their sides.

"Oh, there you are," one of them said. "Could you spare us a drink of water?"

Mrs. Moulton was surprised that her legs would carry her. She walked ahead of them into the kitchen and pointed to the wooden bucket on the table by the window.

"It's very fine water, Mother," the one who had spoken in the doorway said as he passed the gourd dipper to a companion. "But there's not enough to go around. Where is the well?"

She pointed a shaking hand at the back window. He handed the bucket to a redcoat who looked like the rest except that he had no sword or epaulets.

"Go fill it."

The young officer looked at Mrs. Moulton.

"I don't suppose you'd have anything like a spot of rum around? Now, would you?"

His voice was gruff but his manner was almost boyish. She noticed the pink in his cheeks, but she was sure he was callously evil. She took the stone jug out of the cupboard and handed it to him.

He held his ear to it and shook it, and fished a silver dollar out of his pocket, dropped it on the table.

"We'll be taking some of your chairs out front," he said. He picked one up and started for the front door. "You might bring out some mugs."

There were only a half dozen men at first, and they made themselves comfortable on the grass. Mrs. Moulton brought them her four crockery mugs and then two from her best pewter. She gathered they were in charge of the men who were searching the village for colonial supplies. From their conversation, as she fluttered in and out of the house in response to their demands for tea, which she didn't have, ("all right then, coffee") for more mugs as other officers arrived, she learned that they had had trouble with the militia in Lexington and that they had been compelled to kill some of them.

A group of soldiers had gone into the town house next door. They rolled out sixteen new gun carriages. More officers were coming up and making themselves comfortable on anything they could find to carry out of the house and sit on. The calls for water were more than she could keep up with. They rode their horses onto the grass and brought hay from her neighbor's barn to feed them. There were "fifty or sixty of them in and out of the house."

The gun carriages had been stacked beside the town house and set afire. She saw the flames soar up and lick at the dry clapboards.

Mrs. Moulton had been praying under her breath. Now, watching the flames ignite the town-house siding, she prayed even harder. She spoke to the officers sitting around her best table on the grass.

"Your men—they are setting the town house on fire! Can't you do something?"

"Now, Mother," one of them said. "Just be agreeable and no harm will come to you."

"But the town house! The town house is on fire!"

"Now, Mother—" One of them laughed and reached for the bucket she had just brought from the well.

She jerked it away from him and ran and emptied it on the flames. She knew she was "taking my life in my hands, as it were." But, suddenly, a desperate courage came to her as she saw the flames spread up the side of the building. She ran to the young officer who had been the first to speak to her.

"If you don't put it out right away, it will be too late! And all the houses around it will burn! You must! You must!"

He smiled at her. "Oh, all right, Mother."

He stood up and called to a passing squad of grenadiers: "Attention, men! Put this fire out! Be fast about it!" *

Six companies of infantry had left the Common with Captain Parsons to destroy the provincial stores at Colonel James Barrett's farm, two miles out of town. Parsons posted one of them, under Captain Walter Laurie, at the little plank bridge over the Concord River north of the village, to safeguard his return. He dropped two more off along the way and marched with the rest to the Barrett farm, two miles on the other side.

* See Notes, page 244.

Ensign De Bernière, walking with Parsons, said the colonel's big barn was stocked to the rafters with everything from cannon and gunpowder to salt fish. He had seen it with his own eyes only a month ago. But when they got there all they found was a few cannon wheels.

The men fanned out and examined everything from the haystack to the smokehouse. They could find nothing more. None of them thought to look for cannon barrels in the freshly-plowed field.

The elderly Mrs. Barrett received Parsons and his aides graciously but coolly. When the soldiers stacked the cannon wheels before the barn and started to set them afire, she promptly went to the captain and told him there was no sense in burning the barn, too. Parsons ordered the wheels rolled into the road and burned there.

She went with him into the attic and stood quietly aside while his men poked at the feather beds piled against the walls. There were kegs behind them filled with cartridges, others with flints and balls, but Parsons took the stern-faced old lady's word for it that there was nothing but the winter bedding.

The officers were hungry and said so. She set out food for them. They tried to pay her. She shook her head.

"We are commanded to feed our enemies," she said tartly.

One of them tossed his money into her lap. She brushed it back at him.

"This is the price of blood," she said.

THIRTEEN

Even captain laurie, taking his station at the north bridge while Parsons went on to the Barrett farm, did not escape being hoodwinked by a patriot.

The Concord militia under Major Buttrick had taken their time withdrawing north of the village. They came down from the high ground behind Elijah Jones's house and went over the bridge as Parsons and his six companies of redcoats came into sight on the road from the Square.

Laurie saw the provincials straggle up the road that forked to the right on the other side of the river and climb the long slope of Punkatasset Hill. With their muskets cradled in their arms or swinging at their sides, he thought they looked more like a queue of rustic hunters than men in arms. They were still only about a hundred and fifty. Climbing the hill ahead of them were groups of women and children from the village.

The young officer let his men fall out. Some of them went back to the Jones house, on the other side of the road, and gathered around the well to take their turn at the moss-crusted wooden bucket. A few leaned on the bridge railing, looking down into the rippled darkness of the little river. Others wandered along the bank playfully jabbing their bayonets at the frogs that leaped away in front of them.

Laurie saw Parsons march up the road that forked to the left along the river bank and drop off two companies at a small hill between the bridge and Punkatasset. Soon the rest of the detail was out of sight around a bend. He thought he had never seen a more beautiful spot: the slow river curving between its canebrake banks; the rounded hills covered with bright new foliage; the

114

patchwork of brown and green fields; the narrow roads winding away, seemingly to nowhere.

The women and children who had been climbing Punkatasset had disappeared among the trees near the summit. The retreating provincials were drawing together in a field high up the slope. Suddenly Laurie came to rigid attention. Running out of the woods to join the men in the field were others, so many of them that the assemblage was soon twice its original size. And still they came.

He shouted to a sergeant to call the men back. As the company was forming a man on horseback came down the road from the village and started across the bridge. The infantrymen barred his way.

Laurie grabbed the bridle rein.

"Where might you think you are going?" he asked.

The man had on a long black coat and freshly-oiled boots. A limp white neckcloth was tucked under his chin. He looked down at the young officer and a smile slowly dimpled his leathered cheeks.

"I am a physician," he said, "and I am on my way to visit one of my patients."

"How do I know you are not a rebel, and going to join those yonder on the hill?" Laurie demanded.

The man's face became grave.

"I do not trouble myself with the disputes of the country," he answered. "Nor do I in any shape belong to the militia. I have a sick woman, a very sick woman, waiting for me up the road. Now may I pass on?"

Laurie stepped aside and waved him on his way. The man cantered up the road that curved to the right around Punkatasset Hill. As he reached the foot of the slope, he turned in his saddle and waved back to Laurie. Then he wheeled his horse sharply and galloped up the hill to the rebels massing at the edge of the woods.

Laurie had no time to regret his trustfulness. The provincials, he discovered, were starting down the slope in double file. There were more than four hundred now. They suddenly looked quite military, marching in step, their muskets slanted on their shoulders.

He lined up his company on the side of the bridge that faced the hill. Thirty-two men! A ridiculously small number, he realized, compared with the double file coming down the hill. He was glad to see that the two companies Parsons had left a short distance away had also seen the provincials approaching and were pulling back to the bridge. Even so, they would still be less than a hundred. And that long column twisting down the hill! Where could they all have come from?

Lieutenant Alexander Robertson, Laurie's aide, was on horseback. Laurie told him to ride to the village as fast as he could and report to Colonel Smith.

"Ask him to send grenadiers to support me in case of their attacking," he said.

By the time Robertson returned, the provincials had reached the low hill the two British companies had just left. They stopped there. It was about four hundred yards away, separated from the bridge by meadows and a stretch of swampland that the road crossed on a narrow causeway.

Robertson reported that Colonel Smith thought the three companies should be able to handle the situation. However, he had agreed to send two companies of grenadiers. He had told Captain Lumm, a member of the Mitchell patrol that had captured Revere the night before, to ride out with Robertson and look things over. When Lumm saw the size of the provincial assemblage, he raced back to tell Smith he had better hurry the re-enforcements.

Lieutenant Sutherland was with Laurie at the bridge now. So were Lieutenant Barker and Ensign Lister. Sutherland had barely escaped being cut off by the provincials. Since he was a volunteer, he could go where he pleased. He was with one of the two companies Captain Parsons had dropped off on the other side of the bridge. When Sutherland discovered that Parsons had gone on to the Barrett farm, he set out after him. A company officer obligingly assigned two men to go along. They were passing Punkatasset Hill when one of the regulars looked back.

"Sir!" he yelled. "The company of the 4th are retiring!"

The 4th was one of the two companies Sutherland had just left. He saw now that both companies were hurrying to the bridge. The reason was clear. The long column of provincials was coming down the slope. The head of the column was mounting the low hill close on the heels of the retreating British.

Sutherland realized that the two regulars and he were an easy target for the double file of provincials passing down the slope. The nearest ones were within pistol range.

"It struck me," he said, "that it would be disgraceful to be taken by such rascals, and I made the best of my way for the bridge, never out of reach of musket shot of this party."

Ensign Lister, the other young volunteer, watched Sutherland and the two soldiers come across the open fields. For the second time that morning, he wished some of these officers who outranked him had had his experience fighting Indians in the Niagara area. There was Sutherland walking in the open when a stone wall was not far away!

It was just blind luck, he thought, that the company he had been with on the hill had gotten back to the bridge without being wiped out. They had been within deadly range of the rebels' muskets as they crossed the clearing. He had pointed out to the other officers that by following a slightly circuitous route they could use the stone walls for cover. But he had been overruled.

The ever-critical Lieutenant Barker was standing near Captain Laurie when Sutherland came up. Laurie asked Sutherland if he didn't think it was advisable to withdraw the three companies to the other side of the bridge. Sutherland said, "Definitely yes!" It was a much stronger position to defend, he pointed out.

Barker silently agreed with him. The only trouble was, he thought, Laurie should have done it when he first saw the rebels approaching.

"Then he would have had time to make a good disposition."

Sutherland was the last man to cross the bridge. He set his musket against the railing and took up one of the planks. A squad ran out to help him. Then someone yelled, "Here they come!"

The provincials were marching down the causeway, their fifes playing shrilly.

Sutherland, followed by three men, ran into the field adjoining the bridge on the left. Laurie took a last worried look up the road. There was still no sign of the re-enforcements. He disposed his own company to protect his flanks. The other two he lined up in the roadway, one behind the other, for the maneuver known as "Retreating by Divisions" or "Street Fighting."

Used by soldiers properly trained in it, the method provided almost continuous fire from the front of a column. British divisions at the time were squads of twelve men each. They stood four abreast in three ranks. On the order to fire, the first rank of the front division knelt, the second rank stooped and the third stood erect. All fired at once, and immediately divided, six going around the left to the rear of the column, six around the right. The second division fired in the same manner, split and retreated. By the time it was the first division's turn again, they were re-loaded and ready.

The provincials were close now. Someone fired a musket. Laurie thought it was one of his own company on the river bank. He said, "A general popping from them [the provincials] ensued."

The lead squad on the road opened fire. So did some of Laurie's men on the flanks. Two of the provincials fell. The others came on the run, fanning out as they cleared the causeway. Between the rattle of musket shots, the British could hear the yell, "Fire!" "Fire!" "Fire!" echo up the length of the column.

Sutherland, in the field to the south of the bridge, saw two of the men with him fall. He fired at the charging provincials and was reloading his musket when a ball hit him high on the right shoulder and spun him half around. He got back on the road as the provincials stormed up to the river bank and onto the bridge.

The first squad of the British column in the road had performed its maneuver perfectly. They divided and stepped smartly around the next squad. But now men were falling. The provincials were picking off the epaulets. Only five of the nine officers were still on their feet. A private in the second squad fell backward with blood splashing out of his face. Another doubled over, screaming with pain.

Retreating by divisions, to be successfully executed, required

solid training and rigid discipline. Some of the men had never
practiced it. Even Lieutenant Barker did not know what Laurie
had in mind.

"The companies," he complained, "got one behind the other
so that only the front one could fire."

The second squad discharged its guns in the air and, wheeling
as a unit to the right, ran for the rear. The panic spread. The
others ran after them. Laurie, beating at them with his sword
and shouting, tried to force them back into line. But they dodged
past him, and in a moment all three companies were in retreat.

The provincials were running across the bridge and up the
road after them. Suddenly, around the bend in the road, the
grenadiers came into sight.

Lieutenant Barker understood now why it had taken the grenadiers so long to come to the rescue. Colonel Smith had decided to
lead them himself.

"Being a very fat man," Barker said, "he would not have
reached the bridge in half an hour, though it was not a half
mile to it."

Colonel Smith saw the provincials halt and slowly pull back.
He watched some of them recross the bridge and gather around
the two bodies in the road. Soon there were no others in sight.
There was no use asking for more trouble, he said, and ordered
the column to return to the village.

Back at the Wright Tavern, they counted their casualties. Four
of the nine officers who had taken part in the skirmish had been
wounded. Two privates had been left dead in the field. One who
had been brought back to the village was dying. At least three
others had been severely wounded.

In the confusion Colonel Smith forgot about Captain Parsons
and the three companies that had gone with him to the Barrett
farm.

After a while the Parsons detail returned. Ensign De Bernière
said they had passed within musket shot of a large gathering of
provincials on the low hill just behind the bridge. He guessed
the British column had come into sight so suddenly the rebels had
been too disconcerted to organize an attack. Anyway, they had let
the soldiers pass without making a move. He said, not knowing

better, that the rascals had taken up a plank or two of the bridge. Had they finished the job, the detail couldn't have gotten across and "we were most certainly all lost!"

No one corrected him. By now they were all listening to the horror story Captain Parsons was telling.

When they arrived at the bridge, he said, they saw three British soldiers lying in the field just to the right of it. Corporal Gordon and four men had gone over to examine them. Two were dead. The third one died as the men bent over him. His head had been brutally mutilated, his ears cut off, and he had been scalped alive!

The story spread as fast as it could be retold. The soldiers of the 4th, who had headed the column that had faced the provincials at the bridge, were particularly enraged. It was one of their men, the corporal said.

FOURTEEN

COLONEL BARRETT, THE COMMANDER OF THE CONCORD MILITIA, WAS old and fat, and he was lame. But he could still sit a horse as well as any man. He had left his home long before the Parsons detail arrived there. On his way to the village, he had met a mounted messenger who told him his men were retiring to Punkatasset Hill. He joined them there.

He saw that Captain Isaac Davis had already brought most of his company from Acton and that Captain William Smith and a number of the men from Lincoln had arrived. More militiamen were steadily coming up the slope from every direction. They came from Bedford, Billerica, Chelmsford, Carlisle, from Littleton and Stow and Westford. Barrett had never seen so many of his compatriots in one assemblage. The clearing at the edge of the wooded summit was almost filled with them.

He was worried about the stores still hidden in the village. If trouble came every ounce of them would be needed. And the fifty-five barrels of cured beef and seventeen thousand pounds of salt fish in the shed and cellar of Elisha Jones's house! The British company at the bridge was much too close to it for comfort.

There was some smoke rising from the direction of the town square, but it didn't look as if the fires were of any size. What was more disturbing was the story that some of the men who had just ridden in from Lincoln were telling. Word had reached them that the British had massacred a number of the militiamen in Lexington; had shot them down for no good reason, no reason at all! The British had stormed onto the Lexington parade like mad dogs, the Lincoln men said.

Barrett called a council of war. His aide, Major Buttrick, and

Captain Smith of Lincoln said they were ready to march down and drive the British away from the bridge. Captain Davis of Acton said, "I haven't a man that's afraid to go!"

Barrett told the company officers to have the men load their muskets. "And have them see to their flints," he said. "Replace any worn ones."

Joseph Hosmer, the Concord adjutant, was looking out over the bridge at the steeples and roof tops above the village square. He had seen the smoke spiral up when the Liberty Pole was chopped down and set afire, and again when the barrels of wooden utensils were burned. Now a much darker column arose and blotted out the town-house belfry.

"They're setting the village on fire!" he yelled. "The town house is burning! Will you let them burn it down?"

Colonel Barrett said: "March to the bridge and over it. But warn your men not to fire on the king's troops unless they fire first."

Captain Davis took his Acton company to the far end of the clearing and formed them in double file. Captain Smith and the Lincoln men fell in behind him. The two young fifers, Luther Blanchard and John Buttrick, stepped out in front, playing "The White Cockade," and the long column started down the slope.

Old Colonel Barrett sat on his horse surrounded by a few of the village elders, watching the men march away. It seemed to him that only a few years had gone by since he and these men left with him had been marching like those younger ones. It was strange how quickly things change. Then the men in the scarlet uniforms had been their friends.

Young Amos Barrett, the Colonel's nephew, was in the company third in the file. He didn't know whether he was frightened or not. Somehow, he couldn't seem to get enough breath into his lungs. There was a strange, stinging sensation in his legs, as if they might suddenly go weak under him. He wondered what he would do if he suddenly came into hand-to-hand combat with one of those men with a glistening bayonet on the end of his musket. By God, he wouldn't give ground! No, sir! Not an inch!

He's use his musket for a club! That's what he'd do! He'd knock
the bayonet right out of that fellow's hands!

As the Acton company reached the small hill between Punkatasset and the bridge, the sixty-odd redcoats Parsons had left
there retired in front of them. The provincials stopped to reconnoiter. They watched the British march across the bridge and
form in the road and on the river banks on the other side. They
saw Lieutenant Sutherland pry up one of the planks of the
bridge.

"They're taking the bridge down!" Major Buttrick shouted.
"If you're all of a mind, we'll drive them away from it! They
shouldn't tear that up!"

The road ahead curved around the base of the hill and met
the other fork in front of the bridge. They started down it. Major
Buttrick was in the lead with Captain Davis and Lieutenant-
Colonel John Robinson of Westford. The front company had
reached the fork and swung toward the bridge. Amos Barrett
counted three gun flashes on the opposite shore. The balls
splashed into the river near him. Then there was a general firing.

"Their balls," he said, "whistled well."

A man near him was clipped on the arm. He yelled, "Hey!
They're firing jackknives!"

Captain Timothy Brown, a devout churchman who lived near
the North Bridge, had never sworn before in his life. But when a
bullet sang past his head he spoke from impulse: "God damn it!
They are firing ball!"

At the front of the column, two men crumpled to the ground,
dead. They were Captain Davis and a young private in his company, Abner Hosmer. Several others were wounded, including the
boy fifer, Luther Blanchard.

Major Buttrick leaped high, swinging his sword.

"Fire! For God's sake, fire!"

The order traveled like a reverberating echo up the line.
"Fire!" "Fire!" The men broke out of formation, charged around
each other, leveled their muskets and blasted away.

The British volleyed again. But this time Amos heard the
balls whistle overhead and knew they had fired too high.

As the regulars broke and retreated, the provincials charged onto the bridge. They kept on, but pulled up near the Elisha Jones house when they saw the grenadiers come around a turn in the road and take in the fleeing infantrymen.

Some of the men drifted back across the bridge and gathered around the bodies of the two dead Acton men. Major Buttrick led the rest into Jones's pasture and deployed them behind a stone wall close to the road. He walked behind them, stooping out of sight of the British.

"If they come up," he said, "don't fire until I give the order. Fire two or three times before you retreat. Wait until they come close enough, until I give the order."

Amos Barrett settled himself on his knees and laid his musket in a crevice in the wall. He looked up and down the line. He thought there were at least two hundred of them here. They would give the damned redcoats a pretty hot reception. At least, they could kill every one of the officers in front. He looked down the road, straining his eyes to pick out the epaulets.

For ten minutes the British infantrymen and their rescuers moved about in the road. Then, while the provincials watched from behind their wall, the officers gathered in front and studied the countryside through their field glasses. The soldiers fell into formation.

Amos Barrett's finger tensed on the trigger. Any moment now! Why was Buttrick waiting? They were close enough already. He had his eyes on one of them. The tall fellow over to the left, with the fancy sword at his side. He aimed slightly to windward, level with the officer's head. At this range he ought to take him just below the shoulder.

Still the order didn't come. Young Barrett's finger ached, but he dared not take it off the trigger. Any moment!

Down the road, one of the British officers suddenly shouted a command. The column about-faced, and marched off toward the village. Barrett settled glumly back on his heels. Why hadn't Buttrick ordered them to fire while he had the chance? After a while, he stood up and stretched the ache out of his legs. He saw that the smoke had stopped rising from the Town Square. So the British were not burning the village, after all!

Some of the men around him slipped off to their homes or to

their families hiding in the woods on Punkatasset Hill. Some who had been wounded sat on the ground and, with their jackknives, cut strips from their shirts to bandage themselves. Others clustered around Elisha Jones's pump—the same one that the British had been drinking from a few minutes before—and passed around the bucket of wonderful cold water.

Major Buttrick finally got his men into formation again. He marched them up a cart track to the high wooded ground back of the Jones house, from where they could look down through the brush and from behind the stone walls at the British in the village.

Elisha Jones now came out of his house and watched the British disappear up the road. He went back and looked at the bullet hole in the wall beside the door. It was exactly level with his head. A close call, indeed! he told himself.

He had taken his wife and two young children to the cellar when he saw the British come up the road to the bridge a good hour ago. He had barred the door and hidden with them behind the barrels of beef and kegs of salt fish. But when he heard the heavy firing outside, he could stay quiet no longer.

He grabbed his musket and charged up the stairs, his young wife screaming hysterically after him and the children running at their heels in terror.

Looking out, he saw the British retreating past his house. A wounded soldier stumbled along, looking back every few tortured steps with fright-pallored face. Another sagged in the helping arms of two companions. He ran to the bedroom window and shoved his musket out to get at least one shot at the enemy. His wife grabbed the musket barrel with both hands and twisted it away from him.

"Do you want them to burn our house down?" she cried.

Jones, disarmed, strode glumly away. He opened the door and watched the last of the regulars hurry past. One of the stragglers saw him and fired from the hip. It wasn't a bad shot. A bit more to the left and it would have taken Jones in the head.

The Reverend William Emerson was a stout patriot but also a

very frugal man. He stood outside the back door of the manse, looking down across the field as the British massed at the bridge and his neighbors came down the hill toward them. His attention was momentarily distracted when he saw that the village youth he had hired to chop firewood had struck his hatchet into the block and was also staring. He was a dull-witted lad and Mr. Emerson saw no reason why he shouldn't keep on working.

"You, there!" he called. "Go back to your chopping! That is what I am paying you for!"

The bridge was just across his field, no more than a hundred yards away. He heard a few scattered shots and then saw the red flare as the British volleyed. A cloud of smoke hung for a moment over the soldiers and drifted slowly toward the bridge. Weren't the patriots going to answer? Why didn't they fire? Why? Why? The moment seemed forever before he saw the gun flashes across the river.

In his excitement, as he watched the provincials charge after the retreating regulars, he forgot about the young woodchopper. And, despite the pastor's stern admonition, the lad forgot about him. The hatchet in his hand, he ran across the manse field after the provincials. He passed the two redcoats sprawled dead in the new grass, their mouths agape, eyes staring skyward.

The third one was directly in his path, lying on his face near the wall. As the youth got near him, the soldier raised himself painfully on his hands, staring wild-eyed at him. In a sudden fit of terror, the boy swung down with the hatchet. The soldier groaned and sagged back on his face. The boy struck again, and again. He backed off, panting, and ran on after the provincials. On the way, he threw the bloody hatchet into the brush by the roadside.

FIFTEEN

COLONEL SMITH WAS A HARD MAN TO PERTURB, OR HURRY. HE DID not think the incident at the bridge was much more than a brush with a country mob. Of more concern to him at the moment was what could have kept Lord Percy and the re-enforcements from joining him long before now. A twenty-one mile march. If they had started at any reasonable time after his messenger got there, they should have been here hours ago.

The soldier who had been mortally wounded died and was buried in the village. The army surgeons treated the other injured, and two chaises were confiscated for them to ride in.

Occasionally a few armed provincials were spotted on one of the elevations to the east of the Square, and the officers sent a detail to chase them.

It was noon, two hours after the battle at the bridge, when Smith finally ordered the detachment to fall in and start back for Boston.

The wounded, in their commandeered chaises, rode with the grenadiers guarding them. The light infantry fanned out to the left. The millbrook in its open plain protected the column on the right. Everything appeared peaceful. Smith expected it would be an uneventful march. The fifes and drums were silent. The sun rode in and out among white patches of clouds. The wind blew in the men's faces, crisp and edged with the tang of spring. It was a beautiful day.

Then the column came to Meriam's Corner, a crossroads a mile from the Square. The ridge on the left ended abruptly here. At its foot, the road came in from Bedford and Billerica to the northeast. A few rods farther toward Lexington, a small plank bridge crossed the millstream.

Out of sight in the woods up the ridge, the provincials under Major Buttrick had been moving parallel with the British column. Those who had gone across the bridge to take care of the dead had rejoined the men from behind the stone wall. More had come in from Carlisle and from Maynard.

During the long wait in the brush, every man had finally heard the details from Lexington and had had time to brood over the death of the dynamic leader of the Acton company, Captain Davis, and his neighbor, Private Hosmer. They were in an angry mood. As the British started across the millstream bridge, they struck again. Their first shots, from the ridge, were too far off to do any harm. But they kept coming closer.

These men who had faced down the British regulars at the North Bridge crept across the rough terrain of woods and pastures. They came dodging from tree to tree, crouching behind the stone walls. There was no organization that could be recognized. No officers were leading them with drawn swords and ringing commands. Major Buttrick was just another man with a musket. So were Colonel Robinson and Captain Smith. They came fighting the way the Indians had fought their ancestors.

Down the Bedford Road to their left came the company from Reading and, not far behind it, the men from Billerica. Running ahead of the Reading company was its twenty-three-year-old captain, John Brooks, a country physician getting his first taste of battle. Close behind him was the Reverend Mr. Foster, the Reading pastor.

In the clearing where the roads crossed, Foster saw the British column. The van was already across the little bridge. After the pace Captain Brooks had set, the British appeared to him to be marching very slowly. The Reading and Billerica men fired and dodged into the fields. The men on the ridge were close in now. Foster saw a number of the regulars fall at the crossroads. Some of them got up and stumbled on. A few lay still. Suddenly he saw the British halt and face about. They fired a volley. The balls sang through the trees. A trickle of leaves and branches fell.

General Thomas Gage, painted by John Singleton Copley. *Reproduced through the courtesy of its present owner, Colonel R. V. C. Bodley, of Newburyport, Mass.*

Paul Revere, from the painting by John Singleton Copley. *Courtesy, Museum of Fine Arts, Boston.*

General Joseph Warren, by John Singleton Copley. *Courtesy, Museum of Fine Arts, Boston.*

John Hancock, by John Singleton Copley. *Courtesy, The City of Boston. Photograph, courtesy, Museum of Fine Arts, Boston.*

Samuel Adams, by John Singleton Copley. *Courtesy, City of Boston. Photograph, courtesy, Museum of Fine Arts, Boston.*

John Adams, after a portrait by John Singleton Copley. *Courtesy, Museum of Fine Arts, Boston.*

General William Howe, from a miniature of the British school, 18th century. *Courtesy, Frick Art Reference Library.*

The Engagement at the North Bridge in Concord *(see Notes, page 246)*

The Battle of Breeds Hill *(see Notes, page 246)*

AN EXACT VIEW of THE LATE BATTLE AT CHARLESTOWN June 17th 1775

The Battle of Lexington
(see Notes, page 246)

A View of the South Part of Lexington
(see Notes, page 246)

Amos Barrett was coming down the ridge close to the crossroads. He had just fired when he saw the British halt and face about. He dodged behind a boulder as they volleyed. Joseph Hosmer was crouching behind a tree to his right. There was a provincial and sometimes two behind almost every tree or rock. The British infantrymen ran toward them. They raced away up the slope.

The column was moving again. Some of the provincials waited until the end of it had passed, then crossed the road and closed in on their right.

At the Corners two British regulars lay dead in the grass. The road was littered with gear discarded or lost by the wounded: several muskets, cartouche boxes, helmets. There were wet blotches in the dirt. Barrett put his finger in one of them. It came up red.

He ran across the fields until he came up on the right side of the column. After a while it was harder to find a tree or spot behind a wall within range that wasn't already taken by a compatriot. What was worse, he discovered, you had to be on the alert every second. British flankers were ranging out farther to the sides. They came in squads, and if you waited too long to pick off one of them the others would run you down. Barrett saw it happen to Captain Jonathan Wilson of Bedford.

Daniel Thompson of Woburn also paid with his life for daring too far, and Nathaniel Wyman of Billerica.

The Framingham company arrived and deployed in the fields. Captain Nathaniel Cudworth came with his men from Sudbury. Major Loammi Baldwin brought a hundred and eighty from Woburn.

At Lincoln, halfway between Concord and Lexington, Captain Parker and the men who had stood up to the British on the Green that morning, came down the road and deployed around the regulars. Jedidiah Monroe, who had been wounded that morning, was among them. He got one shot at the men who had killed his neighbors, and then a British musket ball finished him off.

At Fiske's Hill the road began its slow descent into Lexington. A group of provincials got ahead of the column and lay in wait behind a rail fence. They spotted an officer on a high-strung bay, waving his sword and shouting at the men to keep their ranks. Several of the minutemen fired. The horse reared and the officer fell off. His mount bolted straight for the rail fence. One of the provincials ran after it and caught it. He found a brace of richly mounted pistols on the saddle. Major Pitcairn's name was embossed on the holster.

Twenty-five-year-old James Hayward, of Acton, had left his father's house early in the morning with a pound of gunpowder and forty balls to march with Captain Davis. His pockets were considerably lighter now. At the foot of Fiske's Hill, after the British had passed, he went into the yard of a farmhouse for a drink of water. He had set his musket against the well casing and was drawing up the bucket when the door opened and he saw the scarlet and white of a British uniform. He grabbed his gun as the Briton leveled his.

He heard the soldier yell, "You are a dead man!"

"So are you!" Hayward answered.

Both fired. The British infantryman fell dead. His bullet plowed into Hayward's groin. He lived eight hours.

Colonel Smith's flankers were not having much luck. For long stretches the woods closed the road in on both sides. The stone fences were built high to keep the cattle and horses from wandering off. They shielded most of the marchers from the middle of their waists down, but they also provided cover for the rebel snipers. When the squads of flankers took out after them, they dodged away in the brush. The pastures and tilled fields were spotted with huge boulders and clumps of trees. Except when they spotted the flare of a gun, there was no way for the infantrymen to tell which of them the angry provincials were hiding behind.

The houses stood close to the road. They appeared deserted, but occasionally, after the column passed, a musket or two flashed at the windows. When the flanking parties ran back and searched them, they found no one.

Lieutenant Sutherland, his shoulder wound thickly bandaged, was riding in one of the chaises. From the time the column left

Meriam's Corner, it seemed to him the rattle of musketry from
the roadsides and the near slopes of the hills got steadily worse.
Several balls plowed into the sides of the carriage. Then one
smashed the rim of a rear wheel. The wheel caved in and the
carriage dragged tilting along the road until another bullet
wounded the horse. Sutherland borrowed a mount and rode
horseback the rest of the way.

He was impatient with Smith for having procrastinated so long
in Concord. They could have started back two hours earlier, he
told himself. Then these savage rascals would not have had time
to mobilize any strength. But now that they were in this mess, he
didn't know what Smith could do except keep the detachment
doggedly moving toward Boston.

He saw that the men were beginning to panic. Battling an
enemy that stubbornly declined to stand up and be shot at in the
established European manner, they were squandering their fire
knocking bark off trees and chipping stone fences. The column
had increased its pace. Some of the grenadiers started to run.
Officers swung at them with their swords, shouted them back into
line.

The flankers were dropping along the roadsides to catch their
breath.

In Lincoln a musket ball hit Colonel Smith in the leg. It was
a flesh wound, and a tight bandage stopped the bleeding. Before
they got out of the village, eight regulars were killed.

Down the road a ball went through Ensign Lister's right elbow.
He kept walking for a while. But the elbow was bleeding badly
and the pain got worse. He saw Colonel Smith borrow a horse
from a marine officer, and hurried up. He showed his crippled
arm to the colonel and asked if he might have the horse. Smith
gave it to him and limped along on foot.

Lister soon noticed that the balls were more numerous up
there than nearer the ground. Smith must have made the same
discovery, he thought. He dismounted and walked beside his
horse.

The regulars had left Boston with seventy-two cartridges in
their cartouche boxes. By the time they reached Fiske's Hill,

where Major Pitcairn lost his mount, many of them were out of ammunition. The rest were running low.

The mounting number of wounded clinging to the horses and the one chaise that was left got in the way of the frantic grenadiers. Colonel Smith, limping painfully and pressing his officers to keep the column together, had lost all hope that Lord Percy was coming to his rescue. As the woods receded and the houses of Lexington came into sight, the men started to bolt. Their officers ran in front of them, trying to keep them in control. They pulled out their pistols and threatened to kill those who ran past them.

Colonel Smith might have surrendered, if there had been an organized command to surrender to anywhere in sight. He knew it could only be a matter of minutes before the entire detachment got out of hand.

Then, mysteriously, the American fire fell off. The center of Lexington lay before them. It was two o'clock and the April sun burnished the back windows of the meetinghouse and traced lengthening shadows on the deserted Green.

An unbelievable sound roared over the diminishing rebel musket fire: the thunder of a six-pounder! The terrorized British troops saw up the road what at first seemed a mirage: a long scarlet swath sparkling with the play of sunlight on bayonet steel. Above it, the standards of three famous British regiments—the King's Own, the Royal Welch Fusiliers and the 47th—snapped in the wind.

On the hilltop to the left, the fieldpiece spoke again. A dark funnel of smoke lifted above the trees. The men stared. A burst of cheering rolled down the column.

Lord Percy had arrived!

SIXTEEN

PERCY'S BELATED ARRIVAL RESULTED FROM A PERFECTLY COORDI-
nated chain of staff blunders. Back in Boston, the night before,
everything had been done properly and according to rote. General Gage had not waited for Colonel Smith's call for re-enforcements. After Lord Percy had come back from the Common and
told him the citizens knew the purpose of his expedition, he
promptly put out orders for the First Brigade, under Percy, to
muster at four in the morning and march to Smith's support.

The order was dutifully carried to the brigade major's quarters.
He was out for the evening. When he came home late, his servant
forgot to tell him there was a letter on the table.

Four o'clock arrived, and no brigade. At five, the express rider
galloped in with Smith's appeal for re-enforcements. An inquiry
was held. A messenger was sent to the major's. He rubbed the
sleep out of his eyes and read the order on the table.

At six o'clock, part of the brigade fell in on the parade. They
waited for the first battalion of marines who, with the royal
artillery, were to go with the column.

No marines.

Another inquiry.

The marines said they had received no order. The officer re-
sponsible for sending it insisted they had. It developed that he
had addressed it to Major Pitcairn and it had been left at his
quarters in North Square. Pitcairn was with Smith. The officer
had been told that, but it had slipped his mind.

So it was nine in the morning, instead of four, before the
brigade got under way.

They took the long road, across Boston Neck and through

Roxbury. The reason: the boats that had ferried Smith's detachment across the Charles were still on the other shore, waiting his return.

There was no need for stealth any more. The brigade marched smartly along the country roads and through the villages to the strains of "Yankee Doodle," almost nine hundred men in spick-and-span scarlet and white, and two burnished brass fieldpieces.

In Roxbury, a schoolboy ran alongside the earl's white horse singing the ancient "Ballad of Chevy Chase," which described the death in battle of one of Percy's noble ancestors. Percy was cynically amused to find anyone among these yokels literate enough to know the song.

From the derisive shouts of boys and occasional old men in barnyards and doorways, the absence everywhere of men of military age, he sensed there might be trouble ahead. It was apparent that the country had been thoroughly alerted.

The head of the column passed little Nabby Blackington grazing her family's cow by the roadside. The cow suddenly took it into its head to cross the road. It strolled into the bristle of slanting bayonets, dragging Nabby at the end of the rope. The soldiers obligingly halted and let them through.

At Cambridge, it looked as if the British were in for trouble. The selectmen of the town had had the planks of the Great Bridge over the Charles River taken up. The column came to a halt. The Charles was a sizable stream.

Then they discovered that the planks had been conveniently stacked along the bank on their side!

They were relaid and the column went on.

A baggage train of two wagons loaded with provisions and extra ammunition for the fieldpieces had been sent out after the brigade, under the guard of a sergeant and twelve men. It was waylaid by the provincials in Menotomy. When the wagons tried to escape, the provincials shot two of the men and several of the horses. The guard fled and the wagons were captured.

George Leonard, a well-to-do Boston Tory, went along with Percy as guide. He was riding a spirited horse and, since he knew the country so well, sometimes galloped far ahead of the brigade.

Beyond Menotomy, he saw three provincials coming up the road. The one in the center was limping on one foot with his arms around the shoulders of the other two. They had three muskets between them, one of them carrying the injured man's beside his own. Leonard asked them what had happened. He hurried back to Percy with their story.

The injured man, he said, told him he had been shot by the king's soldiers on Lexington Green. When Leonard asked why, he said, "Some of our people fired upon the regulars, and they fell on us like bulldogs and killed eight and wounded nineteen."

Leonard said the man added that it was not his company that had fired first, "but some of the country people on the other side of the road."

The other two, said Leonard, had confirmed the man's story. One of them had remarked, "I suppose now the regulars will kill everybody they meet with."

Lieutenant Frederick Mackenzie, the middle-aged adjutant of the Fusiliers, who had helped his two companies embark the night before, was in the van of the Percy brigade. When they were a mile from Lexington he began to hear musket fire in the distance. It grew in volume as they moved down the slope into the village.

The brigade passed the Monroe Tavern. The meetinghouse and Green came into view. The firing in front of them was so heavy now that Percy halted the column. He deployed it across the road and sent one of the six-pounders to the summit of a hill on the right; he put out flanking parties.

Lieutenant Mackenzie saw groups of armed provincials moving around the meetinghouse. Others were dodging behind the stone fences up the slopes.

The blast of the fieldpiece, an unfamiliar sound to the men on the Green, scattered them. Then Mackenzie saw Smith's grenadiers coming on the run down the road on the far side of the village. They ran past him and sprawled along the stone walls, panting with their tongues out.

"My God!" Mackenzie heard an officer near him say, "They remind you of dogs after the chase!"

The provincial firing had stopped. But it wasn't for long. As

Mackenzie helped shepherd Smith's wounded to the rear, scattered shooting broke out from behind a wall off to the right. He saw groups of rebels moving cautiously down the ridges. Some of them numbered nearly fifty. The cannon fired again, and the groups scattered behind trees and boulders.

Percy had the Monroe Tavern taken over for a field hospital. William Monroe, the proprietor, had been with Captain Parker's company on the Green in the morning and was now somewhere in the fields waiting for another shot at the British. He had left John Raymond in charge. Raymond was also a minuteman, but a bad leg had temporarily put him out of service.* The officers had him bring out rum for the wounded who sat or lay on the floors of the taproom, the parlor and kitchen, waiting for the army surgeons to extract bullets and bandage their wounds.

Ensign Lister's elbow was paining him almost more than he could bear. Surgeon's Mate Sims examined it and cut out the ball. He wasn't very comforting. The ball had shattered the joint, he said. He wrapped it the best he could, but the pain was as bad as ever.

Back outside, Lister looked apprehensively up the slopes. An artilleryman had told him Percy had brought only seven rounds apiece for the two fieldpieces. It would take more than that, Lister was sure, to keep the rebels back for long. Already he could see signs of activity among the trees up there. At first he thought it might be his overwrought imagination. But then, unmistakably, he saw a line of muskets slanting behind a stone fence. He saw a figure dart from one boulder to another, two others moving in a clump of trees.

At the head of the brigade, Lord Percy was listening to Colonel Smith's account of the day's misadventure. He consulted with Major Pitcairn and Lieutenant-Colonel Bernard, in charge of the grenadiers.

The tall young duke of Northumberland had a good head and a solid background of battle training. He was thirty-two and had been in the army since his sixteenth birthday. He had served with Duke Ferdinand of Brunswick in the Seven Years' War, had

* See Notes, page 244.

fought at the Battle of Minden, where the infantry had scored a spectacular victory over the French cavalry. But there was nothing in the European warfare he knew, with its pageantry, its precisely marshaled troops in bright uniforms and burnished accoutrements, its standards proudly raised, to guide him here.

He discarded precedent and went to work. He ordered strong flank guards up the slopes to keep the rebels out of range. Studying the terrain from his white charger, he decided that Deacon Loring's tidy stone fence edging the road to the Green was a good hiding place for snipers. He dispatched squads with sledges to dismantle two hundred yards of it.

Smith's men had been fired on from houses and barns. Percy had the deacon's house and outbuildings set afire. The widow Mulliken's house and her son's watch and clock shop were too close for comfort. So were another dwelling and shop. He had them burned.

He saw figures lurking around the meetinghouse and ordered one of his fieldpieces to send a round shot through it.

His officers were being driven relentlessly. He sent back word repeatedly to the tavern to hurry the dressing of the wounded. He had carriages rounded up and rushed to the rear. There was a sixteen-mile march ahead, down country roads that wandered, cowpath fashion, through long stretches of woods, between brush-spotted hills fringed with stone and rail fences, past scattered villages; all of it enemy territory. He wanted to be on his way.

Despite everything the flanking parties could do, the rebel firing was picking up on both sides. Lord Percy thought it was getting rather heavy. Lieutenant Sutherland told him it was nothing compared to what these rebels could do and had done on the road from Concord.

It was just after three-thirty, hardly more than an hour after Percy's arrival, that the long British column fell in and started marching back to Boston. Smith's exhausted troops walked in front. Percy put five of his companies on their right flank, "where," said Sutherland, "most danger was to be apprehended." Three companies were on the left. The wounded rode in the center. Mackenzie's fusiliers and Pitcairn's marines alternated as rear guard.

With Percy now in full command, Colonel Smith rode with the other wounded officers. Ensign Lister, walking beside his crowded carriage, realized that it hadn't taken the country people long to get over their fear of the cannon. Percy's attempts to keep them at a harmless distance weren't working out. He had ordered the flanking parties to range far to the sides. But with Lexington behind them, the woods and hills closed in again and the flankers weren't able to clear all the rebels out of gun range.

The sun rode in and out of the white cloud masses. The wind still whipped briskly out of the east. Every time the advance troops fired at the natives dodging away in front of them, choking smoke rolled back through the ranks.

The windows of the farmhouses hugging the road were shuttered, their chimneys still. Occasionally, a cow lifted its head to stare from a barnyard, a flock of geese or chickens waddled leisurely out of the marchers' path.

Percy's scouts searched every house before the column reached it. They were sullen, angry men. The story they had by now all heard of the scalping of a dying soldier at Concord confirmed their belief that the elusive rebels, sniping from every possible cover, were a mob of savages. When they found any hiding in a house, they cut them down with their bayonets. But many of the houses they searched appeared empty, and yet, after the British passed, the windows suddenly came alive with musket fire.

An officer whose squad had painstakingly searched one of the farmhouses was hurrying his men up the road after the column when he heard a crackle of muskets behind him. He turned and saw three faces behind the guns leveled at them from a window. The one in the middle was a young woman! The squad rushed back and bayoneted all three.

Mackenzie's fusiliers and the marines, bringing up the rear, were suffering the heaviest casualties. Fresh groups of rebels were constantly coming up the road from Lexington and scattering behind the houses and barns in their wake. Some of the houses had been set afire by the advance guard, and the troops passed them in safety. An officer urged Percy to send men with torches into every house. But Percy said there wasn't time. He was keeping the column moving at a steady three-mile-an-hour pace, and with luck they would just barely reach Cambridge by sundown.

He was getting worried about ammunition. His brigade had left Boston with thirty-six rounds per man. The way the soldiers were wasting it in their frenzy, he doubted it would last.

They were coming into Menotomy now, almost halfway home. The long, straight main street, with its two rows of unpainted wooden houses, its church steeple and tall town house, its taverns with their brightly-painted signs swaying over the doorways, wore a Sabbath stillness. But only until the column moved down between the houses. Suddenly, every fence corner and tree clump and wall in the pastures and fields around and behind the houses and barns flashed gunfire. Men stumbled onto the roadside grass and lay there struggling. Some got up and were helped along by their companions. Others stretched out and lay still. Horses reared and neighed wildly. One of those who fell and did not get up was Private Gibson, the young grenadier whose wife worked for Mrs. Stedman in Boston's Winter Street.

The flankers rushed at the patches of gunsmoke in the fields. The provincials were so many now that not all of them got away. The soldiers shot some of them, plunged their bayonets into others. They stormed into the taverns and houses and dispatched everybody they found there. One squad cornered ten men in a house and killed them. Another killed eight. The young officer in charge was astounded at the unyielding defiance of the trapped rebels. Seven of them were cut down. The eighth stood cursing at them "with the rage of a true Cromwellian" to his last breath.

Still there was no letup in the attack. Nor was there any for the rest of the way.

SEVENTEEN

WHILE LORD PERCY'S SIX-POUNDER WAS SCARING THE MEN AT LEX-
ington a leader finally arrived to direct the scattered provincial
companies that, up to now, had been doing very well on their
own.

General William Heath had come up the Boston Road in the
wake of the Percy brigade. On the outskirts of Lexington he had
cut across the fields and galloped onto the Green as the last of
Smith's exhausted regulars ran up the road to their rescuers. He
was thirty-eight years old, stocky and bald-headed. What hair was
left around his ears was sandy brown. His pale face was taut
with determination.

Heath's military experience until today had been strictly parade ground. As a young man in Boston he had become captain
of the Ancient and Honorable Artillery Company. When trouble
started with England he was chosen colonel of the Suffolk
militia. In February the Provincial Congress had named him one
of the colony's five generals. The others were Artemus Ward,
Seth Pomeroy, John Thomas and John Whitcomb.

He was a member of the Committee of Safety that had met the
day before at the Black Horse Tavern in Menotomy. On his way
home to Roxbury at sunset he had passed the group of British
officers General Gage had sent out in advance of Smith's detachment. The fact that they were riding away from Boston at that
hour made him suspicious.

Heath was therefore not very surprised when, early the next
morning, an express rider awoke him with the news that the
British had crossed to the mainland and were marching on Concord. He saddled his horse, visited briefly with other members of

the Committee of Safety and set out after the regulars, riding the back roads by way of Watertown since he surmised the British would have the Lexington Road posted.

At Watertown, he found a company of militia falling in to march to Lexington. He ordered them, instead, to go to Cambridge, dismantle the bridge over the Charles River there and build a barricade of the planks on the south end. It was to be the second time that day that the Cambridge bridge was unplanked, but the Watertown militia, who reached it after Percy's column had passed, made a better job of it than the town selectmen of Cambridge.

General Heath rode on and, near Lexington, met Dr. Joseph Warren.

Warren, the dedicated Boston firebrand, last of the intellectual leaders of the rebellion to risk his neck staying in the city, had gotten word by express that morning of the massacre at Lexington. He had recently been appointed chairman of the Committee of Safety, but he had no military commission. He did have a hearty appetite for adventure.

As soon as he got the message he mounted and rode casually through the British-controlled streets of Boston to the Charlestown ferry.

The guard Gage had posted the night before had been removed. As Warren boarded the boat, he waved a greeting to a compatriot.

"Keep up a brave heart," Warren said. "They have begun it. That either party can do. We'll end it. That only one can do."

In Charlestown he met Dr. Thomas Welsh, a fellow patriot and one of the village doctors. Welsh went with him while he visited the town selectmen to make certain they would be ready if the British came back that way. Then they rode on together.

The two physicians came in sight of the rear of Percy's brigade as it wound out of the Cambridge farmlands into the Lexington Road. At a crossroads called Watson's Corner, two regulars who had fallen behind had spotted the aged Mr. Watson saddling his horse. It was just what they needed to catch up with the brigade. Warren and Welsh saw the farmer standing straddle-legged in his barnyard, his heels dug in, straw hat in one hand, a bridle rein in the other, holding onto his horse with all his failing strength. The two soldiers were pulling on the other rein.

Dr. Warren unlimbered his two pistols. He charged into the barnyard and drew a double bead on the two redcoats. If they didn't get on their way, and fast as they could leg it, he announced, he'd blow both their heads off. They went.

Farther along, Warren suggested that they try to ride past the British column, but a rear guard with fixed bayonets barred their way. Dr. Welsh had had enough excitement for the day and turned back. Dr. Warren rode on and soon met General Heath coming out of a side road.

When Heath and Warren reached Lexington, the provincials had been temporarily driven back by the sight of Percy's sparkling warriors and the thunder of the cannon on the hill. Heath rallied them and attempted to regiment them under his command.

But these men from the villages and farms of Massachusetts who started the American Revolution that day neither needed nor understood an over-all command. The majority of them had come in blazing fury to destroy the enemy that threatened to tear away their liberty and had, they thought, wantonly butchered the few of their fellow-provincials who had dared to stand up to them. Some, particularly among the younger ones, had come for the excitement, and they were as deadly as the rest.

Like the men of Acton, most of them had never been to Boston and seen the soldiers of their king. These redcoats, with their evil-looking knife-edged bayonets and cannon that crashed like August thunder were invading monsters out of another world. It was either destroy or be destroyed.

They soon discovered that the cannon weren't as devastating as they sounded. Those who were running short of powder and balls replenished their supply from the meetinghouse. From every direction, on the roads and across the fields, re-enforcements were still coming in. Heath and Warren galloped out to meet them, gave their officers a quick fill-in, and sent them off behind the stone fences and trees to join their compatriots creeping Indian-fashion into gun range of the scarlet invaders on the Lexington Road.

The message relayed from one church bell to another, by the

alarm guns and express riders, had spread to every village of the great commonwealth of Massachusetts. The men of Middlesex, the county of Lexington and Concord, suddenly found themselves re-enforced in the fence corners and pastures and underbrush by grimly firing groups of strangers from Suffolk County, and Norfolk, Plymouth, Essex.

The majority of them were afoot. One who wasn't was Mr. Wyman of Woburn, a veteran of the French and Indian War. Mr. Wyman had been tagging the British ever since they left Concord, but neither he nor his big white horse showed any signs of tiring. His long gray hair streaming out behind him, he galloped through the brush, now coming up on the British left flank, now on the right. When he got into range of either the column or a squad of flankers, he pulled up his horse, swung off, laid his musket across the saddle, took deliberate aim and fired. Invariably a redcoat doubled over.

With the flash of the gun, the white horse spun around. Mr. Wyman jumped back into the saddle with the alacrity of a young buck and galloped out of range. After a short breather, he came out of the brush from another direction.

In Menotomy he almost dared too far. He charged across an open field, and as he stepped off and fired a mounted patrol took out after him. Doubled low over his horse, he streaked off with his pursuers close behind him. Somehow, as he rode, he managed to ram a fresh charge down the musket barrel, sift a priming charge into the pan.

He swung around and, still at full gallop, brought the gun down on the riders behind him. Instinctively, they reined back. The gun flashed, and one of them slowly slid out of his saddle.

Deacon Joseph Adams was standing at his back door when the British came down the main street of Menotomy. His wife was in bed with her eighteen-day-old baby. His other five children were also in the house. The deacon knew that anyone with the name Adams was suspect. Furthermore, he was known for his energetic support of the patriot cause.

He ran across his barnyard and vaulted a stone wall. A British advance squad took out after him, firing as they ran. Deacon Adams raced away behind the wall, the balls whining over his head. He dodged into the Reverend Samuel Cooke's barn and burrowed a hole for himself in the haymow. The soldiers rushed in after him. They prodded the hay with their bayonets but failed to find the deacon.

Three of them returned to the house. They went into the bedroom and one pushed the bed curtains aside with his bayonet.

"For the Lord's sake!" Mrs. Adams cried, "don't kill me!"

The soldier who had opened the curtains stared at her and said, "Damn you!"

One of his companions spoke in a quieter voice: "We will not hurt the woman if she will get out of the house, but we will surely burn it."

Mrs. Adams' two eldest daughters helped her get dressed and wrapped a blanket around the baby. They went with her to the corn crib beside the barn and arranged a pile of husks in the corner so she would be comfortable. Then they joined two of the other three children in the back yard. They yelled for Joel, their young brother, but got no answer.

Joel, nine years old, had crawled under a bed. When one of the soldiers discovered him and said, "Come out from there, boy," Joel clung to the rope webbing over his head. "No," he said. "You'll kill me."

The soldier poked under the bed with his bayonet.

"No, we won't. Come out of there!"

"Yes, you will," Joel insisted.

This went on until Joel finally stuck his head out and decided the redcoats were just ordinary men after all and not the murderous monsters he had feared. He tagged along behind them as they searched the rooms. When they stopped to examine the church's silver candlesticks and community service stored in a dresser, Joel warned them:

"Better not touch that. Pa'll give you a licking if you do!"

One of them said they'd chance that, and they began stuffing what they could into their haversacks and pockets. When they had finished their search, they agreed they'd better set the house on fire so the rebels couldn't use it after they left. They piled chips from the wood box in the middle of the living room, broke up a couple of chairs and tossed a shovel-full of coals from the fireplace onto the pile.

They told Joel he'd better get out now, too, and left. But Joel got a bucket from the kitchen and put out the fire with two helpings from his father's barrel of home brew.

When the deacon came home, after the British had passed on, he discovered the soldiers had made a neat haul. Itemized, it came to the value of sixteen pounds, sixteen shillings, eightpence.

Another looter was not so fortunate. One of the provincials, creeping around the rear of a house, looked in an open window and saw a redcoat sitting before the secretary, pilfering the drawers. He laid his musket on the sill and took careful aim. The woman of the house found the dead soldier there when she came home that evening. She thought at first he was taking a nap, his head nestled on his arms, until she saw the blood on the floor.

The Cooper Tavern, down the road from Deacon Adams' house, was usually deserted in the late afternoon. It was the time Rachel Cooper did a last bit of tidying up and her husband, Benjamin, checked the stock in his bar. This afternoon they had two customers. They were Jabez Wyman, who did odd jobs for the village pastor, Mr. Cooke, and his brother-in-law, Jason Winship.

Benjamin Cooper had just served them another round of flip and was rinsing the pitcher when he heard the muskets up the road. His wife and he took a quick look out the door and ran back into the taproom. Cooper yelled to the two middle-aged flip drinkers that "The redcoats are coming!" He opened the trap door to the cellar and helped his wife down. "Come and hide!" he called as he started down after her.

Wyman wiped the foam off his mustache with the back of his hand. "No," he said. "Let us finish the mug. There is plenty of time."

A British patrol charged into the taproom. Wyman and Winship staggered to their feet and squared away with their half-empty tankards. But drunken bravery was no match for bayonets in the hands of angry men to whom every house had become an enemy fortress. The two died quickly.

Meanwhile, outside, the battle fury mounted. Nearly eighteen

hundred fresh provincials joined the attack as the British fought
their way through the village. They came in from Roxbury,
Brookline, Dorchester, from Watertown and Sudbury. Two companies of minutemen and three alarm companies, a hundred and
fifty in all, arrived from Danvers. They had covered the sixteen
miles in four hours, running part of the way.

General Heath rode among his countrymen, calling out orders
that few of them understood and fewer still obeyed. Dr. Warren
on his big, froth-streaked bay charged from one group to another,
yelling encouragement. General Heath saw a British musket ball
tear away the pin that held Warren's earlock in place. Warren
laughed and shook his head, and rode closer.

Spurring on the men of Menotomy was the Reverend Samuel
Cooke, their pastor. His text of a few Sundays before still ran
bell-sharp in their memory. He had taken it from Nehemiah:
"Be not ye afraid of them; remember the Lord, which is great
and terrible, and fight for your brethren, your sons, and your
daughters, your wives, and your houses."

He had told them: "There appears no other choice left us
but either tamely to sit down and surrender our lives and property, our wives and children, our religion and consciences, to the
arbitrary will of others, or, trusting in God, to stand up in our
own defense."

One of his parishioners was crusty, seventy-nine-year-old Samuel Whittemore, whose house stood under two ancient elms not
far from the Cooper Tavern. Whittemore, a tall, gaunt man
with a tobacco-stained white beard, a militia officer in the French
and Indian War, had watched Smith's detachment march
through the village in the moonlight on its way to Concord.

Whittemore hadn't cared much for the British when he'd
fought beside them in the wilderness. He thought they were
uppity and overbearing. The gradual increase of tension between
America and the empire since then had solidified his distaste for
them.

He surmised they would be coming back this way and sent his
grandson, Amos, sixteen, to the attic to bring down his battle
paraphernalia from the old leather trunk under the eaves. It

consisted of a rusty musket, two long-barreled pistols and a sword.

Amos helped him repair the lock on the musket. They spent the rest of the forenoon oiling and polishing it and the pistols, and putting a new edge on the sword.

In the early afternoon a carriage came from Lexington carrying Lieutenant Edward Thornton Gould of the King's Own, who had been wounded at the North Bridge. A group of villagers captured the carriage and took the wounded officer to Ammi Cutter's house.

Soon the word spread that the rest of the British were on their way back. Fires were dampened. The women and the men too old to go off with the militia hurriedly hid their few valued possessions in wells and soap barrels or buried them in the fields. They collected their children and left for the farmhouses of friends over the fields.

Samuel Whittemore's wife tried to persuade him to come along to the safety of their son's house near the Mystic River, but he wouldn't budge. He sat silently on the front stoop, honing away at his sword, until she gave up pleading. She did succeed in making young Amos come with her, insisting he had to help take care of the younger children.

When Samuel decided the sword was adequately edged, he strapped it on, stuck the two pistols into the top of his pants, shouldered his musket and marched off.

He was barely ahead of the British column as it came down the slope into the village. A clanking one-man arsenal, he strode past the Cooper Tavern about the time that Cooper and his wife were going to the cellar. Just beyond the church, he climbed over a stone wall and settled himself and his weapons behind it.

As the British column and its flankers reached the church, Samuel Whittemore scanned the front rank for epaulets. He laid his musket across the wall, took aim and fired. An officer collapsed.

He rammed a fresh charge down the barrel, fired at another epaulet. He unlimbered the two pistols and knocked off one of five soldiers charging down on him with their bayonets. In close quarters, he fired the other pistol. In all he accounted for three British regulars.

Then they were on him. A musket ball tore away his cheek-bone and as he fell the soldiers rammed their bayonets into him and clubbed his head with the butts of their muskets until they were satisfied he was dead.

He lay, bloody and still, until the battle had passed and his neighbors came and picked him up. They carried him into the Cooper Tavern. The village surgeon, Dr. Tufts, took a long look at the thirteen bayonet holes in his shoulders and chest, the ugly bullet wound in his head, and said there was no use wasting time treating the old man. He was as good as dead. But he dressed his wounds, nevertheless, and Samuel Whittemore slowly came back to consciousness and recovered.

One thing he never forgot: during the long months of convalescence, his wife never let a day pass without saying, as she changed his many bandages or spooned soup into his mouth, "Now, don't you wish you had done as I wanted you to?"

His infuriated, "No! By God!" apparently never convinced her. He died eighteen years later, at ninety-eight.

Jason Russell, fifty-nine and lame, lived in the same part of the village as Samuel Whittemore. When the alarm came that the British were approaching, he got his family together and started across the fields with them to an out-of-the-way farmhouse. But as he limped along he brooded, and when they got halfway there he stopped and said he was going back. His wife begged him not to. The children cried and tried to pull him along. But Russell had made up his mind.

Back at his house, he built a barricade of shingles across the gate facing the road. Ammi Cutter, his neighbor, came from his house across the brook and warned him he was playing with death, pleaded with him to come away with him. Russell's answer was short and final.

"No. An Englishman's house is his castle."

He cocked his flintlock and sat back behind his barricade watching the smoke and dust and the spatterings of flame as the head of the British column fought its way down the road. A few rods to the west of his house, the road came around the side of a hill. Members of the newly-arrived companies of minutemen from Danvers and Beverly had come around the other side of the hill and were crouching in wait for the column to come into sight. As they were leveling their guns, a squad of British flankers charged up behind them.

The Danvers and Beverly men bolted across the road, leaped Russell's fence and ran into his house. Russell limped after them. Two bullets caught him as he reached the doorway and he sprawled dead across the threshold.

The British squad leaped over him and caught ten of the provincials in the south room. They put a quick end to them with their bayonets. Eight others had managed to get into the cellar. A regular started down after them, but a provincial bullet caught him in the shoulder and spun him back. The regulars shouted down the stairs for the provincials to come up and surrender. They got no answer. Every time one of them moved near the stairs a musket roared below.

The British finally gave up and left.

Down the road another British flanking party came up behind a group who had gotten into a walled enclosure and piled up bundles of shingles for added protection. The British killed seven of them.

Nearby, Dr. Eliphalet Downer, who had just arrived from Roxbury, saw a soldier coming at him with his bayonet. Dr. Downer was one of the few provincials who possessed a bayonet. He parried the regular's thrust and slashed with his own blade. For a few furious seconds they dueled in the grass beside the road. Then Dr. Downer got his blade in over the regular's and plunged it into his chest.

In the middle of Menotomy the two British six-pounders had gone into action again. The balls whistled down the road, tearing up sections of stone fence and burying themselves in a ditch bank or pasture lot.

John Tufts, coming across the fields from Somerville to get into the fight, heard the cannon blast and saw the clouds of smoke cover the van of the marching column. He stared fascinated as a ball tore a great limb off an elm tree beside a nearby house. The door of the barn behind it burst open and a girl ran out, screaming. She ran towards young Tufts, but when she saw him she stopped and stared at him in terror. She turned and fled toward the British column.

Tufts raced after her and caught her at the pasture wall. Stray bullets were whining past them. He grabbed her and threw her down behind the wall, held her close, stroking her tangled hair and talking softly until he quieted her.

They stayed there until the British column and the provincials swarming around them had passed. Then he let her sit up. She was very pretty, he saw. About eighteen, he guessed. The hysteria had left her eyes, and they were a warm gray. He pushed the tangle of dark hair away from her face and smiled at her. She slowly smiled back.

"Can you do things with your voice besides scream?" he said. She nodded.

"Well, try."

"Well—," she said. Then, finally: "I guess I was frightened."

"You were that," he agreed.

"I was home alone," she said. "Father and my brothers had gone off to fight the regulars. I thought I would be safe in the haymow. But when the shooting came closer I got scared. And then—then that awful roar. It sounded as if it was right outside. And I heard it hit the tree. I thought— I don't know what I thought. I just ran."

Her name, she said, was Elizabeth Perry.

"And yours?" she asked.

John Tufts didn't do any fighting that day. He took Elizabeth across the pastures and up the hill to the George Prentiss farmhouse, crowded with other families of the village who had flocked to it for safety.

Mrs. Lydia Price was among the crowd of women and children in the Prentiss farmhouse. Her Puritan modesty was shocked when she saw her neighbor Perry's pretty young daughter coming up the path with a stranger who carried a musket in one hand and had the other arm crooked under Elizabeth's.

But she was still too shaken to give it much thought. A rumor had started that the Negro slaves of the neighborhood were rising up and were going to murder the defenseless women and children while the British finished off their menfolk. Suddenly, coming up the path, they saw big, black Ishmael, the slave of Mr. Cutler.

One of the women called out, her voice harsh with fear: "Are you going to kill us, Ishmael?"

Ishmael stopped in his tracks, mouth agape.

"Lor-a-massy, no, ma'am!" he said. "Is my missis here?"

With Elizabeth Perry safely deposited among her friends, young John Tufts hurried off after the British. He caught up with the other provincials in Cambridge and went into camp. But in a few days he was back—to make sure, he said, that Elizabeth hadn't suffered any bad aftereffects from her adventure. A few days later he was back again. This time he just had a little time to kill. The next time he didn't bother making up an excuse. Elizabeth knew why he had come, and so did he.

They were married within the year.

With the British column descending with the sun on Charlestown, the women of Menotomy came back to their homes. One found that the British had raked coals from the fireplace into the middle of the floor and stacked the furniture on top of it. A clothesline strung with wet wash hung over it. Providentially, the blaze burned the clothesline and the wet clothes fell and smothered the fire.

At the old John Adams house, Mrs. Adams came home to find a dead British soldier on her doorstep. In the front room another lay on her bed, seriously wounded. She made him as comfortable as she could, brought him hot milk and food, but he died while she was trying to feed him.

Mrs. Samuel Butterfield found two wounded soldiers in her beds. One was a provincial soldier named Hemmenway from Framingham. The other was a British officer. She nursed them both without discrimination. Hemmenway soon recovered and went home, but the Briton's wound was more serious. In a few days British headquarters in Boston sent out medical supplies and nurses under a flag of truce and turned Mrs. Butterfield's house into a one-man hospital.

A truculent neighbor thought Mrs. Butterfield was carrying

tolerance too far. He called her a Tory and said she was harboring an enemy. He said he was going to come in and kill the wounded officer.

Mrs. Butterfield stared him down.

"Only a coward would want to kill a dying man," she told him.

EIGHTEEN

Once the british were out of menotomy, the distance between the silent houses widened again, but in their place
reappeared the pasture walls and wood lots that made as good
cover for the attackers. Lord Percy's flankers fanned out again,
but their ammunition boxes were ominously light and the drive
was out of their legs.

By now the sixteen hundred regulars were outnumbered nearly
two to one. Lieutenant-Colonel Barnard, in command of the
grenadiers, rode with the wounded. Lieutenant Joseph Knight,
of the King's Own, lay dying in one of the carriages. Both were
casualties of the rough fighting in the long village street.

Sound strategy by Lord Percy at the right moment saved the
British column from the annihilation that appeared its destiny.
He had given every indication that he was going to follow the
road through Cambridge by which he had marched from Boston,
over the Charles River bridge, now unplanked and fortified by
the provincials. Instead, as the troops rounded Prospect Hill, he
cut sharply to the east and took the road that led over the neck
of land between the Mystic and the Charles into Charlestown.
The maneuver even pleased the carping young subaltern, Lieutenant Barker.

"We threw them!" he exulted.

Once onto the narrow strip of marshland and clay pits that
served the village of Charlestown as a common, the British were
at last safe from their hornet-angry assailants. The Mystic River
fenced them on the left, the Charles on the right. From the
harbor of Charlestown, clustered around the foot of Breed's Hill,
the big guns of the men-of-war pointed protectingly over their

heads. The houses they passed were dark. As a tired squad approached one of them, a face appeared at a downstairs window. The soldiers fired and rushed in. The house was deserted except for a boy lying dead under the window. He was in his early teens. There was no gun in sight.

As General Heath saw the British rear guard pass onto the Neck, he and Dr. Warren galloped up the road behind them and wheeled their horses. Darkness was closing in and the flaring muskets of their countrymen lighted their faces fitfully. General Heath stood in his stirrups and shouted for the provincials to halt. It would be suicide to go on, he told the company commanders who gathered around him. They had gone as far as they could.

While he was talking an officer charged up and briskly identified himself. He had been sent by Colonel Timothy Pickering of Salem, commander of the Essex militia. Colonel Pickering, he said, had just arrived on the other side of nearby Winter Hill with seven hundred militiamen.

General Heath nodded glumly and said that that was fine. But they were a half hour too late. If they had arrived that much sooner, the British could have been cut off at the Neck.

"We could have destroyed them," he said. "Why are you so late?"

The officer said, "The colonel had some matters to attend to. We got a belated start."

Colonel Pickering had missed being the hero of the day. The thirty-year-old perfectionist and amateur drill master who had saved the Salem arms from a previous British expedition, had insisted on finishing some work he was doing as clerk in the office of the Salem recorder of deeds before putting his Essex regiment on the road. The Danvers and Beverly companies of his command had not waited for him and had gotten into the fighting while the British were still in Menotomy.*

General Heath assembled the militia officers at the foot of Prospect Hill. He ordered sentinels posted across the Neck and

* See Notes, page 245.

patrols organized to guard the Charles River waterfront through the night. Any movement of the enemy, he warned, was to be reported instantly to him at headquarters, which he was setting up in Cambridge. Those who weren't assigned to night duty, he said, should march to Cambridge with him and "lie on their arms."

He looked out over the dark multitude that filled the fields around him. The thought came to him that he was in the presence of a miracle! The force of sixty-odd minutemen who had faced the British at Lexington in the dawn had grown by sunset to more than three thousand!

Charlestown, on its jug-shaped peninsula, was a village in panic as the battle foamed into the Neck. Since Dr. Warren had ridden through on his way to Lexington in the forenoon, tension had been growing. Schools had been closed. Most of the men of fighting age had hurried off after the doctor. The women had warned their children to stay within calling range. Some had tossed their best possessions into gunny sacks—the piece or two of cherished silverware, the table pewter, the iron cooking pot and skillet. They had filled other bags with bread and the sausage and hams in the smokehouse, and trudged off with their families to relatives or friends in the country. But most of them had stayed in the little wooden houses that hugged the hard-packed streets between the waterfront and the pasture-fenced slopes of Breed's Hill.

Early in the afternoon, General Gage had sent word to the selectmen that he would have the ships' guns set the village on fire if any more armed men were caught leaving.

The news had spread of the massacre at Lexington. It was told that the Cambridge bridge had been dismantled and the British troops would have to come back through Charlestown. Stories of British atrocities passed from house to house, and grew in the telling.

At the Cooper Tavern in Menotomy, it was said, two innocent, senile gentlemen had been brutally bayoneted to death, their heads beaten in and their brains splashed on the floor and walls. More than a hundred musket balls had riddled the tavern.

Deacon Adams' wife had been driven from her bed with her newborn child and the house set on fire.

Groups gathered in the village, among them a few militiamen who had been dissuaded by Gage's warning from leaving town. Dr. Prince was standing with some of his neighbors in the road when a man in a long civilian coat came riding across the Neck and pulled up in front of them. He asked, casually, "What's the news, fellow patriots?"

Dr. Prince thought the rider's face looked familiar. When someone answered that there wasn't anything very new, the man spurred his horse. He spurred too hard, and as the horse plunged forward the rider's coat ballooned out, revealing the scarlet and white of a British uniform.

The men with muskets standing with Dr. Prince snapped them to their shoulders. Dr. Prince, on the impulse to save a man he knew from being killed, yelled, "Don't shoot! He's my friend, Small, a fine fellow!"

As the rider galloped toward the ferry, Dr. Prince had some fast explaining to do. It was Small, all right—Major John Small of His Majesty's Army!

One of the doctor's neighbors pointed out angrily that, since the officer had come from the direction of Lexington, he was probably a messenger on his way to Boston from Lord Percy. All Dr. Prince could say was that he had not thought of him as an enemy at the moment, but as a personable young officer he had met and liked.

Near sunset distant firing was heard. A frightening rumor had fanned through the village: "The British are massacring everybody in their path!"

Families hurried across the Neck, hugging the mud flats along the Mystic on the right to the penny ferry to Malden or the Medford bridge beyond it. Others ran to the clay pits on the far side of Bunker Hill. Many stood in the doorways of their homes, helpless with fear.

Captain Jacob Rogers' house was on one of the back streets of Charlestown. He had made up his mind early in the day that he wouldn't leave his family to the mercy of the British, even though he was an officer of the militia. His children were young, and there was his wife's sister dependent on him, too.

Late in the afternoon there was no longer any doubt that the British would retreat through the village. Men had ridden out and galloped back with the news that the embattled column was turning off the Cambridge Road and swinging toward the Charlestown peninsula. Rogers put his family in the chaise and drove to the Neck. A neighbor was filling a cart with children. It seemed to Rogers that a vehicle carrying children surely wouldn't be molested. He put his own brood in with them and watched the driver whip the horses down the road.

As he started after them in the chaise with his wife and sister-in-law, he saw musket flashes far ahead. A man standing on the roadside yelled, "My God! They're shooting at the young ones!"

Rogers put the whip to his horse. He had reached the narrow part of the Neck when he saw his neighbor, David Waitt, riding toward him. Waitt pulled up short and grabbed the bridle of Rogers' horse. He steered the chaise off the road.

"Quick, Jacob!" he shouted. "The troops are coming onto the Common. They're shooting at everybody in sight!"

Still holding the bridle, he led the carriage across the fields toward Bunker Hill. The cart with the children, he said, had gotten off the road and was going across the flats toward the Mystic. He had been close by when it had been fired on. He was sure none of the children had been hit.

Rogers drove to his father-in-law's pasture on the top of Bunker Hill and tethered the horse. As he helped the women out, he saw the British coming up the slope only forty rods away. The two women lifted their long skirts and ran with Rogers across the pasture. They met the tailor, Hayley, and his wife coming toward them from the village. Hayley didn't know the British were on the hill. He had his musket on his shoulder. The British spotted it and opened fire.

He flung the gun away and they all raced down the slope. Rogers thought the musket balls sounded like angry hornets around his head. He expected to see his wife or her sister drop at any moment.

The nearest house was that of Mr. Townsend, the pump maker.

They found it filled with women and children. Rogers left his wife and her sister there and walked down to the village center with several of his neighbors to see what was happening. It was dark now. On the way they met another neighbor coming up the street. He said it was getting quiet in the village. The officers had gone through the streets calling out that the women and children should stay indoors. The soldiers were going from door to door asking for rum. The people were gladly handing it out to keep from being mistreated.

Rogers went into the tavern by the town house. It was crowded with officers. He had never seen so much confusion. They were all calling for drinks. The frightened innkeeper and his wife were scurrying among them, passing out mugs as fast as they could, but it seemed to Rogers they would never catch up with the demand. To his surprise, the officers didn't appear hostile. They were exhausted, and apparently so glad to have reached safety that all they wanted was the luxury of a stiff drink.

He found his house had not been harmed. Returning to Mr. Townsend's, he brought his wife and her sister home. They were about to go to bed when a neighbor came with the news that Mrs. Rogers' fourteen-year-old brother had been killed by the redcoats as they came into the town. Somehow, he had become separated from his mother and the other children, the neighbor said. He had gone back to the house on the Neck and was standing at a window when the British came by. That was where they had found him: under the window in the front room, with a ball through his forehead.

Early next morning, Rogers got his horse and chaise from the hill and went searching for his children. Some rascals, he discovered, had stolen the seat cushion and cleaned out the toolbox. A camp of British troops covered the far slope of Bunker Hill. A heavy guard had been thrown across the Neck. A sentry directed him to Brigadier-General Robert Pigot, who was in charge. Rogers found a number of other Charlestown fathers waiting ahead of him. General Pigot said he would have to send to headquarters in Boston for permission to let them go out and hunt for their children. Rogers waited. It was getting dusk when the word came.

At the penny ferry he learned that the cartload of children had crossed there. He rode on toward Malden, stopping at every farmhouse along the way until he got to the village and found them at the home of his friend, Captain Waters.

NINETEEN

IN THE OLD BURIAL GROUND ON BOSTON'S COPP'S HILL, BRITISH OFFI-
cers stood among the gravestones of the city's Puritan founders
in the dusk and trained their field glasses on the distant cloud
of gunsmoke and dust. The sun set at half past six, and now the
muskets flickered like fireflies on the northwestern horizon.

General Gage, hardly able to believe the reports that were
coming in, ordered the rowboats of the men-of-war in the harbor
rushed to the Charlestown water front. He had General Pigot
muster five hundred re-enforcements.

"My Lord," he wrote to Percy, "Gen. Pigot will pass over with
a Reinforcement and fresh ammunition. The Boats which carry
him may return with the Grenadiers and Light Infantry who
must be most fatigued and the wounded."

By half past seven, the gunfire had died out as the rear of
Percy's column reached the protection of Bunker Hill.

By eight, the wounded were being moved through the village
to the water front.

Among the first to reach the waiting boats was young Ensign
Lister. The pain from his shattered elbow now stabbed deep
into his shoulder. It seemed more than he could take at moments.
The cold salt water splashing off the gunwales soaked through
the dried blood. It set his teeth to chattering. He wondered if he
would ever be able to use the arm again. At least he would live,
he consoled himself. That was apparently more than Lieutenant
Sutherland could be sure of. The way Sutherland had been fretting over the wound in his chest, he did not expect to get over it.

Lister had never realized before how far it was from the Common to his lodgings at Mrs. Miller's. He hurried through the

dark, silent streets shaking with a chill and sick at his stomach. When he saw the many faces that turned to stare at him as he came into the Miller sitting room he wished he had slipped quietly in the back way. But he needed something hot in his stomach. The rum they had served him at the tavern in Charlestown had worn off long ago.

Besides the Millers and Mr. and Mrs. Funnel, the genteel middle-aged Tory couple who had moved in from the country, there were a number of anxious-faced women in the room. They made a great fuss over him, but mostly they wanted to hear about the day's happenings.

He told Mrs. Miller he had to get warm first of all. They gave him a chair by the fire and wrapped a blanket around him. Mrs. Miller made hot tea for him from the kettle on the hearth. He recognized some of the women around him as wives of officers he knew. When he assured them that their husbands had come through unhurt, their faces relaxed. They helped him off with his boots, poured fresh tea into his cup. One with sure, gentle hands unwrapped the bandage on his arm and washed the wound with hot water into which she had stirred a handful of dried herbs. Another tore an old flannel petticoat into strips for a fresh bandage.

They all knew Lieutenant Sutherland, and when Lister said he had been wounded in the fight at the bridge the room was suddenly silent. Then one of them asked in a barely audible voice whether the lieutenant had been badly hurt.

"Pretty badly," Lister answered. "I suppose he's dead by now."

There was a thump behind his chair and several of the women said, "Oh!" One screamed. A very pretty young woman lay on the floor in a faint. She was Lieutenant Sutherland's wife.

One of the women scolded Lister gently.

"You should not have said that unless you were sure," she said.

He answered indignantly, staring back at the reproachful faces around him, "I didn't know she was here."

Ensign Lister spent a sleepless, pain-racked night, the first of many to come. Like others of the wounded in Boston, and in the colonial camp, he knew that a simple gun wound could mean months of torture, possibly even slow death if infection set in.

The next day an army surgeon came and examined his arm, shook his head gravely over it. He advised Lister to drink a cup of hot tea made of Jesuits' bark every two hours, day and night, "to prevent mortification."

The arm swelled to three times its normal size, turned dark, festered. The young ensign lay in his room, the blinds drawn, alone during the day except for Mrs. Miller's visit every two hours with the cup of Jesuits' bark tea and the army surgeon who dropped by for brief calls every few days. But the doctor was a busy man and there was not much he could do except watch and hope that the wound would eventually heal by itself.

On one of his early calls he had given Lister a stiff shot of rum and, while the young officer screamed with pain, cut long slashes in the angry-looking, swollen flesh to expose the bone and let out the pus. On May 9th he brought along another surgeon and they consulted whether or not to amputate the arm. They decided, fortunately, to wait a few days more.

It was not until two months later, July 15th, that Lister could finally write to his father in England that the arm was now slowly getting better. The elbow would be permanently stiff, he said, but he was getting back the use of his fingers.

Sutherland, meanwhile, had recovered. And the widow of the young grenadier, Gibson, was on a transport going back alone to her home in Ireland. She had stood all that night of April 19th at the water's edge, the cold wind whipping at her long skirt, watching the men come back in the boats, running up as close to the boats as the guards would let her to scan the blurred faces in the moonlight. As the men filed past, her voice worn hoarse from repetition, she had called to them: "Private Gibson. Have you seen Private Gibson?"

Finally one of them had called back, "He's dead, Ma'am."

As the boats came in the British tabulated their casualties. Seventy-three had been killed, a hundred and seventy-four wounded. Twenty-six were missing.

The American casualties, they were to learn from Tory informers, were: forty-nine killed, thirty-nine wounded, and five missing.

Lord Percy was in one of the first boats that left Charlestown that night. The *Somerset's* fastest oarsmen rowed him to Boston Common. A button was missing from the Earl's coat, snipped off by a Yankee musket ball in Menotomy. His tired face was dark with gunsmoke and dust, his uniform mud-blotched where the waves had drenched it in crossing.

He hurried up the slope to Province House and into the up-stairs room where General Gage was waiting. The general's us-ually impassive face wore deep lines of frustration and shock as he listened to his aide's story.

The realistic young earl gave him a blunt and enlightened account of the day's debacle and the dedicated mood of rebellion he had encountered. He admitted he had suddenly acquired a solid respect for the men he had previously dismissed as "sly, artful rascals, cruel and cowards."

It was after midnight when Percy left Province House. He was still too keyed up for sleep, so he got off a letter to his friend, Adjutant General Edward Harvey in London.

"Whoever looks upon them as an irregular mob will find him-self much mistaken," he said. "They have men amongst them who know very well what they are about, having been employed as Rangers against the Indians and Canadians; and this country, being much covered with wood, and hills, is very advantageous for their method of fighting.

"Nor are several of their men void of a spirit of enthusiasm, as we experienced yesterday, for many of them concealed them-selves in houses and advanced within ten yards to fire at me and other officers, though they were mortally certain of being put to death themselves in an instant.

"You may depend upon it, that as the rebels have now had time to prepare, they are determined to go through with it, nor will the insurrection here turn out so despicable as it is perhaps imagined at home. For my part, I never believed, I confess, that they would have attacked the King's troops, or have had the perseverance I found in them yesterday."

The candles burned low in the crystal chandelier over the big walnut desk in Gage's study long after Lord Percy had left. Through the wavy glass panes of the windows looking out over the Common, the general could see the twinkle of a long row of campfires along the opposite shore of the Charles.

They were the fires of independence. Between the dawn and darkness of that April day, Great Britain had lost control forever over her American colonies.

The Cambridge campfires burned all night, and all night new recruits came in. They came with muskets slanted on their shoulders, cradled in their arms or slung Indian-fashion at their sides; with ancient horse pistols in their belts. Some, who did not own guns, came swinging pickaxes and shovels.

"If we can't fight," they said, "we can dig."

They had no uniforms, only the clothes they wore in the fields or in their village shops: the checkered shirts, the thick-soled half boots, the leather or homespun woolen breeches, the weather-faded tricorn hats.

There were young men among them with down on their chins and the pimpled faces of adolescence, and old men with shaggy, tobacco-stained beards and rheumatic legs.

They crowded around the men who had gotten in their licks against the "damned redcoats," listened silently to the talk of hairbreadth escapes and hand-to-hand encounters on the road from Concord. Now and then they lifted their faces to stare broodingly at the scattered pin points of light and the black skyline of the British citadel across the river.

Those who had the foresight to bring along a cut of bacon or a sausage shared it with the others. The people of the farms and the villagers of Cambridge handed out loaves of bread and a ham or bacon from their smokehouses.

The regiments and companies that had been in the fighting had become hopelessly entangled. In the circles around the fires there were few who knew more than two or three of their companions. Company captains and lieutenants spent half the night picking their way across the dark fields and pastures, the burial grounds and churchyards, walking from campfire to campfire to stare at the faces in the yellow light.

They called out to the men they recognized or thought they did: "Ezekiel, come along." "Hey, Samuel." "Moses? That you?" "Halloo, John." Old names out of the Bible and the short, familiar names of today: Aaron, Abel, Agijah, Abner, Amos, Elias, Isaac, Jedidiah, Jonathan, William and Joe.

At last the reshuffling of faces around the campfires was over. The men piled on more fence rails and brush and lay down on the cold ground with whatever cover they could find: an armful of straw or hay, the lucky ones under a horse blanket "borrowed" from a nearby barn. Many of them had no cover at all.

Soon after midnight the men were roused by the guns of one of the patrols. An armed schooner was coming up the river. General Heath thought it was the start of an attack, until he saw that the ship was alone. He decided it was merely on reconnaissance. The tide was out and as the men crowded the shore it grounded on a sand bar far out. A few waded into the canebrake and fired their muskets at the men they could see working frantically with poles in the ship's prow. Heath called them back. They were wasting precious powder, he said. The ship was well out of range.

He stood watching with the rest until the tide came in and the schooner slid away. If there were only a cannon in the camp! Just one cannon!

Daybreak brought with it a major crisis: how to provide enough food to feed nearly five thousand hungry men! Heath delegated squads to visit every house in the village and collect everything edible they could. The Harvard College kitchens were emptied of their cooking utensils. A butcher turned over several carcasses of pork and beef he had ready for the Boston market. At Roxbury, a supply of ship's bread on its way to the Brititsh navy was confiscated.

The meetinghouse had been turned into a hospital. Most of the benches had been stacked outside. The others had been pulled together and planks laid over them for operating tables. Dr. Eliphald Downer, who had killed a redcoat with his bayonet in Menotomy the afternoon before, came to the doorway and stared with fatigue-shadowed eyes at the men crouching around

the kettles over the campfires. Major John Brooks, the young
Reading physician who had led his company into the fighting at
Meriam's Corner, came and stood beside him. They had been up
all night, bandaging arms and legs, cutting British musket balls
out of flesh. They had no stomach for breakfast.

General Heath assigned a company from Dedham to go back
up the road to Concord and see that all the dead were buried.

And in Acton, four miles from Concord, the widow of Captain
Isaac Davis, her brown hair parted in the middle, combed tight
to her head, moved silently about the little upstairs bedroom,
her restless hands straightening a window curtain, picking a
piece of lint off the counterpane of the high four-poster bed,
smoothing out a crease in the pillow under her husband's head.
She had tried putting the rocker beside the bed and sitting there,
but it was too low to see anything but his profile and the hands
crossed on his chest.

In the dark Sabbath clothes she had put on him it seemed to
her he might have lain down for a nap, as he so often used to do
while she finished off dinner after their return from church. He
looked so serene, so young still and full of quiet strength. She
remembered how he had looked back at her just before they
marched off. "Take care of the children," was all he had said. He
was about to speak again, but he turned abruptly and marched
off. She kept wondering what it was he had wanted to say.

When the coffins were finished, they were going to bring Abner Hosmer's body to the house, and James Hayward's. There
would be a single funeral service for all three. Hosmer, they said,
had been killed at almost the same instant as her husband. Young
Hayward, who had shot it out with a British soldier at the pump
near Lexington, had still been alive when they brought him
home. He had died last night with a sudden convulsion and
moan of agony.

Concord had had the battle, but the dead were from Acton.

TWENTY

GENERAL ARTEMUS WARD WAS IN BED IN HIS HOME IN SHREWSBURY, suffering with bladder stones, when the express rider brought the news of Lexington and Concord. Ward was a big man, fat and florid-faced. A descendant of one of the original Boston Puritans, graduate of Harvard, he had risen to colonel in the provincial militia during the French and Indian War and had served with Abercrombie in the '58 debacle at Ticonderoga.

He had originally taught school, but had given it up after a few years for the more profitable business of running a general store. An easygoing man, a slow talker, his main interests next to making a living for his big family—there were eight children— had been town politics and the local militia. From the beginning of the trouble with England he had given his spare time to organizing and drilling his Shrewsbury neighbors. When the Provincial Congress, in February, had appointed general officers, he had received senior rating.

Now, as the express rider galloped on, he got out of bed and into his uniform. Gritting his teeth against the stabbing pains that raked his bowels every now and then, he mounted and rode to Cambridge, surrounded by his minutemen neighbors. Along the way they fell in with other companies coming in from the side roads. From Marlboro on, the road was ground to dust by the footsteps of those who had gone before them.

Near Boston, an occasional carriage overtook them, filled with the family and bundled possessions of Tories hurrying to the security of Boston. Coming the other way were other carriages and wagons—mostly wagons—crowded with women and children and old men, and their bedclothes and trunks. These were the families of patriots who were leaving Boston and the perimeter of villages that had become a sprawling armed camp overnight.

In Cambridge, General Heath had set up headquarters in the white clapboard house of Jonathan Hastings. When Ward arrived, Heath turned over the command to him as senior member of the Massachusetts military staff. They settled down to the massive task of trying to shape into a military organization the scattered thousands of old and young and middle-aged men with their fowling pieces and squirrel guns, shovels and axes, who were still tramping in from every corner of the province.

Dr. Joseph Warren, his shirt sleeves rolled back, waistcoat unbuttoned, labored with the two generals. So did the brilliant, urbane Marlborough Street surgeon, Dr. Benjamin Church, Jr. As members of the Committee of Safety with Warren as president, they represented the government of the colony. Church was also a member of the Provincial Congress, now gathering in Watertown.

Paul Revere was on hand for "the outdoor business," as he called his express riding. Another post rider, Israel Bissel, was already galloping down the long main highway hugging the coast line through Providence, New London, New Haven and New York to Philadelphia, carrying Warren's bitter account of the British actions to the continental leaders getting ready to convene their second Congress there.

Waiting for Dr. Warren to finish writing an appeal to the towns of Massachusetts for immediate and all possible help, Revere watched Dr. Church working furiously at his paper-littered table. One of the doctor's stockings was smeared with dried blood. It had spurted on him, Church explained, when the man crouching beside him was killed in the fighting near Prospect Hill.

Revere was glad he had never told anyone his suspicion of the talented patriot ringleader and surgeon. He had been tempted to several times during the last year when he discovered that information turned in by his Committee of Mechanics, in their secret meetings at the Green Dragon, had mysteriously leaked to the British. Only his thirty mechanics and tradesmen, all men he knew and trusted, and the eleven-member Committee of Safety, to whom their reports were sent, knew what was said and done in the closely-guarded upstairs room at the inn. Yet the patriot son-in-law of one of the Tories who worked for General Gage had warned him repeatedly that someone was keeping the British informed of their activities. Dr. Church occasionally dined with one of the British officers at a Tory inn in Boston. Revere had doubted his story that he was cultivating the officer to get information.

But now, Revere told himself, he would have to look among the other members of the Committee of Safety for the betrayer. A man who would risk his life for the cause was surely devoted to it.

As oxcarts and wagons brought in the provisions and war supplies that had been hidden in Concord and Worcester, Groton and Sudbury, General Ward extended his lines from Charlestown on the north down the coast line, some fourteen miles, to Roxbury, where the British-fortified neck of land connected the southern tip of Boston with the mainland. Except for the seaward side, Boston was hemmed in by a ragged line of fiery-eyed provincials building themselves shelters with everything from boards and sailcloth to brush plastered together with mud, their arms warily stacked within easy reach.

The roisterous men from the Boston wharves, the shipwrights and riggers, the sailmakers and ropewalkers, out of work and living on what they could scavenge since Gage had closed down the port, had slipped across the bay during the night and were enthusiastically lending their skills, sewing canvas into tents, sawing boards and logs for huts.

When General Ward learned that the last of the British troops had pulled out of Charlestown, he posted strong patrols in the village to watch the ferry lane. Fatigue parties set to work in Roxbury building redoubts from which the cannon brought from Concord and Worcester could cover Boston Neck. General Heath moved into them with four regiments.

Colorful frontier warriors from Connecticut and New Hampshire were now marching their regiments to the primitive barricade around Boston.

One of them was fifty-seven-year-old Colonel Israel Putnam of Pomfret, Connecticut. "Old Put" had had little formal schooling, but he knew at first hand the survival secrets of the wilderness and the skulking ways of Indians on the warpath.

He had been a scout with Rogers' Rangers. He had been captured by Indians in '55 and tied to a tree. The Indians had piled fagots high around him and were setting them afire when a rescue party arrived. He had been shipwrecked in a hurricane off Cuba.

He had the round, deeply-creased face and white hair of a well-fed squire out of an English comedy. He was fat but still filled with driving energy, and he was immensely popular with his men. The tavern he operated as a side line on his farm in Pomfret was the village hangout for reminiscing ex-soldiers of the war with France and the young men of the newly-organized militia. A year ago, when Boston had begun to feel the pinch of the British blockade, he had driven a flock of sheep, the gift of his fellow-villagers, the eighty-odd miles to the city.

Now he was traveling the same twisting country roads, with the minutemen of Pomfret and the farmlands around it marching at his heels.

From Londonderry, New Hampshire, came another of Robert Rogers' French and Indian War scouts. He was Colonel John Stark, a captain in the tough Rangers that had bested the Indians at their own tricks and dished out a hefty measure of their own. A lean, hard-muscled man, reserved and stubborn-minded, he had grown up on the frontier, in an area where life was harsh and primitive and consisted mainly of fishing and hunting and fighting Indians. He had been with Abercrombie in his bloody defeat at Ticonderoga and with Amherst at the capture of the fort, a year later, and at Crown Point. Up to now he was best remembered for a forty-mile trek he had made through deep snow in the winter of '57 after a day-long fight and night march, to bring rescue to a scouting party besieged near Lake Champlain.

Massachusetts had its own memorable leaders coming into camp: Colonel William Prescott, the tall, forty-nine-year-old farmer from Pepperell with the quiet knack for making his courage contagious; General Seth Pomeroy, tall as Prescott, still at sixty-eight strong as an Indian buck, frontiersman and famous hunter in his younger days, now a gunsmith in Northampton.

These were the men the militia crowding into the Cambridge

camps looked up to with almost religious devotion. There were nearly twenty thousand of them now. They were a queer breed, independent, opinionated, sentimental and tough as boot leather, as ready to fight for their prejudices as for their homes and children.

Within a few days their rage against the British army they had driven back across the river lost its edge and they began to worry about their farms and families: how their wives were making out with the stock and the children, the fields that needed sowing, the unfinished harness or pair of boots or unground grain for a neighbor. The mud was hardly dry on some of their lean-tos when they began to drift back home, casually shouldering their muskets and walking off down the road, singly, in little groups, even companies. Why stick around when there was so much to do back home and things looked pretty quiet here?

The desperate Provincial Congress at Watertown, unable to wait for the Continental Congress to come to a decision on supporting Massachusetts against a British attack, authorized enlistment of the militia into a provincial army. It dug into its scant treasury for money to pay the soldiery and offer bonuses to officers who signed up their companies for the rest of the year. It set up printing presses to turn out currency. Paul Revere, once more the skilled craftsman, engraved the plates.

While he tooled away at the design Revere thought again about Dr. Church and the blood on his stocking. He remembered the next day. It was Friday, late in the afternoon, and several members of the Committee of Safety were meeting with Dr. Warren in his room at the Hastings house. Revere had just come in and laid a dispatch on Warren's desk. He heard Dr. Church say, so quietly that he wasn't sure at first he had heard him correctly, "Dr. Warren, I am going into Boston tomorrow."

Dr. Warren said, staring at him, "Are you serious, Dr. Church? They will hang you if they catch you in Boston!"

"I am serious," Church answered. "I am determined to go at all adventure!"

"But why?"

Dr. Church looked down and pulled at one of the buttons on his waistcoat.

"It is a personal matter," he said. Revere saw a touch of color on his cheeks. "Purely personal."

Dr. Church had left his attractive wife back in the house on Marlborough Street. She was English and her dresses showed accomplished taste. He had married her during the year he had spent in London finishing his surgical training. But Revere knew, as did most of the others in the room, that the debonair and witty doctor was interested in another woman he had also left behind him in Boston: his American-born young mistress.

After a strained silence, Dr. Warren said, "Well, if you are determined, let us at least find some business for you there. No one knows better how badly we need medicine for our wounded. Do you think you could bring some back with you?"

"I shall surely try my best," Church answered.

Revere saw him ride off the next morning. He came back Sunday night. He said wearily as he took a few packages out of his saddlebag, "This is all the medicine the damned British would let me bring out."

He had had a trying time. When he arrived at the enemy lines on Boston Neck, he said, they had arrested him and taken him to Gage. The general's aides had questioned him until he thought he could endure no more of it. But he had managed to tell them nothing that they didn't already know. Afterward they had locked him in a room in the barracks. He had been allowed only one short visit to his home, and then it was with an officer guarding him.

It had sounded plausible to Revere. But this afternoon he had met a friend who had only recently left Boston. He was Deacon Caleb Davis.

The deacon told Revere that the Saturday after Lexington he had received a peremptory summons from General Gage "on a matter of business." When he arrived, he was told to wait in the antechamber.

"The general," his aide explained to the deacon, "is in private conversation with a gentleman."

It was a good half hour before the study door opened. The gentleman who walked out with Gage was Dr. Church. They were talking in low, confidential tones. When Dr. Church saw Deacon Davis he was plainly startled.

"His face became very red," said the deacon, "and after briefly acknowledging my greeting he hurried away. I talked to others who saw him that day, and they said that Dr. Church arrived at Province House in a chaise and walked up the steps more like an important visitor than a prisoner. He went where he pleased the rest of the day, attended only by one of Gage's aides, a Major Caine."

He would pass the deacon's story on to Dr. Warren when he saw him tonight, Revere decided. But what could they do about it? If Dr. Church was betraying the patriot cause he would surely have a glib explanation on hand. Actually, the story he had told on his return jibed roughly with the deacon's. He had said he had been taken to Gage, and he had had a guard.

Revere wished he could slip into Boston and see how Rachel and the children were making out. According to Billy Dawes, they were all well, at least; and so far nobody had tried to harm them.

The man who had helped Revere carry the message to Lexington was the only one of the leading patriots who still had no trouble getting in and out of Boston. In his favorite disguise as a dim-witted but amusing bumpkin, Dawes wandered through the lines on heavily-fortified Boston Neck as he pleased. He had managed to get his wife and children settled with friends in Watertown. Their family silver and other cherished possessions they had buried under the Anne Street house and hidden in the cistern. Whatever they could dispose of they turned into gold coin. It was left with his sister, who was remaining in Boston.

Once a week, Billy Dawes drifted onto the Neck and hob-nobbed with the British sentries who knew him for a ne'er-do-well who was always slightly inebriated and good for a laugh or two. They swapped banter with him for a while, then ignored him. His long farmer's coat, his soiled waistcoat and leather breeches had cloth-covered buttons wherever there was a possible spot for one. The sentries considered it one of his many eccentricities. When Dawes reached the house in town, his sister removed the buttons, snipped open the cloth cover and took out the wooden molds. She replaced them with gold coins and sewed them back into place.

Next day, in Watertown, Dawes' young wife, Mehitable, removed the coins and replaced them again with wooden molds.

While the stalemate lasted, the days dragged in sedentary dullness for the sentries on the Neck, the British standing at their fortified gate, the Americans at their road blocks just out of gun range. There was a brief interlude one afternoon in early May. A carriage arrived at the provincial barrier. It was no ordinary carriage, but an English coach lavishly ornamented in gold, and the woman inside was beautiful and dressed in wine-colored satin. Strung out behind was a caravan of phaetons, chaises and loaded wagons. An escort of provincial troopers came with it.

The officer in charge of the guard had never seen anything so elegant. He looked at the woman's pass, stamped with the seal of the Provincial Congress, and, in a sudden flush of Yankee stubbornness, refused to honor it. One of the troopers rode to Cambridge and came back with Dr. Warren. Warren scolded the officer and apologized to the pretty woman in the coach.

She was Lady Frankland, and the wagons were loaded with hay and corn, three canopy beds and their bedding, six sheep, two pigs, a crate of chickens, a keg of pickled tongues, hams and cured veal, seven trunks, and two barrels and a hamper of household goods. She had appealed to the Congress to let her move from her estate, Frankland Hall, at Hopkinton outside Framingham, to her town house, the old Clark mansion near the Revere home.

To urbane Dr. Warren and the members of the Congress she was the wealthy widow of Sir Harry Frankland, the personable one-time collector of the port for Massachusetts. But to the Puritan housewives of Boston she would always be "that Surriage woman," spoken with narrowed eyes and a cold frown of disapproval. Her poignant love story was not fit, they said, for the ears of children.

Sir Harry was a young man when Britain sent him to Boston as collector of the port soon after the war with France ended. As he walked into a Marblehead inn one night, a young serving girl on her knees scrubbing the taproom floor had to move her pail out of his path. She lifted her eyes.

The young baronet looked down, and his life was never the same again. This was the loveliest face he had ever seen! It was an exquisite cameo, a miniature by Peale, framed in dirty suds!

When Sir Harry returned to his Boston mansion the next day, Agnes Surriage went with him—her status: servant. Combed and scrubbed, dressed in the best imported silks the bachelor baronet could buy, she promptly attracted wide-eyed attention whenever she left the house. Sir Harry hired a tutor for her and let it be known that his intentions were purely altruistic: to educate the pretty little unfortunate he had rescued from a gray life of drudgery.

But soon there was no hiding it any longer: Sir Harry had a mistress.

Agnes Surriage, however, had more than a pretty face and animal charm. She learned fast, not only the social graces, but how to keep Sir Harry enchanted. In a few years, while they were on a tour of Europe, he threw propriety to the wind and married her.

Sir Harry died a few years later and Agnes, Lady Frankland now, inherited his estate, including one of the finest of the old mansions in Boston and the baronial country seat at Hopkinton.

The Puritan mothers of Boston thought there ought to be a moral somewhere in all this, but it was difficult to put a finger on it. Agnes Surriage had done very well for herself.

TWENTY-ONE

WHEN THE BRITISH EXPEDITION RETREATED INTO CHARLESTOWN, the night of April 19th, Gage sent re-enforcements across the Charles under Brigadier-General Pigot. He ordered them to throw up a redoubt and dig trenches across the neck, intending to hold the village as his northern outpost. The next day he had the works demolished and withdrew the last of his troops into Boston.

Through their field glasses, Gage and his officers watched the massing provincial army drill and build its encampment. At night they counted the line of campfires, a string of tiny red beads glinting on the long perimeter across the river and bay.

Gage was as fearful of an attack on his garrison in Boston as the provincials were that he would send an expedition against them. Bewildered by the totally unexpected turn affairs had taken, he got little comfort out of the reports of his spies, that there was hardly any military order in the swelling American camp. They seemed to be able to fight very well without it.

Most of the officers had been billeted in private homes, comfortably out of range of the ripe body smells and packed quarters of the barracks. The provincial uprising now brought the discomforts of war sharply home to the smartly caparisoned men in epaulets. Gage ordered that they were to sleep with their men.

But by May the campfires were no longer visible across the Charles at night. From his spies and Tory informers Gage learned that the twenty thousand provincials had dwindled to seventy-five hundred. Those who remained were in improvised shelters hidden by the lush foliage.

Gage had moved his heaviest warships into the Charles. The

Somerset with its sixty-eight guns still guarded the ferry lane from Charlestown. The *Lively* and *Falcon,* both mounting twenty guns, were on either side of her. The *Glasgow,* twenty-four guns, was anchored farther upriver.

Fearing the people of Boston would rise behind his lines if the provincials attacked, Gage sent word to the town's selectmen that all privately-held arms would have to be turned in to headquarters, tagged with the names of their owners so they could be returned when the unpleasantness was over. On the appointed day, seventeen hundred and seventy-eight muskets were surrendered, six hundred and thirty-four pistols, nine hundred and seventy-three bayonets and thirty-eight blunderbusses.

In return, Gage promised that inhabitants who wished could leave the city and take their transportable property with them. He received from the camp across the river, in exchange, an agreement to let the Tories from the interior move their effects into Boston.

The agreement was no sooner made than Gage regretted it. General Timothy Ruggles, the bluff leader of the Boston Tories, pointed out the danger in it. Once the patriot families were out of the city, there would be nothing to keep the rebels from setting its clustered wooden houses afire with the incendiary shells called carcasses or by patrols slipping across the water at night.

So Gage quickly wrapped the issuance of permits to leave in a tangle of red tape. Women and old men stood in long lines up and down Marlborough Street outside Province House. The lines did not move all day. At dark the people went back to their homes, to come back and stand again the next day. Rachel Revere was among them, and waited with slowly fading hope like all the rest.

Life had become almost as trying for the British garrison. The men were now on salt rations, since the only supplies they could get had to come in by ship from ports less hostile far down the coast. Fresh meat became such a luxury that some unfeeling rascals slipped up on General Pigot's little black cow at night and cut off her tail for stew.

Both the garrison and the citizens of Boston were running out of firewood for cooking, since farmers were no longer bringing any in. Fences disappeared, and even the wooden casings around the wells. Gage issued stern orders against stealing wood. But the soldiers in the fatigue details sent out to collect tree limbs for the defenses known as fascines developed a way to get around that.

Having stripped a tree of the branches that were the right size, they casually cut off a few more. Then a few more after that. Soon nothing remained but the bare trunk. What possible good was that? So they cut it up and surreptitiously peddled it to waiting civilians.

But the high command had something more important to worry about just now. Sentries at the Neck and the members of fatigue squads who ventured too close to the scattered trees and bushes beyond the lines were being silently picked off in broad daylight by enemies they couldn't see.

For a provincial to expose himself by the flare of his musket from such hiding places was suicide. He would be cut down by a British volley before he could take a step toward safety. But the weapons doing the damage weren't muskets. They were bows and arrows in the expert hands of Indians who hid in the high foliage of a tree or behind a bush and dispatched their deadly shafts without the telltale disturbance of a leaf.

The British didn't know where they had come from, but they wished they'd go back home.

As May yellowed the forsythia and nudged the orchards into bloom along the Charlestown-Cambridge-Roxbury perimeter, an institution that had performed a major miracle for America slipped quietly into history. The minutemen, the volunteer farmers and villagers of Massachusetts who had rushed from their homes to drive the British back into Boston, became a part of the past. Some had gone back to tend their land or reopen their shops. The rest had enrolled for eight-months' service as full-time soldiers in the provincial army.

They still chose their own company officers, their captains and lieutenants and ensigns; and the company commanders elected the field officers, the majors, lieutenant colonels and colonels. Discipline was a commodity as scarce as good cannon.

A captain ordered one of his men to get another pail of water.

"Get it yourself, Cap'n," the private told him. "I got the last one."

A company commander who had been the village barber back home obligingly tucked a blanket around one of his men's neck and gave him a haircut in front of the company tent. A row of privates sat to one side patiently waiting their turn.

The Reverend William Emerson of Concord visited the Cambridge headquarters and found it "diverting to walk among the camps."

He found the shelters as varied as the dress of their occupants. It amused him to see how each reflected the general character of the men who lived in it. Some were constructed of boards, some were no more than four poles covered with sailcloth. Others were made of stone and turf, or of brush plastered with mud. He found a few that showed loving care and painstaken construction. The doors were set in sturdy timbers. The windows were framed in wreaths of braided twigs.

The Indians had their own camp of primitive lean-tos. They were of the Stockbridge tribe in the western end of the province. There were fifty of them, and they came as minutemen, filled with a fine enthusiasm to help do in their old enemies, the British. But the provincials distrusted them, particularly those from the interior who had grown up under the dark terror of border warfare. To them the only good Indian was a dead one. The Indians soon sensed the hostility and drifted back home.

For a while there was so little activity in the provincial camp that Corporal Amos Farnsworth of Groton looked forward to Sunday services as the highlight of the week. He liked particularly the sermon he heard the second Sunday in May. The minister took his text from the second epistle of Paul to Timothy: "Thou therefore endure hardness, as a good soldier of Jesus Christ."

That was exactly what he was doing, Amos told himself: sleeping on the hard ground in a drafty lean-to, standing guard duty till his feet ached worse than they did after plowing, and never getting quite enough to eat. But he had listened to General Ward's speech about how important it was to keep the damned redcoats from making slaves of the people, and had enlisted for

the rest of the year. He wished, though, that soldiering wasn't
such a dull business.

The third Sunday in May the tempo suddenly picked up.
There were a number of islands around Boston, laid out in
pasture lands and meadows. On one of them, Grape Island, south
of the city, the British had stored hay for their horses. They sent
two sloops and an armed schooner to pick it up. Private Farnsworth was in one of the three companies General Ward sent to
meet them. There was a brief encounter, and the British retreated. The provincials burned the hay. They destroyed eighty
tons and loaded the cattle on the island aboard a lighter
and took them to camp.

Off Chelsea, north of Boston, there were two large islands, Hog
and Noddle's, lying close together and separated from the mainland by a narrow channel only three feet deep at low tide. The
farms on them were stocked with cattle and sheep. The Americans knew the British were feeling the pinch of shortened rations,
and decided it was time to remove temptation.

The Saturday after the Grape Island encounter, General Ward
sent an expedition to take the cattle off the two islands and destroy whatever fodder they couldn't remove. Private Farnsworth
was seeing action again.

The Americans landed first on Hog Island and brought off six
horses, twenty-seven cattle and four hundred and eleven sheep.
They went back and were crossing Hog Island to Noddle's, the
farther out of the two, when the British spotted them and sent
forty marines aboard a schooner and a sloop to drive them off.
The provincials managed to set a barn filled with salt hay on fire
and a house. They killed a number of cattle and horses and drove
the rest in front of them as they retreated to Hog Island. There
the marines caught up with them.

Amos Farnsworth lay in a ditch with fifteen others and
watched the marines come on the run across the marsh. When
those in the lead were within squirrel-shooting range the provincials fired. Four marines fell. The rest crouched in the tall
grass and fired back.

None of the provincials was hurt. They continued shooting
from the security of their ditch, and the marines retreated. By

sunset, Farnsworth and his company were back with the rest of the detachment. They crossed to the Chelsea mainland. Meanwhile more marines had arrived in boats from the men-of-war in the harbor and landed on Noddle's Island, in easy gun range of the mainland. From the American camp came General Putnam and Dr. Warren with re-enforcements.

The British schooner came in close and opened fire with her swivel guns. Putnam had brought two cannons with him, and put them to work. The battle lasted until eleven that night. The schooner ran aground then, and as the Americans closed in the British abandoned her. Toward morning, a party of twelve provincials boarded her. They took off her guns and sails and set her afire. The British had withdrawn to Boston. Twenty of them had been killed and fifty wounded. The Americans hadn't lost a man. Only four were wounded.

Corporal Farnsworth offered up a brief prayer.

"Thanks be unto God," he said, "that so little hurt was done us when the balls sung like bees round our heads."

The next day both camps settled back to watching each other. The British occasionally threw a few cannon balls across the river. Provincial headquarters offered a small reward for bringing in the balls. They thought it would help the men to overcome their fear of them. It did more. It provided diversion for the officers, watching the men race across the fields and fight each other for possession of the balls. It also caused some casualties. When a ball landed and started to bounce and roll, the men ran ahead of it and stuck out a foot to stop it. Occasionally an eighteen-pounder had retained more momentum than was apparent, and a crushed foot resulted.

The Committee of Safety's spy ring still operated smoothly inside Boston. It reported the arrival of transports loaded with re-enforcements, increasing Gage's garrison to about sixty-five hundred. It sent out word on May 25th that the thirty-six gun *Cerberus* had docked at Long Wharf with three of England's best-known generals aboard; William Howe, Henry Clinton and John Burgoyne.

Repeatedly it passed along warnings that Gage, now that he

had the sizable force he had been waiting for, was planning to send out expeditions to fortify the two elevations from which Boston could be bombarded by the colonists: Charlestown Heights, overlooking the city's North End, and Dorchester Heights to the south, from which cannon could sweep the entire city and harbor.

The spy network also reported that the three newly arrived generals had a low opinion of the provincial army; one of them in particular, "Gentleman Johnny" Burgoyne, the most colorful of the three. Something of a dandy, Burgoyne at fifty-three still had a trim figure. He was a daring gambler, a politician, a dramatist of sorts, a London drawing-room favorite, a soldier of distinction.

Upon his arrival, it was said, he inquired, "What is the news?"

Told that Boston was surrounded by ten thousand provincials, he asked, "And how many regulars are there in Boston?"

When he heard there were five thousand, he threw up his hands.

"What! Ten thousand peasants keep five thousand king's troops shut up! Let *us* get in, and we'll soon find elbowroom."

As reports kept coming to the Committee of Safety that the British were getting ready to move on the two heights, the general staff in Cambridge got busy on plans for extending the American defenses. They agreed that Prospect and Winter Hills, just beyond Charlestown Neck, had to be strengthened to protect the Cambridge camp from the north. Something should be done about the Dorchester area.

General Putnam and Colonel Prescott were particularly anxious to fortify Bunker Hill, just inside the Charlestown peninsula. It would serve to draw the British onto ground where they could be met on equal terms, they argued. The army, Putnam pointed out, was getting restless. He had great confidence in it. Put them behind breastworks, he promised, and they'd make a good showing.

"The Americans," he said, "are not afraid of their heads, though very much afraid of their legs; if you cover these, they will fight forever."

General Ward and Dr. Warren were against the Bunker Hill

proposal. The army was not in condition, they argued. It needed more cannon and powder. Besides, such a maneuver might bring on a general engagement, which was more than should be risked so soon.

"I admire your spirit, and respect General Ward's prudence," Warren said to Putnam. "We shall need them both, and one must temper the other."

The argument went on. Warren paced the room. He came back and leaned his arms on the back of his chair.

"Almost thou persuadest me, General Putnam," he said. "But I must still think the project a rash one. Nevertheless, if it be adopted, and the strife becomes hard, you must not be surprised to find me near you in the midst of it."

On June 14th the Provincial Congress appointed Dr. Warren a major general. The same day word came out of Boston that Gage had fixed the morning of the 18th for his attack. He would send a detachment first to occupy Dorchester Heights, then another to take Charlestown.

The next day the Committee of Safety secretly passed the resolve:

"Whereas, it appears of importance to the safety of this colony, that possession of the hill called Bunker's Hill, in Charlestown, be securely kept and defended; and also, some one hill or hills on Dorchester Neck be likewise secured; therefore, resolved, unanimously, that it be recommended to the council of war, that the above mentioned Bunker's Hill be maintained, by sufficient forces being posted there; and as the particular situation of Dorchester Neck is unknown to this committee, they advise that the council of war take and pursue such steps, respecting the same, as to them shall appear to be for the security of this colony."

BOOK THREE

FRIDAY, JUNE 16TH, WAS SUNNY AND WARM. AMOS FARNSWORTH WAS homesick. The ripening hay in the Cambridge meadows and the blossoms wilting under the fruit trees reminded him of his father's farm in Groton. He was finding camp life painfully dull again. He hadn't done a lick of work all morning.

Early in the afternoon orders came for his regiment to be prepared for a march at six o'clock. No further details were given out. At sunset they fell in on the parade and stood with bared heads while a minister prayed over them. It was dusk when they marched off. Private Farnsworth's husky neighbor, Colonel Prescott of Pepperell, was leading them.

The council of war had decided to get the jump on General Gage. Acting on the Committee of Safety's resolve, they had drafted explicit orders and put Colonel Prescott in command of the expedition. About twelve hundred troops were assigned to him, including a fatigue party of two hundred Connecticut men equipped with all the intrenching tools in the camp, and a company of artillery with two fieldpieces. Prescott was under strict orders to keep the purpose of the march a secret until they had passed over Charlestown Neck.

The column started at nine o'clock. Prescott, in his uniform of buff-colored breeches, long blue coat and three-cornered hat, walked at the head with Colonel Richard Gridley, the army's chief engineer, who would lay out the fortifications. Captain Samuel Gridley was in charge of the artillery company and Captain Thomas Knowlton of the Connecticut men. Two sergeants preceded them with masked lanterns.

At the neck they were joined by General Putnam and his aide,

young Major Brooks of Reading. Colonel Prescott sent Corporal
Farnsworth's company into the village to stand guard. Captain
Nutting, their leader, set up headquarters in the dark town
house. The others slipped away down the empty streets and scattered around the waterfront houses to watch the ferry landing
and the men-of-war in the river.

Since April 19th, Charlestown had been almost deserted.
Only a few of the more courageous had remained in their homes
with the guns of the British warships on one side of them and the
provincial army camped on the other.

The village was on a roughly globular peninsula about a mile
long and a half-mile across at its widest place, facing Boston.
There were two sizable hills on it. Bunker Hill was just inside
the Neck. It was a hundred and ten feet high, with a rounded
summit. On the east, it sloped almost to the bank of the Mystic.
On the west, the road into the village ran along its base, with the
bay and a millpond beyond it. Stone and rail fences marked it
off into pastures and hayfields.

At its southern base the land sloped up again to another hill.
It was only seventy-five feet high and had steep sides. It was gen-
erally known as Breed's Hill, for the owner of one of the largest
pastures on it. It was also known as Green Hill, for another tenant, and Russell's, for the man who owned the pasture on the
summit. Along its eastern base the land was rough and marshy
and spotted with clay pits and brick kilns. The houses of Charlestown, some six hundred, nearly all of wood, clustered along its
western foot.

After Prescott sent the detail down to the village, he marched
the rest of the detachment onto Bunker Hill and drew up on the
slope facing the harbor. Over the next hill they could see the riding lights of the men-of-war in the Charles. Behind them, the
church steeples of Boston stood dark against the stars.

Prescott now called the field officers around him and revealed
his orders. There was a long consultation. The orders were clear
enough. It was Bunker Hill that was to be fortified. But now that
they were on the ground, some of the officers thought the summit
of the hill in front of them, being that much nearer Boston,
would better serve their purpose. They argued that it was all one

general elevation and they were the best judges of where the fortification should be built. Colonel Gridley of the engineers sided
with them.

An officer said, "But the order specifies Bunker Hill and not
Breed's."

"Breed's?" another in the group answered. "Never heard of it.
Bunker Hill. Yes. But Breed's. Who's Breed? It's all just a hill."

Colonel Gridley said he wasn't against erecting works on
Bunker Hill. In fact, there should be, as soon as they'd finished
the main fortification; for defense in depth in case they had to
fall back.

Colonel Prescott was getting impatient. Time was running out.
He was certain the British would open fire on them as soon as the
light became strong enough to spot the earthworks. These were
raw troops. No matter how fired they might be with patriotism, it
would be impossible to make any sort of stand with them in an
open field against Gage's heavy artillery and seasoned regulars.

When one of the group observed that it was going on midnight
and nothing had been done, a field officer peremptorily announced it was time to get onto the forward hill and start digging.
Colonel Prescott led the men to the summit of Breed's. They
stacked their arms and piled their rations and blanket rolls on
the ground. Colonel Gridley took a pick and scored the rough
outline of an oblong redoubt in the sod. It was about ten rods
long and eight wide. He marked a line eight rods down the
slope to the left for a breastwork.

The pickaxes and spades were distributed and the men fell to
digging. Half of them dug for an hour, and then changed places
with the other half who had been standing guard. Their only
light was from the stars in the clear, windless sky. Orders were
spoken in muted voices. The men with picks dug with short, ex-
ploratory strokes to avoid the sharp ring of steel on a suddenly
discovered stone.

Colonel Prescott threw his uniform coat and tricorn hat on
the ground and wielded a pickax with quiet fury. Back in Pepperell, the tall, hard-muscled farmer had cleared many a sled load
of rocks from his land. Now, with deft, practiced strokes of the

pick, he loosened the ground around them and pried them up for the men to heave onto the slowly rising parapet.

He sent an additional party into Charlestown to help patrol the water front. He knew that a belt of sentinels lined the Boston shore across the river. Closer by, their riding lights bright, their masts black stencils against the stars, rode the British battleships: the *Somerset* off the ferry landing, the *Falcon* off Morton's Point, the *Lively* between them, the *Glasgow* and *Cerberus* in easy gunshot. If, in the vast, almost oppressive stillness of the night, the watches aboard heard the men working on the hill, all would be lost.

Twice he left the works and went down into the village with Major Brooks to reconnoiter. They walked to the river edge and stood in the shadow of the ferry shed, listening to the drowsy voices of the watch on the ships calling out at intervals, "All's well!"

Now, much too soon, the light was beginning to gray over the Boston skyline. The men were still digging furiously. Prescott was back among them, his officer's uniform replaced by a broad-brimmed hat and a loose brown coat called a banian.

General Putnam had left soon after the men started digging. He had returned several times during the night to watch silently from the sidelines. With the energetic Prescott getting every possible ounce of effort out of the men, he saw no reason to meddle. He returned to the provincial lines around Winter and Prospect Hills just beyond Charlestown Neck.

General Ward was at headquarters in Cambridge with Dr. Warren and the other members of the council of war.

The redoubt and breastwork were only partly finished. The redoubt looked like the excavation for an average house. On the side facing Boston the dirt and stones had been piled into a rude parapet six feet above the floor of the fort. At the rear a narrow exit had been dug. The breastwork had been extended almost a hundred yards to the left.

The sky over North Boston took on a rosy pallor. Suddenly a cannon roared. A spurt of flame lighted briefly the hull and rigging of one of the men-of-war in the river. A white cloud of smoke plumed skyward, and a cannon ball whined over the heads of the men in the redoubt.

The watch on the *Lively* had spotted the swarm of men working on the top of Breed's Hill. Her captain had put a spring on her cable and opened fire.

Colonel Prescott saw his troops instinctively drop their pickaxes and shovels and crouch down.

"Keep digging!" he shouted. "Keep digging, men!"

He grabbed a spade from the hands of one of them and flung earth up onto the parapet.

"Keep digging! They can't hurt us in here!"

The sky was brightening fast. Now the *Lively* had opened with all her guns. The *Somerset* joined in, and the *Falcon*. From Copp's Hill, in Boston's North End, one of the land guns opened fire.

A ball crashed into the works and killed one of the men. Asa Pollard, of Billerica, a subaltern, ran over to Prescott with the news.

"What should we do with him?" he asked.

"Bury him," Prescott answered.

"Without prayers?" The officer was aghast.

"Without prayers," Prescott answered. "Just bury him."

A minister in the company started preparing for a burial service. The dead man's friends gathered around him, Prescott ordered them to get back to their work. The minister and Prescott had a brief set-to. If they were going to stop for a burial service every time a man was killed, said Prescott, they might as well pull out now. He finally gave in, when the minister promised to make it brief.

Now that they had been discovered, there was no further need for patrols in Charlestown. Prescott ordered them back onto the hill. When Corporal Farnsworth got there the cannon balls were churning up the sod on every side. He ducked into the redoubt and walked over to where his friend, Peter Brown, a company clerk in the regiment, was leaning on his shovel. Private Brown said he didn't mind admitting he was scared. He was also mad, he said. Working in the darkness, the men had no way of knowing what an exposed position they had been ordered to fortify. There was treachery somewhere, said Brown. Either that or flagrant oversight by the officers.

Colonel Prescott realized that his green troops were getting panicky. He climbed to the top of the parapet and stood there, in his broad-brimmed hat and long brown coat, his back to the enemy, calmly inspecting the excavation below him. One of his captains, sensing his motive, climbed up beside him. Together they strolled along the top of the parapet, gesturing, talking as casually as if there were not an enemy gun within miles of them.

The men watched them, wide-eyed at first. A few swung their shovels and cheered. Prescott and his companion ignored them as pointedly as they did the cannon balls. And the men, touched with a new courage, went back to their digging.

Prescott had them build a platform of earth and wood around the sides of the redoubt to stand on. He dispatched a messenger to have water sent up. It was getting hot and the little that had been brought along was gone.

The blasting of the ships' guns rattled the windows of Boston and awoke the populace with a start such as they had never had before. Many of them, still in their nightcaps and shifts, crowded the rooftops, staring through the morning mist at the belching ships and the puffs of dust raised by the balls as they dug into the slopes of Breed's Hill.

Admiral Graves, standing at the bedroom window of his house on Beacon Hill, took a long look through his field glass and ordered the cannonading stopped. He hurried into his uniform and went up Marlborough Street to Province House.

General Gage was at a back window with his American councillor, Col. Willard. He handed the glass to Willard.

"Who is the tall man walking on the parapet?" he asked.

Willard recognized his brother-in-law, Colonel Prescott. He remembered his last visit to the Prescott house in Pepperell several months ago. They had argued most of the evening, the Tory Willard and Prescott, the Whig. Willard was concerned because his brother-in-law had taken over command of the local regiment of minutemen. If Prescott should be found in arms against the

king's government, Willard pointed out, his life and estate would
be forfeited for treason.

"I've made up my mind on that subject," Prescott answered.
"I think it probable I may be found in arms, but I will never be
taken alive. The Tories shall never have the satisfaction of seeing
me hanged."

Gage tapped Willard impatiently on the shoulder.

"Do you recognize him?"

"He is my brother-in-law, Colonel Prescott," Willard answered.

"Will he fight?"

"Yes, sir. He is an old soldier, and will fight as long as a drop
of blood remains in his veins!"

Gage took back the glass and stared at the tall figure calmly
walking back and forth on the parapet.

"The works must be carried," he said.

He called a council of war.

They sat around the long walnut table: Gage, Howe, Clinton,
Burgoyne, Lord Percy. Gage sat at the head, Howe at his right as
next in command. General Clinton urged that a strong force
be embarked at the Common and, under the protection of the
shore batteries and the ships' guns, rowed to Charlestown Neck.
Landed in their rear, the provincial retreat could easily be cut
off. Burgoyne agreed. So did Lord Percy.

Gage was against it. Such a maneuver, he said, was both un-
military and hazardous. The British force would be placed between two armies, one of which was strongly fortified and the
other stronger in numbers. The British force could be destroyed
completely.

Howe vigorously agreed with him. A frontal attack was the
only one to be considered, he said. Those peasants on the hill
could never stand up to an assault by the king's well-armed and
disciplined regulars.

Orders were sent to the kitchens on the Common to start cooking rations for a large force. Glasses were set out and a bottle of
Madeira passed around. General Timothy Ruggles, tall, gray-
haired, explosive and profane, a former royal jurist and now
leader of the Boston Tories, got into the debate. As commander
of the Loyal American Associators, the militant organization of

Massachusetts citizens who sided with Britain, he hotly supported Clinton.

Gage listened patiently to all of them. Howe had the right
idea, he said finally. A show of force was needed. These rebel
farmers and shopkeepers had to be taught a lesson they wouldn't
forget. They had to be shown that they could not tamper with the
might of the British army.

General Ruggles stalked out of the meeting, his face dark with
frustration. So this was the kind of blundering God-damned
leadership the crown was depending on to crush the American
rebellion! Surely, the good people of the province who had staked
everything they possessed, their futures, possibly even their lives,
on their loyalty to King George and parliament, deserved something better. As he crossed the lawn of Province House a royalist
friend hailed him. Was there any news from the council of war?
Ruggles stared at him with angry eyes. Yes! There was news!
News of the worst kind!

"It will cost many lives to attack in front," he shouted, "but
the English officers will not believe the Americans will fight!"

The windows of his house looked out over Boston Common.
Soldiers were standing in tightly-packed groups on the parade
and in the open spaces between the barracks. Through the trees
he could see the rigging of the frigate *Glasgow*. He climbed to the
flat roof. When he opened the trap door he saw that it was already crowded with his friends and neighbors, the women tightly
clutching the hands of their children, the men wearing the white
sleeve band of the Loyal American Associators.

General Ruggles made his way among them to the coping on
the riverside. The sun had burned the morning haze off the
water. A fair wind blew out of the west, but the day was already
sultry and hot. The tarred seams of the roofing stuck to the soles
of his boots. He stared out over the Common, and again his eyes
narrowed with anger at Gage and Howe.

Directly in front of him, her prow pointing up river, lay the
man-of-war *Glasgow*, the larboard battery of her twenty-four
guns facing across the bay at Charlestown Neck. Just beyond her,
near the western shore of the Charlestown peninsula, was the
twenty-gun transport *Symmetry*. Downriver to his right, he could

see the mighty *Somerset,* with her sixty-four guns, straddling the
ferry lane between Boston and Charlestown, the frigate *Falcon*
on one side of her, the *Lively* on the other. Like dark bugs on
the water, two floating batteries were putting out from the Common.

He thought: a hundred and forty-four ships' cannon, plus the
guns of the floating batteries! Enough to blow the entire tatterde-
malion provincial army off the earth! And what were Gage and
Howe doing with them? The battleships' sails were furled, their
anchor chains slanted taut into the water!

The Charlestown peninsula lay bright green in the late morning sunlight. The wide stretch of shore line facing Boston rose
at the far, southeastern end to a low elevation called Morton's
Point, an area of rail-fenced pastures. The houses of the village
dropped to the water edge from the ferry landing at the south-
western tip and curved around the base of Breed's Hill in the
center of the peninsula. Beyond Breed's Hill was the highest
elevation, Bunker Hill, and beyond that the narrow neck that
connected the peninsula to the mainland.

On the summit of Breed's Hill he could see the redoubt the
provincials had built during the night, and to the right of it a
long, straight slit in the earth that was a breastwork. Tiny figures
were visible in both fortifications, throwing spadefuls of earth
onto the parapets. The green pasture lands around them were
scarred with brown pencil strokes where the British ships' cannon had gouged the earth.

The ships' guns were silent. Apparently Gage had had his
reasons for stopping the cannonading. Ruggles gave up trying to
figure Gage. Of more concern to him now was the sudden appearance of dark masses on the slope of Bunker Hill, re-enforcements
moving toward the redoubt and the breastwork.

He became conscious of a sudden swelling of sound around
him. For a moment it seemed he was hearing the wind whispering again in the pines on his abandoned estate back in Hard-
wick. Then he realized it was the murmur of many voices. He
looked around. Every housetop as far as he could see was crowded
like his own with spectators staring out over the water at the ant-
like activity on the two Charlestown hills. They filled the roofs

tiered up the slope of Beacon Hill, on Tremont Street and Sudbury, around the burial ground on the summit of Copp's Hill.
Every window framed staring faces. Men and boys clung to the
chimney pots and the steep sides of the church steeples. He wondered if any event had ever had so great an audience. Boston had
become one massive grandstand.

Well, Gage and Howe would put on a show for them they
would never forget, he told himself, a show embellished with all
the sparkle and pageantry of regimental pennants rippling in
the sunlight, burnished files of bayonets, brass cannon spurting
fire, massed ranks in scarlet and white—the mighty British army
on the field of battle.

Many would die, and many others would be brought back
moaning in agony. That was as certain as the fact that it was all
unnecessary. He had no love for his countrymen up there on the
hill. But he knew they would fight. How much better it would be
to land the expedition behind them on the Neck, the way General Clinton had suggested, cut off their retreat and starve them
into submission. There was enough wind for the men-of-war to
move in from both sides and enfilade the narrow connection to
the mainland so no man could pass over it and live. Gage's argument that the troops would be in danger of attack from the rear
was nonsense. The guns of the British frigates would cut down
the entire provincial army, decimate it, if it tried to come to the
rescue of those men who had so stupidly exposed themselves to
entrapment on the lowest and nearest of the two Charlestown
hills. But Gage wanted a show of force. He had to demonstrate
to these misguided colonists that the mighty army of Great
Britain must not be challenged by a mob of yokels.

Ruggles looked at the men and women and children crowding
his roof. Nearly all of them were expatriates who, like himself,
had been compelled to leave their homes in the interior knowing
that they might never be able to return, that the land their ancestors had cleared out of the wilderness, the houses filled with
treasured possessions were possibly lost to them forever. Many
were already dependent on the charity of friends in the city. He
could understand the taut look in their faces as they watched and
waited. If Gage would only strike hard enough! Once the rebel

concentration in the exposed earthworks on the hilltop was wiped
out, the whole might of the British army could be thrown against
their depleted camp in Cambridge. Supported by the ships' guns,
they could destroy the rebel stores and headquarters, fire their
encampments and send them flying for their lives. The rebellion
would be crushed, and these people around him could go back
and pick up their pleasant lives again on their farms and in their
village shops.

It was nearly noon before the troops started to fall into marching formation on the Common. General Ruggles had gone downstairs and brought up his field glass. The rectangular redoubt on
Breed's Hill, he saw, was still unfinished, but it looked formidable
to a frontal attack. He guessed from the fact that only the tallest
of the provincials' heads were visible inside that the floor was at
least six feet below the top of the parapet. Steps had been built
around the sides for the men to stand on while they fired. The
breastwork had been extended about a hundred yards along the
crest of the hill to the right of the redoubt. Another, much
shorter barricade had been thrown up between the left side of
the redoubt and the cartway along the edge of the steep slope
into the village.

Only a scattering of re-enforcements was coming across Bunker
Hill now, but the redoubt and trenches appeared almost filled.
He saw that the intrenching tools had been stacked behind the redoubt. An officer on a bay horse galloped up the slope, and after
a short discussion with a man in a brown coat Ruggles saw him
point his sword at the tools. Men scrambled out of the redoubt.
For the first time that day a smile crossed Ruggles' face as he
watched them run off toward Bunker Hill with the picks and
shovels.

"Some of those fellows aren't as dedicated to rebellion as I
thought they were," he said to the men around him.

The troops on the Common were now marching off in platoons
toward the North Battery and Long Wharf. They walked with
the flat-footed gait of men carrying a heavy load. Ruggles stared
at the bulging packs on their backs. The intricacies of British
military thinking baffled him. Why had Gage insisted that each
man carry enough provisions and supplies for almost a week's

expedition? The packs and gear they were toting must weigh at least eighty pounds!

After a long wait Ruggles saw two floating batteries round the North End and head toward Morton's Point. Strung out behind them came some forty barges and boats filled with scarlet uniforms. He guessed there must be at least fifteen hundred of them. They waded ashore at the point and fell back into formation. Ruggles saw General Howe, who was in charge, study the rebel fortifications through his field glass and confer with General Pigot, his next in command. The empty barges came back across the river. The men unslung their packs and sat down to eat their dinner.

The only sound was the distant crackle of the two floating batteries that had crossed from the Common hours ago and were now anchored in the bay on the western side of the peninsula. They were sending an infilading fire across Charlestown Neck. Occasionally the cannon on the *Glasgow* or the *Symmetry* chimed in with an explosive shell.

The sun burned in a cloudless sky. It was oppressively hot on the roof, but Ruggles doubted that a single person had left his place. The men around him had taken off their coats and hung them on the coping. The women hushed their fretting children, mopped their wet faces with their skirts.

It was after two o'clock before the barges left the North Battery again, loaded with the re-enforcements Howe had called for. There were some seven hundred of them, grenadiers and light infantrymen, and Major Pitcairn with his marines. They landed to the left of the original force, close to the water-front houses of the village. While the two forces were uniting Ruggles again trained his glass on the redoubt. The New England flag now floated over the parapet. It had a blue field with the red St. George's cross on a white background in the corner. In the top right section of the cross was a tiny pine tree.

More re-enforcements were moving over the Neck now and coming down the slope of Bunker Hill into the redoubt and breastwork. The officer on the bay horse was galloping back and forth between the redoubt and Bunker Hill. Ruggles saw a detachment leave the breastwork and run to a stone and rail fence that sloped down to the Mystic along the foot of Bunker Hill. Groups of provincials coming over Bunker Hill hurried down to join them. Others marched into the breastwork.

Howe had now formed his force into two divisions that spread in long ranks across the foot of the peninsula. He commanded the division on the right, General Pigot the one on the left. Ruggles noticed that Howe's valet was close behind him wherever he went, lugging a heavy basket from which several longnecked wine bottles protruded. Well, he thought, a general must have his refreshments with him at all times.

At a signal from Howe a blue flag was hoisted. Suddenly the guns of all the ships in the river opened a devasting bombardment. The floating batteries joined in, and the six-pounders that Howe had brought along. It was a thunder the like of which Ruggles had never heard before. The roof on which he was standing trembled with the shock. He could see the sunlight shimmer on the windows down the street.

The *Glasgow* and *Symmetry* in the bay along the western side of the peninsula and the floating batteries close to the shore were pouring a furious stream of round and chain shot and exploding shells onto the Neck. The *Somerset* and *Lively* and *Falcon* and the floating batteries off Morton's Point were blasting away at the earthworks on Breed's Hill. From Boston's Copp's Hill howitzers and cannon joined the bombardment. A great cloud of smoke, dark near the ground, cotton-white where the sunlight washed it on top, covered the harbor.

For a moment longer Ruggles could see the British troops standing ready to advance, a thick swath of scarlet and white stretched across the green pasture lands from Morton's Point to the edge of the village. Then he lost them behind the tumbling piles of cannon smoke.

On the Charlestown waterfront, General Howe had sent his artillery pieces ahead with orders to concentrate their fire on the breastwork. After a few rounds, they stopped. He sent an officer to find out why. The officer came back and said an unfortunate mistake had been made. As the general knew, the guns were six-pounders. The ammunition chests had been filled with twelve-pound balls.

"Tell them to change to grape," Howe shouted.

But before the fieldpieces could get near enough to the rebel defenses for grapeshot to be effective their wheels mired in the soft ground.

———————

TWENTY-THREE

COLONEL PRESCOTT, LOOKING OVER THE PARAPET OF THE REDOUBT, watched the British ranks get under way a mile down the slope. He tried to estimate their number. At least two thousand, he thought; probably more. Every one of them a seasoned, disciplined veteran. Against them, he had a hundred and fifty raw volunteers in the redoubt, another two hundred in the breastwork, and between four and five hundred behind the rail and stone fence.

He had had a rough day. The men who had come with him had had no sleep since the night before and had dug from midnight until noon. Many of them, knowing nothing about warfare, had neglected to bring along the rations that had been passed out to them. The others had finished theirs. The dust raised by the picks and shovels and the cannon balls gouging the earth around the works had made the men thirsty, and the water was soon exhausted. His repeated pleas for a fresh supply had been ignored. Finally a few barrels of beer had arrived. They had been emptied long ago.

After the first cannonading from the British ships had stopped, Prescott's officers had urged him to send a messenger to General Ward at Headquarters, asking that the detachment be relieved by fresh troops. Prescott answered angrily he would never consent to that.

"The enemy will not dare to attack us here," he said. "And if they do they will be defeated. The men who have raised the works are the best able to defend them. Already they have learned to despise the fire of the enemy. They have had the merit of the labor, and should have the honor of the victory."

The officers went back to their men. But after supervising the digging for a while they called for a second council of war. Again they warned Prescott that the men were worn out. No refreshments of any sort had come through. They were in no condition for fighting.

Prescott still insisted he would not let them be relieved. But he agreed to dispatch a messenger to General Ward to ask for additional troops and supplies.

Major Brooks was assigned and hurried away to Headquarters. He discovered that General Putnam had already persuaded Ward to send Colonel John Stark and part of his New Hampshire regiment to the fortifications. Ward refused to send any more. Until he learned the British intentions, he said, he could not consent to a further weakening of the Cambridge defenses. For all he knew, Gage might attack Cambridge to destroy the colonial stores.

Finally, the Committee of Safety stepped in and persuaded Ward to send in the rest of the New Hampshire troops.

At the same time the Committee of Safety called on the Committee of Supply for "four of the best riding horses" to carry dispatches the two miles between Breed's Hill and Headquarters.

Supply replied that it had no horses available. The Provincial Congress had ordered twenty-eight delivered to the committee, but only ten had arrived. They were all in use.

So the messengers continued to walk back and forth between the fortifications and Cambridge.

General Putnam rode up to the redoubt shortly before noon. The men had finished digging, and the intrenching tools were stacked back of the works. He told Colonel Prescott they should be sent back to Cambridge while there was still time. He didn't want them to get lost.

"If I send any men away with the tools," Prescott said, "not one of them will return."

"Every one of them shall return," Putnam answered brusquely. He looked down at a group of his Connecticut men standing near the picks and shovels they had just finished using. "My lads, these tools must be carried back."

An order was never obeyed with more alacrity. Moreover, General Putnam's voice had carried better than he realized. Men leaped out of the redoubt and joined the group around the tools. Some took one shovel, some two. Some fought each other for a pickax. They raced down the slope with them.

Colonel Prescott was right. None of them came back.

At twelve o'clock the men in the redoubt and breastwork saw the scarlet patches form on Boston Common. After a while, the boats and barges rounded the North End and bore down on Morton's Point. In the bright sunlight, they looked like a path of red petals on the water.

Colonel Prescott thought the procession was heading toward the Mystic side of the peninsula to flank his works. He ordered Captain Knowlton to take his Connecticut troops out of the breastwork and fortify a stone fence topped with rails that extended from the Mystic along the base of Bunker Hill some distance to the rear of the redoubt and parallel to it. He sent two fieldpieces with them.

The Connecticut men hastily collected the rails of other fences and stacked them in front of the stone and rail wall. The hay in the field behind them had been cut the day before and lay in piles drying in the sun. They gathered it in their arms and stuffed it in the foot-wide space between the newly-laid rails and the stone and rail fence.

Coming to their support as the British flotilla landed on the beach were Colonel Stark and his New Hampshire troops. The enfilading fire from the floating batteries as the men started across Charlestown Neck worried Captain Dearborn, who was walking beside Stark. He suggested they had better make a run for it. The weather-browned old frontiersman said, "No. One fresh man in action is worth ten fatigued ones."

He kept them marching at their regular pace through the fury of whining shells. Crossing Bunker Hill, he joined forces with the Connecticut troops. While Knowlton's men gathered hay to strengthen their wall, Stark led his to the Mystic shore and brought back rocks to pile on top.

Soon Colonel James Reed's New Hampshire regiment joined

them. The artillery moved into the open area between the rail
fence and the breastwork.

Dr. Warren had started the day with a throbbing headache.
As president of the Committee of Safety, he worked as long as
he could, studying the dispatches being brought in from the
redoubt, persuading General Ward to send more men to Prescott's support. But the pain finally became so intense that he
had to go to his room and lie down.

At two o'clock he heard a messenger gallop up outside his
window at the Hastings House and shout to the sentry that the
British were landing on the Charlestown peninsula. He got up
and, mounting his horse, set out for Breed's Hill. As he was leaving Cambridge village he met General Seth Pomeroy, the aging
scout and Indian fighter from Northampton. Together they rode
across the Neck and up the slope of Bunker Hill. There they
separated. Warren went to the redoubt, Pomeroy to the stone
and rail fence.

As Warren entered the fort he saw Colonel Prescott walking
along the raised platform, talking to the men leaning their muskets on the parapet.

"They'll never make it, boys," Prescott was saying. "Let them
come. We'll knock them down when the time is ready. Just hold
your fire. Don't waste it."

Dr. Warren said, in the voice that had often reached to the
far corners of Old South Church at patriot rallies: "Have you
room for one more, Colonel?"

Prescott remembered that Warren had been recently commissioned a major general. He came down and offered to turn over
the command to him.

Warren shook his head.

"I shall take no command here," he said. "I came as a volunteer, with my musket, to serve under you, and shall be happy to
learn from a soldier of your experience."

The men recognized him. Some of them swung their muskets
over their heads and cheered. Warren climbed up and walked
along behind them.

"Room for one more here?" he asked. "Where is there a good spot to shoot from?"

General Pomeroy had much the same answer for Captain Knowlton at the stone and rail fence. He tapped the stock of the musket in his hand.

"I came to use this. Where do you want me?"

It was three o'clock, and at last the long scarlet line was advancing. In the provincial earthwork the officers crouched behind their men. "Powder is scarce and must not be wasted," they warned. "Aim at the waistbands." "Aim at the handsomest coats." "Pick off the commanders." "Fire low." "Wait till you see the whites of their eyes."

Colonel Prescott walked along the platform of the redoubt.

"Don't fire till I tell you," he warned. "Wait till I give the order." With his sword he pushed up the musket of a man who seemed about to pull the trigger. A few others, seeing the British discharge their guns as they sweated up the slope under their heavy packs, couldn't resist firing back. Prescott indignantly struck up their guns, shouted at them to "Keep your heads!"

At the stone and rail fence, General Putnam was having the same trouble. He threatened to cut down the next man who disobeyed him. "Men, you are all marksmen," Private Philip Johnson heard him plead. "Don't one of you fire until you see the whites of their eyes."

Now the British ranks, their faces glistening with rivulets of sweat from the long climb in the hot sun, were only fifty yards from the redoubt and breastwork, and the fence down the slope.

"Fire!" Prescott shouted and swung down his sword. "Fire!" yelled "Old Put." The word passed from officer to officer. Fire! Fire! Fire!

A long slash of flame flared from one end of the provincial defenses to the other. A cloud of dark smoke billowed skyward.

The scarlet ranks crumbled. British regulars fell against each other, screaming with sudden pain. Others sprawled on their faces and lay still, or bent over and sighed a last full-lunged sigh. Some clutched their waistbands and staggered a few strides down the slope before they fell. Others ran.

Colonel Prescott saw General Howe standing alone within

pistol range of the stone fence. A circle of officers lay writhing on the ground around him. The British general followed his retreating troops back down to the shore. Some of his men had fled into the boats that had brought them across. Prescott saw officers swinging at them with their swords to make them come back.

Slowly the British line formed again. On the slope before the earthworks a scarlet swath lay on the green pasture land. The British marched doggedly toward it. The first time, their progress had been slowed by the rail and stone fences they had had to climb over. Now there were the bodies of the dead and the screaming wounded underfoot.

They passed the scarlet line, firing as they climbed. But their bullets merely churned up the dirt of the provincial defenses.

A new assurance had come to the men behind the fortifications. They had routed the king's trained regulars! Had sent them scurrying in retreat!

This time they held their fire like veterans.

"See that officer over there. Let's pick him off."

"I'm taking the fat one with the pug nose."

They leaned their muskets on the fence rails and the earth of the parapet. And they waited.

Now the regulars were only thirty yards away. Again the order went down the lines. Fire!

A second scarlet windrow of dead and wounded lay across the pastures and meadowlands. Some of the Americans ran yelling out of the defenses and started after the retreating redcoats. Their officers shouted them back.

General Johnny Burgoyne, the part-time dramatist and literateur, stood with General Clinton on Copp's Hill in Boston, watching through his glass. He realized he had never witnessed anything to compare with this.

The ancient burial ground he was standing on was filled with officers and privileged citizens. He looked around at the crowded roofs, the faces in the church-steeple windows. It was undoubtedly, he told Clinton, the greatest spectator event in history.

Howe had signaled for the battery on the hill to fire the village of Charlestown so the rebels couldn't flank him. The cannon sent carcasses, iron-ribbed frameworks filled with combustibles and covered with canvas, lobbing over the water. Church steeples in Charlestown were folding over and crashing in showers of blazing timbers. Blocks of houses were disappearing under great clouds of dark smoke laced with flames. In the river the men-of-war and floating batteries were spewing sheets of fire, the tall masts and tightly-wrapped spars of the ships swaying in recoil. On the slope beyond, like two carelessly dropped scarlet and white ribbons on a green cloth, lay the British dead. Just above them were the brown earth parapet of the redoubt and the breast-work. At the foot of the slope, like a swarm of red ants, the regulars were scurrying to the boats and barges that had brought them across.

It was, Burgoyne decided, "one of the greatest scenes of war that can be conceived."

General Clinton, seeing the regulars repulsed for the second time, left Copp's Hill on the run. He jumped into a boat at the North Battery and ordered the crew to row him across as fast as they could. He joined Howe and Pigot as they were reforming their lines for a third assault. General Howe was limping from a bullet wound in his foot. He insisted he could carry on.

Many of the officers who had come across with him were now lying in the scarlet windrows up the slope. The provincials had shown again their talent for picking off the epaulets. The officers who remained were violently divided on whether another assault was called for. Some argued they should try Clinton's plan. There was enough wind now for the ships to maneuver. Bring them up the Mystic. Together with the *Glasgow* and *Symmetry* on the other side of the peninsula, they could close off the Neck, trap the rebels on their hill.

Howe said, definitely no. The honor of the British army was at stake. They had to carry through. Besides, one of the officers had gotten near enough to the redoubt in the last assault to hear a provincial yell, "Watch your powder! It's running low!"

He suggested that Clinton go with Pigot's division on the left. The weak spot in the rebel defenses was the open area between the breastwork and the stone fence, Howe pointed out. No earthworks there. It was undefended except for two fieldpieces that could easily be knocked out of action. He sent orders to the men-of-war to concentrate their fire on the breastwork and slough. The cannon balls soared across the sky and churned up the earth to the right of the redoubt.

That was doing it, Howe said as he saw men scurry out of the breastwork, some running into the redoubt, some to the stone fence down the slope; others racing away toward Bunker Hill. He would take his force to the stone fence again, he said. Pigot would drive for the opening beside the breastwork and storm the redoubt from the right side.

The men had better remove their packs, he said, so they could maneuver better. And, instead of ranks, have them form in files. That way they would be less of a target. He watched the officers drive the men back out of the barges and off the beach where they had collected in frightened groups. It was apparent that they had no stomach for another assault.

The officers ran among them with their pistols drawn, threatening to shoot the first man who disobeyed the command to fall in. They pricked the laggards with their swords. This, Howe told himself, was where discipline paid off. He wondered if that murderous mob of rebels up there would be as manageable if the tables were reversed.

At last the regulars were back in formation. The cannonading stopped. Howe limped in front of them. He had called on them before the first assault to "behave like Englishmen, and as becometh good soldiers." He had told them the rebels had to be dislodged or they would set Boston afire and compel the entire garrison to take refuge on the ships. Now he spoke again, a new, hard edge to his voice.

"I shall not desire one of you," he shouted, "to go a step further than I go myself at your head."

He gave the order to march.

Colonel Prescott hid his anxiety under a show of bluff assurance as he saw the British once more start up the slope. Some of the men in the redoubt with him had used up their last powder. Others had only one round left. The field pieces had retreated to Bunker Hill under the last British bombardment. They had left several cannon cartridges behind. Prescott had them slit open and the powder distributed so that every man had at least one round to fire.

He placed those who had bayonets at the front of the redoubt, the others around the sides and against the rear wall. The ones without bayonets he told to gather up all the stones they could find and pile them at their feet.

"Use them when your powder gives out," he said.

He strode back and forth behind the men on the front parapet.

"Hold your fire," he warned. "Don't waste a kernel of it. We'll drive them back again."

Corporal Farnsworth looked down at the little pile of rocks in front of him. He sorted out the biggest ones and put them on top. At close range, he thought, they might do almost as well as a musket. He wondered why someone back at Headquarters hadn't seen to it that fresh ammunition was sent to them. And why hadn't more re-enforcements come up?

He looked over at Peter Brown and wondered if there wasn't some truth in what Brown had said about treachery behind the lines; at least, he thought, something was wrong. Well, his life was in the Lord's hands. The Lord had seen him safely through other close fixes. If it was His will to do it again—

He heard muffled shouts behind him. Looking over the parapet, he saw a company of Connecticut men coming up the slope. Captain John Chester was running in front of them, yelling to them to hurry.

Captain Chester had just finished dinner in his lodgings at Cambridge when he heard the church bells ringing and a drummer beating To Arms. He ran into the street and saw young Captain Putnam, the general's son, galloping up the road from Charlestown. Chester hailed him.

"What's the matter?" he asked.

Captain Putnam pulled up short and stared down at him.

"Haven't you heard?"

"No."

"Why, the regulars are landing at Charlestown," Putnam said. "Father says you must all march immediately to oppose them."

Chester ran to his room and strapped on his sword and pistol. At the meetinghouse where his company was billeted he found them nearly ready to march. They had just acquired their first uniforms. They were bright blue, trimmed with red. Chester thought they offered too good a target and told the men to put their civilian coats and trousers on over them.

They marched off, heading a parade of nearly all the troops that were still in the area. Chester guessed there were at least three regiments in all. He led his men through the barrage of shot and exploding shells the British were sending onto the Neck. Miraculously, none of his company was hit. But when he reached the foot of Bunker Hill and looked back he discovered that none of the other companies that had marched off with his were in sight.

He stared at the scene around him, hardly able to believe what he saw. Although there was no sign of the enemy this far behind the lines, every rock and haystack had a group of men crouching back of it. He counted thirty behind an apple tree. Several knots of men were coming from the direction of Breed's Hill carrying off wounded companions. In every case there was only one wounded man, and more around him than could get a hand on him. One man had twenty trying to help him.

A company came toward the young captain, marching rank and file. Chester called to the officer in command:

"Why are you retreating?"

The officer didn't answer.

Chester halted his company.

"Answer me," he shouted, "or it will be at your peril!"

The officer still ignored him.

Chester told his men to cock their muskets.

"Be ready to fire on them when I give the command," he shouted.

The other company stopped short. The officer said lamely he had been told he could go back.

"By whom?" Chester asked.

He didn't seem to know.

"It is a living hell up there," he said. "My men wouldn't stay."

"Command them to," Chester answered. He decided he had

already wasted too much time on the fellow. "Command them to, or I will report you." He signaled his company to resume their march.

As they started down the southern slope of Bunker Hill, the cannonading from the ships in the harbor stopped. He looked around for a commanding officer to report to, but there was none in sight. Breaking into a run and calling to his men to come along, he went up Breed's Hill. Through the opening at the rear of the redoubt he could see men massed around the parapet. He recognized the tall figure of Colonel Prescott in his big hat and brown coat. Prescott had his sword poised over his head, waiting to give the command to fire.

The breastwork beside the redoubt was a shambles. The piled-up earth had been gouged by cannon shot. There were gaping holes where shells had exploded. But it was still a defense of sorts. As Chester started toward it musket balls whined around him. For the first time he saw the British files coming up the slope. They were so close he could have hit the foremost with a rock. He could see the sweat shining on their faces. They were firing as they came. But not a shot came from the redoubt.

Now they were twenty rods away. Above the rattle of their muskets he heard the shouted command, "Fire!" inside the redoubt. There was a roar of gunfire. The leading ranks of the British fell as if they had been swept down by a great wind. The men behind them wavered. Another discharge, but much lighter, came from the redoubt, and more redcoats sprawled on the grass. Officers ran forward, yelling and waving their swords. Others beat at the men, driving them on.

A British major reached the corner of the redoubt and stormed up it, yelling, "Now for the glory of the marines!" A general mounted the other front corner. Officers and men swarmed up behind them. A shower of stones and thrusting of bayonets tumbled some of them back. But others charged up in their places.

The provincials were now rushing out of the redoubt. In the thick gunsmoke and dust, Chester recognized a face coming toward him. It was young Farnsworth.

"Colonel's said we should retreat!" he shouted. Chester's men were firing as they backed away. He saw Dr. Warren come out, warding off a British soldier's bayonet with the barrel of his musket. He seemed in no hurry. His face was set in a determined scowl. He took a few steps and turned back to face the enemy. A musket ball struck him in the left cheek. His head snapped back, and he fell.

Colonel Prescott was among the last out of the redoubt. He came parrying furiously with his sword. A panting regular lunged at him with his bayonet and tore a long slit in his coat. Another got the point of his blade against his waistcoat and slashed it.

The provincials backed down the slope to the foot of Bunker Hill, wielding their empty muskets as clubs. Many of them broke and ran. Captain Chester rallied his men around Colonel Prescott. He saw that the troops at the stone fence were now also retreating, but in good order, firing their last few rounds with unhurried aim.

Men fell around him as the British volleyed from the redoubt and breastwork on the crest and then came charging across the fields. On the summit of Bunker Hill, General Putnam, his white hair whipping around his head, his face pink with frustration and rage, galloped back and forth through the retreating masses, swinging his sword and shouting at them to "Make a stand here!"

"We can stop them yet!" he yelled. "In God's name, form and give them one shot more!"

General Pomeroy, the firelock of his musket smashed by a British ball, waved it over his head and pleaded with the men passing him to stop. But the retreat couldn't be checked. Clubbed muskets were a poor defense against bayonets and gunfire.

Now it was the provincials who sprawled dead and wounded in the tall grass of the pastures. Lieutenant Samuel Webb of Chester's company was sure he would not make it alive to the bottom of the hill.

"Four men were shot dead within five feet of me," he said. "But, thank Heaven, I escaped with only a graze of a musket ball on my hat."

He discovered that the fear of death, which he had forced himself to fight down on coming into the battle, had completely left him. Instead, seeing these men he knew dropping dead or crying out in sudden agony around him, filled him with a dark, helpless fury. He could see that young Edward Brown of his company, backing down the slope beside him, felt the same way. Brown still had the British gun with the bayonet on it he had wrenched away from a regular in the breastwork.

When it came to courage, Webb thought, Brown had more than his share. Webb had been near him in the trench when the British stormed up. He saw young Gershom Smith, standing beside Brown, collapse with a bullet in his head. Brown fired his own gun, then picked up Smith's and fired it. As the regulars leaped into the trench, Brown lunged barehanded at one of them, tore his musket away from him and killed him with it.

The Americans took their heaviest casualties crossing Bunker Hill and the Neck. Private Peter Brown, who had suspected treachery when he discovered the exposed position he had helped fortify on Breed's Hill, had stayed in the redoubt until he saw the British swarming over the parapet.

"I ran for about half a mile," he said. "The balls flew like hailstones."

The British pursuit stopped at the Neck. Captain Chester wondered about it. Then he remembered the redcoats' sweat-shiny faces and loud breathing as they had come over the breast-work. He guessed they were too spent to press on.

It was five o'clock, and the battle of Bunker Hill was over. The provincials took cover behind the two hills, Prospect and Winter, on the mainland. General Putnam galloped to Cambridge Head-quarters and begged General Ward to let him organize a counter-attack. Given fresh ammunition, he said, they could drive the British back to Boston. The enemy force had been cut in half, he pointed out. They were exhausted from their three assaults on the hill in the blistering heat. But Ward did not think it would be wise. The Americans were too disorganized. Besides, he said, there was still danger that Gage would send a fresh force to attack the Cambridge camp.

The men slept on their arms. Sentries patroled the roads from the Neck, watching the string of British campfires on the near slope of Bunker Hill gradually die out. The next day the provincials counted their losses. A hundred and forty had been killed and two hundred and seventy-one wounded. They were sure the British toll had been much heavier.

Boston, from its rooftops, had seen one spectacle. Now, in its streets, it saw another as the barges returned to the Long Wharf with the dead and wounded.

Lieutenant John Clark of the marines had been with Howe's left wing. Now he was back in Boston, and what he saw impressed him as vividly as anything he had gone through on the Charlestown peninsula.

The Tories of Boston had brought every vehicle they possessed to the dock. There were coaches, chariots, single-horse chaises, even wheelbarrows. All the physicians and surgeons in the city were waiting as the barges tied up.

Lieutenant Clark stood in a doorway near his lodgings and watched the casualties start for the hospitals. In the first carriage he recognized a major who was slowly bleeding to death, and three dead captains of the 52nd regiment. The second contained four dead officers, the third six wounded. From his window through the night he could hear the carriages rumble by and the moans and drawn-out shrieks of the wounded. It was late Sunday forenoon before the last carriage passed, bringing the final load of wounded privates.

Peter Oliver, a Boston Tory, found his stomach hardly up to the horrors around him. Walking home from the wharf he met a private whose white waistcoat, breeches and stockings were as red as his coat.

"My friend, are you badly wounded?" Oliver asked him.

The man smiled quietly.

"I have three bullets through me."

He pointed to the places. The one in his abdomen, Oliver knew, would be fatal. But the soldier calmly went on talking. He said the fighting had been very severe. He talked about the battle, calmly, as if he were telling an everyday story. Oliver couldn't listen for long. He saw the gray pallor in the man's face, the blood seeping through his clothing.

"You must hurry to the hospital," he said. "You must hurry."

"Yes," the soldier said quietly. "I suppose I must."

He turned and, still with the quiet smile on his face, walked on.

The British computed their casualties. The one who was mourned the most was Major Pitcairn of the marines. He had been mortally wounded as he led his men over the parapet. Of the twenty-two hundred who had marched up Breed's Hill, a thousand and fifty-four had been shot down by the Americans. Ninety-two of them had been officers. The dead totaled two hundred and twenty-six.

Captain Walter Sloane Laurie, who had commanded the British force at Concord Bridge, was in charge of one of the details sent to Breed's Hill on Sunday to bury the dead. Outside the redoubt he came upon the body of Dr. Warren.

"I stuffed the scoundrel with another rebel into one hole," he said, "and there he and his seditious principles may remain."

In the American camp in Cambridge there was both elation and chagrin. It was wonderful how the untried Yankee troops had stood up to and twice driven back the king's seasoned regulars. Their fierce resistance, it was apparent, had wilted the fighting spirit of General Howe, since all pursuit had stopped at Charlestown Neck. But if things had gone as well behind the provincial lines as they had at the front the third assault would have been overcome and the battle might have been won.

General Ward went his plodding way. The criticism of his failure to get re-enforcements and fresh ammunition to Breed's Hill appeared to leave him unperturbed.

In leadership and communications, experienced officers agreed, much had been lacking. Liaison had been almost nonexistent. The troops of Massachusetts, Connecticut and New Hampshire had performed as individual units. It was clear that each province still considered itself a separate sovereignty. General Putnam of Connecticut pointed out that he had been openly defied by Massachusetts officers when he tried to order them into the action.

Life behind the lines slipped back into its easygoing routine. The barber captain spent a good part of his time giving his men haircuts. Privates, although they had enlisted for the rest of the year, went back home if they felt like it.

The Stockbridge Indians were still in camp. On June 21st, two of them got close enough to the British lines on Boston Neck to dispatch four regulars with their bows and arrows. The next day they got several more. On the 26th, two crept across Charlestown Neck and picked off a sentry on Bunker Hill.

The same day a British patrol attacked the sentries at the Roxbury end of the line. The picket guard turned out and chased them back.

Occasionally a cannon ball crashed into the American defenses, a carcass set a house or barn on fire. The few fieldpieces in the American camp held their tongues. They had no powder to waste.

Meanwhile, however, the Provincial Congress, struggling to provide money and supplies to keep the army together, had received the best news it had heard since the trouble with Britain started. Dispatches brought by express rider from Philadelphia revealed that John Adams had finally achieved what he had focused all his quiet enterprise and energy on since the morning of Lexington.

On June 14th, three days before the Battle of Bunker Hill, he had persuaded the Continental Congress to adopt the troops in Cambridge as the nucleus of a new American Army. The next day, still under John Adams' adept guidance, the Congress had appointed a Virginia military colonel and plantation squire named George Washington the country's commander-in-chief.

BOOK FOUR

TWENTY-FOUR

It was July second, a sunny New England Sabbath afternoon when George Washington arrived at the little college town of Cambridge. Morning showers had laid the dust on the roads and brightened the foliage on the softly-rounded hills. The pleasant red-brick buildings of Harvard College stretched cool shadows across the village square.

He had left Philadelphia nine days before, riding a giant bay stallion. Four other hunters from his stables at Mount Vernon were in his entourage, together with his two secretaries and a staff of officers headed by the volatile, spindly-legged Major General Charles Lee.

John Adams had been in one of the carriages that had accompanied them out of the Quaker city. Washington remembered the wistful look on Adams' pink face as the escort pulled up beside the road and waved them on. He had never met a man more devoted to the cause, more competent and at the same time self-effacing and painstakingly honest. It had been no secret that dapper John Hancock, president of this session of the Continental Congress, had expected to be offered command of the new army as the richest and one of the most prominent patriots in New England. And there was Artemus Ward, already in charge at Cambridge. But Adams had realized that, to obtain the support of the other colonies, someone other than a New Englander must be chosen.

The quiet sadness in Adams' eyes as he waved good-bye. Was it homesickness, Washington wondered, for his wife and children in their farmhouse outside Boston? Or regret that he had to stay behind and toil over papers and listen to the endless debates of

the delegates in the stifling heat of the State House while others
rode off to deal with the enemy? Behind Adams' scholarly ex-
terior, Washington knew, the martial fever burned as fiercely as
it did in anyone in his cavalcade. But it was his sharp legal mind
that the country needed.

A letter in the mail pouch in Washington's baggage told it
better than he could conjecture. Addressed to his wife, Abigail,
and hurriedly scribbled just before Washington set off, John
Adams wrote:

"Such is the price and pomp of war. I, poor creature, worn out
with scribbling for my bread and my liberty, low in spirits and
weak in health, must leave others to wear the laurels which I
have sown."

It wasn't until Washington arrived in New York that an express rider from Cambridge met him with the news that the
provincial army he was taking over had already fought a major
battle with the British regulars in Charlestown and had twice
thrown them back with heavy losses.

He rode harder from there on, cutting the receptions in the
towns they passed through as short as politeness allowed, starting earlier and riding until dark. It was interesting to see the
changing mood of the country as he moved northward. There had
been regiments drilling daily in Philadelphia, among them a
few companies of Quakers who larded their commands with
"thous" and "thys." But most of the devout Pennsylvania
Friends had stuck to their stern principle of nonviolence.

In New Jersey the populace had been almost hostilely pro-
British. New York had been about evenly divided in its sympa-
thies. As someone had remarked, the city itself was "one-third
patriot, one-third Tory and one-third rabble." But as he rode
through Connecticut and into Massachusetts the climate changed.
These people, closer to the scene of British inflexibility and the
dark threat of servitude, were angrily defiant.

A mounted escort and a delegation of cheering citizens met
him in Springfield and went along the rest of the way to Cambridge. The big white house of the president of the college, with
its mansard roof and widow's walk from which Boston was in
easy view across the bay, had been taken over for his residence.

It was all very pleasant. General Ward and his staff were doing everything they could to show their wholehearted welcome. The warm cheerfulness of candlelight reflected from polished walnut and mahogany, sparkling on the windowpanes and the silver service, was a sharp contrast to the rude wayside inns he had been sleeping in.

The next morning, without ceremony, Washington took over command. He toured the camp with Generals Ward, Putnam and Lee, and the disillusionment began. He had never seen such disreputable-looking groups of men as clustered around the untidy lean-tos and shacks staring at them as they rode past. Some of them appeared hardly old enough to carry in the milk. Others, with their scrawny bodies and tobacco-stained beards, looked like grandfathers.

They leaned against the walls of their shelters or squatted cross-legged on the ground, scratching themselves, spitting tobacco juice. When General Lee halted beside one group and asked for the officer in charge a stubble-faced man sitting in the doorway shifted his cud from one cheek to the other and said in a slow, nasal drawl, "He's gone to fetch himself some firewood."

From the New England delegates in Philadelphia Washington had gotten the impression that he was to take over an army of stalwart citizens dedicated to defend their homes and families against the tyranny of their British overlords. He doubted there was a stalwart figure among them. Even the stout, middle-aged Artemus Ward, twisting in his saddle to ease the stabbing pains from the stones in his bladder, looked anything but military.

Tall, soldierly-erect on his spirited hunter, in his immaculate blue and buff uniform, his gold epaulets, Washington realized from their slack-mouth stares that he was an object of rare curiosity to these men. So were they to him. Could these be the people who had sent two British columns reeling back from Lexington, who had stood up to the king's regulars on Breed's Hill until the last charge of powder was gone?

But already he was hearing things about the Charlestown battle that clouded its luster. Some regiments, he was told, had refused to go to the support of the men on the hill. Some had refused to take orders from field officers who weren't from their

own province. Others had broken and run at the first taste of
gunfire on the Neck. Ward was being talked about for his failure
to send in supplies and adequate re-enforcements.

The defenses Washington saw were as disappointing as the
soldiery. The redoubts around Prospect and Winter Hills were
obviously thrown up in careless haste by men with no knowledge
whatever of engineering. One of the best natural defenses, Cobble
Hill, overlooking both Boston and Charlestown, hadn't been
touched.

The few cannon in the camp were almost useless because the
so-called artillery companies had hardly any training in handling
them.

From the summit of Cobble Hill he could tell that the British
were heavily entrenched in Charlestown. From Roxbury he saw
that their fortifications were equally strong across Boston Neck.
If they decided to sally from either point, he wondered how he
could possibly stop them.

Back at Headquarters, more problems badgered him. The simple act of presenting to Israel Putnam the commission Washington had brought from the Congress, appointing him one of the
four major generals—the others were Artemus Ward, Charles Lee
and the wealthy New York merchant, Philip Schulyer—revealed
smoldering jealousies among the ranking officers in the camp.
When word of the appointment got out, another capable Connecticut general, Joseph Spencer, who felt he outranked Putnam,
packed up and went home. Seth Pomeroy, the old Northampton
Indian fighter who had gone with Dr. Warren as a volunteer to
Breed's Hill, had already left in a huff because he thought he
had been overlooked. General John Thomas of the Massachusetts
contingent announced he was going back to his farm because he
had heard General William Heath was going to outrank him in
the new army setup.

Washington delayed further appointments until he had matters
better in hand. His first task, he decided, was to instill subordi-
nation and discipline into the ranks. Since the men had chosen
their own company officers and could elect new ones if they
didn't like those they had picked, he realized it was not easy for

the officers to rule them arbitrarily. But, all in all, he thought, the officers were more to blame than the men.

"They are the most indifferent kind of people I ever saw," he wrote to his brother Lund back in Virginia.

He caught the barber captain giving one of his company a haircut, and promptly cashiered him. He broke five other captains and a colonel for offenses ranging from cowardice in the Charlestown battle to collecting pay for more men than they had on their rolls. Some of the officers, he discovered, had put their children on their company payrolls. Others had sent men home to look after their farms on army pay. He wrote Lund he thought the men in the ranks might make passable soldiers if they had competent officers, "although they are an exceedingly dirty and nasty people."

The "leveling" that had been going on for generations among these New England farmers and village craftsmen, the spirit of equality and independence that had been bred into their nature, were as unfamiliar to the aristocratic Washington as the rock-studded land which gave them a grudging living. Back in Virginia class distinctions were sharply defined. The plantation owners like himself were gentlemen and had slaves to do their manual work. The poor whites were a breed apart. The Virginia militia he had led into the Pittsburgh wilderness with Braddock in the French and Indian War were trained in the British manner. An officer's command was law.

Washington introduced the British penalty of flogging to discourage desertion and insubordination. Infractions of discipline were sternly penalized with fines or sentence to the guardhouse. The fiery-tempered General Lee set an example by breaking the head of a soldier who sassed him. Like Washington, the British-born Lee had never seen anything like the ingrained democracy of these rough New Englanders. He had fought with Burgoyne in Portugal, had been on the staff of the Polish army. He had marched into the wilderness with Braddock. The Mohawks had adopted him and named him "Boiling Water" because of his hot temper. He doubted that this shaby collection of armed citizens could ever be shaped into an army.

One of Washington's greatest handicaps was the easygoing nature of Artemus Ward. Ward rated next to the commander-in-

chief. But it took him forever to get anything done. One of the
first things Washington had asked him to do was find out how
much powder there was in camp. It should have taken Ward only
a few hours, Washington thought. Eight weeks passed. Meanwhile
Washington expected the British to attack at any moment. Ward
kept assuring him there was plenty of powder on hand for both
the artillery and the infantry. At last reports, he said, it was
around three hundred quarter barrels. When the returns finally
came in, Washington learned there were only thirty-two barrels,
barely enough for a round or two of musket fire. If the British
advanced now, he would be helpless to stop them!

Urgent messages to the Continental Congress finally brought
a fresh supply. About the same time news came to Headquarters
that Washington thought was the best he had heard since his
arrival. The enlistments from Massachusetts, Connecticut, New
Hampshire and Rhode Island were being augmented by regiments of riflemen from Pennsylvania, Maryland and his own
commonwealth of Virginia. At last, the American Army would no
longer be made up strictly of New Englanders.

They were a breed apart, these frontier riflemen. Used to the
hard ways of the wilderness, all they needed to get along was an
occasional stream to drink from, a little parched corn and a fair
shot at game. At night they rolled themselves in their blankets
and slept under the nearest tree. The long-barreled guns they
carried with careless ease in the crooks of their arms were as
strange to the New Englanders as their dress of homespun dyed
an autumn-leaf brown, their long fringed coats and deer-tail
cockades. The long barrels of their guns were spiral-grooved and
unbelievably accurate.

The idea of the rifled gun barrel was not new. It had been
developed in Europe as far back as the early seventeenth century.
But ramming the ball into place took long pounding with a
mallet. A Pennsylvania German gunsmith had recently solved
that by using a ball smaller than the gun bore and wrapping it in
a patch of greased cloth.

It still took twice as long to load and fire as a musket. Two
shots a minute was tops, against four or five for the smooth-bore.
But what shooting! The musket's effective range was sixty to a

hundred yards, and not accurate at that. In the Virginia back-woods a village leader appointed himself captain and let it be known he was organizing a rifle company to join the Cambridge army. More applicants showed up than he could take. He decided to accept only the best marksmen. On a tree trunk a hundred and fifty yards away he tacked a board a foot square with a normal-sized nose chalked in the center. Only those whose shots came closest to the nose would be accepted, he announced. But by the time the first fifty had taken their turns there was no nose left!

Captain Michael Cresap's company were entertained by the people of Frederick, Maryland, on their way north. In return they put on a demonstration. Cresap chalked a circle the size of a dollar on a piece of clapboard and nailed it to a fence post a hundred yards away. The men took turns drilling it, some lying on their backs, others on their sides; some firing on the run. None missed. One man held the board at his side and let his brother shoot it out of his hand. Another stood against a tree and put the board between his legs.

When they arrived in camp the southern frontiersmen displayed the same uncanny marksmanship. Marching on the double, they could take snap aim and hit a target the size of a coonskin cap two hundred yards away. They were hunters and Indian fighters, and marksmanship was their stock in trade. Unfortunately for Washington, who expected them to set an example of southern respect for authority, they soon revealed an independence and downright orneriness that outdid the New Englanders at their worst.

Used to the rough, lonely life of the backwoods, many of them thought nothing came up to a good brawl for entertainment, and they provided themselves with plenty of them. They had a healthy thirst, and at fourpence a quart their seven-dollars-a-month pay kept them generously supplied with New England rum. Their fondness for brawling often landed them in the guard-house. When this happened, their companions would come loyally to their rescue, chase the guard and release them.

Individually, they were excellent warriors. Shortly after their arrival, one of the companies was sent on a night raid inside the

British lines on Charlestown Neck. They blackened their faces and in their leaf-brown uniforms quickly faded into the darkness. Creeping along with the silent stealth they had learned stalking Indians and game, they picked off sentries with a skill equaled only by the Stockbridge redskins. They did even better: several of them came back leading British regulars they had pounced on in the dark and bound and gagged.

For a while the riflemen raised havoc inside the British lines with their long-range sniping. But after a few of the more disreputable deserted to the enemy, taking their rifles with them, the British acquired a proper respect for the new weapon and stayed out of range.

It didn't deter the riflemen. They tried the impossible, firing at British sentries and work parties three and four hundred yards away. They wasted so much precious gunpowder that Washington issued orders they were not to go sniping without a pass issued by himself or Generals Lee or Greene.

There were among these southern volunteers earnest young men who from the start saved their fighting for the enemy. One of them was young Private Jesse Lukens of Virginia. He "blushed with shame and indignation" at the behavior of his rowdy companions.

Private Lukens' battalion was stationed at Prospect Hill under the command of the New Englander, Colonel William Thompson. A sergeant in Lukens' rifle company had been thrown in the guardhouse for neglect of duty. When his friends threatened to rescue him, the adjutant grabbed their leader and put him in with the sergeant. The adjutant then went to report to Colonel Thompson. The mutineers promptly broke open the guardhouse and freed their two friends.

Colonel Thompson, a Massachusetts militia leader, was as tough and fearless as any frontiersman. With his lieutenant colonel, he walked into the mob and collared the leader they had just released. They marched him off to the Main Guard in Cambridge, two miles away.

Private Lukens thought that settled it. But in a few minutes thirty-two of the troublemakers came out of their tents with their rifles loaded and set off on the run for Cambridge.

"They swore, by God, they would go to the Main Guard," said Lukens, "and release the men or lose their lives."

Word got to Washington. He threw five hundred men with fixed bayonets around the Cambridge guardhouse and set off with Generals Lee and Nathaniel Greene to settle the matter. The thirty-two, meanwhile, had run off some of their enthusiasm. They holed up in a woods a quarter mile from their starting point. Washington headed the brigade that surrounded them. He ordered the mutineers to ground their arms. When they did, he pointedly sent riflemen from their own regiment to surround them with fixed bayonets.

The thirty-two were locked in the guardhouse, convicted of mutiny and fined twenty shillings apiece. As further penalty, Washington put their entire regiment to work with picks and shovels on the fortifications.

In time, the strict discipline Washington brought to the Cambridge camp converted the riflemen into good soldiers, as it did the New Englanders as well. Washington was developing a growing respect for these men of the northern colonies. Brigadier General Nathaniel Greene, the Rhode Island militia leader and Quaker who became one of his most dependable aides, understood them and passed his understanding along to Washington. They were, Greene pointed out, hard-working, fiercely individualistic folk, each a small landowner or shop proprietor. For generations they had been able to depend on no one but themselves to provide them a living. So they were naturally self-reliant and independent. Even their untidiness here in camp was explainable. Back home they depended on their womenfolk to do the washing and mending. It was strictly woman's work. Since their wives and mothers weren't here to keep them respectable looking, they went back to nature.

There were exceptions. Lieutenant Jabez Fitch of Norwich, Connecticut, was a veteran of the French and Indian War. He arrived in the Cambridge camp early in August with his son, Cordilla. It was a rainy month and the dirt floors of the shelters were soon ankle deep in mud. Lieutenant Fitch bought a load of lumber in Roxbury and laid a plank floor in his tent. He found a woman to do mending for himself and his son, and another to take care of their wash. He dug a well behind their tent.

In spite of his pains, his son came down with camp sickness. A Dr. Waldo visited him and prescribed a strong emetic. It didn't help. The next day, Lieutenant Fitch had in another camp physician, a Dr. How, who mixed what he called a white concoction: hulled barley, cinnamon and burned hartshorn. Before they could feed it to Cordilla, Dr. Waldo arrived and ordered another purge instead.

Fitch's son wasn't getting any better. The next day he called in a Dr. Turner, who fed the patient his cure-all, which he called elixir vitae.

The lieutenant had an added worry. Everybody in the camp who had ever met Cordilla thought it his duty to come and sit with him.

"With the wet weather and mud," said Fitch, "they were as dirty as horses."

In spite of the doctors, his son recovered. Fitch was free once more to spend his spare time finishing off the bunks in his tent and visiting the outer lines to examine Boston and the British defenses through a borrowed spyglass. While he liked his mug of hard cider for breakfast and a half pint of brandy or rum after supper, he spent his pay frugally. His coat was getting shabby and thin in spots, and the nights were growing chilly, but he put off getting it mended. Washington, he heard, was planning to put the army in uniforms, and coats and breeches would be available at cost.

When he learned that Headquarters was buying oxen and paying well for them, he sent word to a neighbor in Norwich to bring his team to camp. The price he received—thirteen pounds, three shillings—made him wonder. The high command, he decided, must have an important reason for wanting oxen.

Only the officers in Washington's circle knew the purpose behind the quiet accumulation of draft animals. The robust forty-three-year-old commander-in-chief was getting restless. Back in Virginia he would have been wearing off his surplus energy hunting foxes and directing the slaves on his vast plantation. The armchair inactivity at army headquarters was hard to take. Unlike the easygoing Artemus Ward, he was a fighter by instinct. If he could possibly do anything about it, he wasn't going to sit out the winter watching the blockaded British in Boston.

But, with only a few cannon in camp, he was helpless to do anything else. The galling thing about it was that there were plenty of cannon in American hands, cannon as large as twenty-four-pounders, and mortars, too. Unfortunately, they were nearly three hundred miles away, across a wilderness of mountains, rivers and trackless forest.

When the word of Lexington and Concord had reached Connecticut in the spring, a New Haven apothecary and former horse trader named Benedict Arnold, captain of his militia company, had hurried to Cambridge. In his horse dealings in the upper reaches of New York, he told the men at Headquarters, he had learned that there were two run-down and lightly manned British forts on Lake Champlain, Forts Ticonderoga and Crown Point, and they were well supplied with good cannon. A small force, the swarthy, black-haired young captain pointed out enthusiastically, could easily capture both. He was allowed to organize an expedition.

When word of it got out another tough frontier warrior, Ethan Allen, leader of the roisterous Green Mountain men of New Hampshire, quickly organized his own expedition. The two leaders quarreled their way through the wilderness, each insisting he was in command. But when they reached the forts they joined forces and captured them without losing a man. They counted their loot: nearly a hundred and fifty cannons and mortars, barrels of flints, a good supply of gunpowder. But Arnold and Allen had no means of transporting the armament to Cambridge. So it stayed there.

Now, at last, Washington had found the man he thought might be able to accomplish the heroic task. He was Captain Henry Knox, twenty-five, round-faced, jovial, two hundred and fifty pounds of hard-packed muscle and bone, a former Boston bookseller who had learned the science of artillery warfare by reading the military manuals he had stocked for his British customers. On his first tour of the camp, Washington had been impressed with the assurance and quiet efficiency of the young officer then in charge of the few cannon in the Roxbury defenses. Since then he had noticed that Knox had a way of getting things done and done right. He had the stamina of an ox and the energy of a colt.

Washington arranged with General Schuyler at Albany to provide men and oxen, and sent Knox off to organize and lead the expedition. Rafts would have to be built to transport the guns down the Hudson and sledges to haul them across the mountains. When they reached Massachusetts, the oxen Washington was acquiring would be waiting to take over.

Meanwhile, the commander-in-chief watched with growing concern the sick lists of the camp. The untidiness of the men was beginning to injure their health. The regimental hospitals were crowded with scurvy cases and dysentery. If an epidemic started, Washington realized, it could wipe out the camp. So he was glad to learn that a capable director general of hospitals had finally been appointed by the Continental Congress. He was forty-one-year-old Dr. Benjamin Church, the prominent Marlborough Street surgeon who, since the death of Dr. Warren, had become chairman of the Massachusetts Committee of Safety.

Dr. Church went to work with the energy of a dedicated public servant. He ordered drugs, commandeered houses in Cambridge, Brookline and Roxbury to convert into additional hospitals. He cleaned up the buildings already in use, some of which he found "a perfect sink of putrescence, filth and disease."

Money for medical supplies as well as powder and arms was getting progressively harder to come by. Washington's war chest contained hardly any silver or gold coin, and the paper currency being printed at Watertown by the Massachusetts Congress had few willing takers. Paul Revere, having designed the plates, was helping with the printing when he wasn't riding express or drafting plans for a desperately needed New England powder factory.

Revere had managed finally to get his family out of Boston and settled in a house in Watertown. He missed Dr. Warren more than he had ever thought he could any man. Not only as a friend. It seemed to him that something irreplaceable had been lost to

the patriot cause with Warren's death. Warren had a way of ac-
complishing things that none of the other members of the Committee of Safety, least of all the brisk, impatient Dr. Church,
could touch.

One day late in September Revere was dramatically reminded
of the conspiratorial days back in Boston when the secret reports
of his Committee of Mechanics to the top men of the patriot
organization had mysteriously been passed along to the British.

A scandal rocked the camp. A coded letter had been intercepted on its way into the British lines. An attractive young
woman from the Cambridge area had carried it to Newport
shortly after the Battle of Charlestown. In Newport she had tried
to deliver it to Captain Wallace of the British man-of-war *Rose*
to be transported into Boston.

She had asked a man named Wainwood, whom she knew and
trusted, to help her get aboard the British warship. Wainwood
was a patriot who posed as a rabid loyalist. He convinced her it
would be impossible for her to board the ship but he would personally deliver the letter for her. When he and a friend examined
it, they could make nothing of it. Its cipher looked to them like
nothing but gibberish. They held onto it.

In September, Wainwood got an anxious note from the girl,
asking why the letter had not been delivered. They thought that
over. Since the girl knew the message had not been sent along, she
must have been in contact since then with someone in the British
camp. Perhaps, they decided, the letter was more important than
they had supposed. They gave it to the head of the patriot organization in Rhode Island, who turned it over to General Greene.
Greene took it to Washington.

A minister in the Cambridge camp who knew something
about cryptography deciphered it.

The letter, addressed to John Fleming, one of General Gage's
provincial supporters, exaggerated the strength of the patriot
army, its supplies and the martial enthusiasm of the colonies.

"I hope this will reach you," the informer wrote. "Three attempts have I made without success. In effecting the last, the man
was discovered in attempting to escape; but fortunately my letter
was sewed in the waistband of his breeches. He was confined a

few days, during which time you may guess my feelings; but a
little art and a little cash settled the matter. 'Tis a month since
my return from Philadelphia; I went by way of Providence, to
visit mother. The Committee for warlike stores (at Providence)
made me a formal tender of twelve pieces of cannon, eight and
twenty-four pounders; they having taken a previous resolution to
make the offer to General Ward. To make a merit of my services,
I sent them down. The people of Connecticut are raving in the
cause of liberty. A number from the colony, from the town of
Stamford, robbed the King's stores in New York, with some small
assistance the New Yorkers lent them; these were growing turbu-
lent. I counted two hundred and eighty pieces of cannon, from
twenty-four to three pounders, at Kingsbridge, which the Committee had secured for the use of the colonies. The Jerseys are
not a whit behind Connecticut in zeal. The Philadelphians exceed them both. I saw twenty-two hundred men in review there
by General Lee, consisting of Quakers and other inhabitants, in
uniform, with one thousand riflemen and forty horse, who, together, made a most warlike appearance. I mingled freely and
frequently with the members of the Continental Congress; they
were united, determined in opposition, and appeared assured of
success."

The writer said provisions were plentiful in the rebel camp,
recruits were coming in daily, the paper money being issued in
Watertown was accepted as readily as hard cash. He asked for a
prompt answer in the same cipher and warned, "Make use of
every precaution, or I perish!"

While the information in the letter was highly exaggerated
(the Jerseys, for example, were anything but fired with patriot
zeal), it was thought likely that this was part of the code. Another
possibility was that the purpose was to warn Gage that this was
not a good time for an offensive.

The young woman who had carried the letter to Newport was
picked up at her home inside the provincial lines. General Artemus Ward brought her to Washington's headquarters riding
behind him on his horse. She was identified as the mistress of Dr.
Benjamin Church. After a night of strenuous questioning, she
confessed that Church had given her the letter.

Dr. Church readily admitted authorship. John Fleming, to whom the letter had been addressed, was his brother-in-law and a Boston loyalist, he said. Fleming had been trying to persuade him to return and join the British camp. He had written the exaggerated account of the strength and spirit of the provincials in the hope it would convince Gage he had better come to terms before he was destroyed.

General Washington sat on the court martial. Dr. Church was brilliant and talented. Besides being a competent surgeon, he was a polished essayist, a fair poet, a persuasive orator. His poems satirizing the British cause had been enthusiastically quoted in patriot circles for years. His speech on the third anniversary of the Boston Massacre, delivered in Old South Church in '73, had been a stirring success.

Now Church called up every gift he possessed to clear himself. He wrote a long, detailed explanation to Washington. He stood up before the court and in the florid manner and flourishes of the time defended his conduct as at the worst a slight indiscretion inspired by patriotic zeal. But his brilliance failed him when he needed it most. He was found guilty of carrying on a criminal correspondence with the enemy.

When the news reached Philadelphia, John Adams was as dumfounded as were the people of Massachusetts who had looked upon Church as one of their leading champions.

"Good God!" Adams said. "What shall we say of human nature? What shall we say of American patriots?"

In Watertown, Paul Revere knew at last how the secret reports of his Committee of Mechanics in Boston had gotten so quickly into British hands. Another question that had often puzzled him was also suddenly understandable: Dr. Church's affluence during the years they had worked together. He knew the Marlborough Street surgeon had not inherited any sizable fortune. His practice was not conspicuously better than that of Dr. Warren, who lived in a simple brown house in crowded downtown Boston. Yet Church had a large country estate beside his fine house in the best part of the city. He entertained lavishly. His English wife and he were among the best-dressed couples in town. And he had enough money left over to support a pretty mistress.

Clearly he had been in the pay of the British for a long while.

Dr. Church, still protesting his innocence, was stripped of his appointments. But when it came to sentencing him it was discovered that the Continental Congress had overlooked the possibility of treason and had not spelled out a penalty. Feeling was so strong against him in Massachusetts by now that it was felt he wouldn't be safe from mob violence in any of its village jails. So he was taken to Norwich, Connecticut, and locked up there.

At Province House in Boston, Generals Gage and Howe learned of Church's arrest with regret. Gage was packing to go back to London. The British ministry, dismayed at the heavy casualties in his mismanaged attack on Breed's Hill, had decided to recall him and give the command to Howe. Gage was glad to get out of a hopeless situation. The stodgy Howe wasn't sure he was going to enjoy taking over. The savage provincial resistance he had encountered in the Charlestown battle had given him a fearful respect for their fighting capacity. If he hadn't been so taken with his new mistress, the charming blonde Elizabeth Loring, whose husband, Joshua, he had conveniently made one of his commissaries, he would have gladly gone back to the gambling tables and drawing rooms of London.

Gage let him read the confidential reports he had been receiving from Dr. Church ever since the occupation of Boston had started, the accounts of the rebel spy network's activities, the detailed data on the arms that had been stored in Worcester and Concord, and on the proceedings of the Provincial Congress. He wrapped them up and packed them with his personal papers to be taken back to London for safekeeping. It was most unfortunate, he said, that Howe would be deprived of his star informer's services just because that little slut of Church's hadn't had the sense to keep from getting caught.

General Howe helped his old friend get his large family comfortably settled on the frigate that was taking them back to London. It was October tenth. The trees that had escaped the fuel collectors on the Common and Copp's Hill had turned brilliant red and rust-brown. Across the Charles, the rebel camp was hidden under a gaudy pallet of autumn colors. Occasional skirmishes between the sentries and raiding parties on the Neck and the Charlestown lines broke the monotony briefly. Now and then the British cannon dropped a few explosive shells into the provincial lines.

Howe had nearly fourteen thousand troops in Boston now. But the salt rations they were limited to by the provincial blockade were sapping their health. Fuel was almost exhausted. He watched with dread as winter settled over the crowded, starving town. It was a poor base for operations against the rebels, he thought. New York would be much better. A friendlier city, from all accounts; more centrally located, too. Control the Hudson River, and he could split off these cantakerous New Englanders from the rest of the colonies and wear down their resistance.

He was still thinking about it when his valet rushed into his bedroom at dawn one gray morning in March and excitedly shook him awake. The rebels, he cried, had fortified the heights of Dorchester, just south of the city, during the night. Their cannon, dozens of them, were pointing down on the entire harbor!

Howe pulled on his boots and breeches. Struggling into his coat as he ran, he climbed to the roof and took a look through his glass. It was unbelievable.

"The rebels," he exclaimed, "have done more in one night than my whole army would have done in a month!"

He had intended to evacuate Boston. Some of the transports were already loading. But now British honor was at stake. To leave this city without a fight, this city which had been the cause of all the trouble, just because it was being threatened by a collection of raw provincial recruits, would be a disgrace to the empire. The damned rebels had gone a bit too far this time.

He ordered Lord Percy to take twenty-four hundred men aboard transports and storm the provincial works as soon as it became dark. During the day he watched the work progress on the hilltops. The ground was frozen, but it hadn't stopped the rebels from erecting redoubts. They had brought up bales of hay and great bundles of tree limbs and built their fortifications of them. They had mounted good-sized guns behind them, brass and iron pieces. In front, along the edge of the steep slopes, were

rows of barrels linked together with chains. The works swarmed
with troops.

In the afternoon it started to rain. Lord Percy got his detachment aboard the ships and started down the harbor. The wind
came up. By night it was blowing a full gale. A landing in the
raging surf was impossible. Worse still, the ships became unman-
ageable.

Wrapped in his greatcoat, Washington stood behind one of the
fortifications of tangled tree limbs and twisted salt hay on the two
highest Dorchester hills and looked down at the storm-swept
harbor and the panorama of Boston beyond it. With him were
the two men he had come to lean on most heavily in the American camp: General Nathaniel Greene, the thirty-three-year-old
Rhode Island commander, who despite a stiff leg and a Quaker
background was one of the ablest officers on his staff, and Henry
Knox, now a colonel, the man who had made the sudden American maneuver possible by his herculean achievement of dragging
more than fifty cannons and mortars across the frozen wilderness
from Lake George to Cambridge.

The purpose of Washington's maneuver was to lure the British
out of Boston for a general engagement or force them to evacuate
the city. It had been mapped with painstaking care. The first
problem had been how to dig earthworks between the dark and
dawn of one night on hills commanding the city when the ground
was frozen eighteen inches deep. Colonel Rufus Putnam, a rela-
tive of "Old Put," had solved that.

"Don't try to dig them," he said. "Put them on top."

He outlined his plan and Washington liked it. It was to get the
defenses ready beforehand, prepare tangled masses of tree limbs
called fascines and twisted bundles of marsh hay. There was an
orchard of more than a hundred trees on the heights. Send men
to chop them down while others hauled the fascines and hay to
the summits. Brace the breastworks with the tree trunks. About
the only digging that would be required, he pointed out, was for
moorings for the fascines and the cannon platforms.

A former Boston merchant proposed another device to General Heath, who sent it along to Washington. It was to set a row

of barrels on the crests of the two hills, just outside the breast-works, fill them with stones and dirt and chain them together. When the British started up the steep slopes, roll the barrels down on them.

The militia of the towns near Cambridge were called in to re-enforce the enlisted army. Barges were collected for an invasion attempt across the Charles River if Howe attacked the Dor-chester Heights in force.

The cannon Knox had delivered were mounted in the re-doubts guarding Cambridge, all except the heaviest ones, which were loaded onto carts to be hauled to Dorchester Heights. The evening of March 4th Washington ordered a general cannonad-ing from the redoubts. The British answered from their emplace-ments on Boston Neck and Copp's Hill. Meanwhile, a work party of twelve hundred men climbed to the summits of the two Dor-chester hills, followed by three hundred and sixty teams of oxen hauling carts filled with fascines, great bundles of twisted hay, and cannon. Squads of axmen invaded the Dorchester orchard and started felling the trees.

The night was clear and cold. The moon came up. Boston lay in plain view below the two summits where the men worked. Fortunately, a haze hung over the water, hiding them from the watches on the ships in the harbor. A northeast wind carried the sound of the axes and picks, the creaking cart wheels away from the city.

At three in the morning, three thousand fresh troops arrived to help with the work. Five companies of riflemen settled them-selves behind the rising breastworks.

The ox teams made three and four trips apiece during the night. By dawn the fortifications were in fair shape. The freshly-cut tree trunks had been sunk into the frozen ground, the tangled brush and hay packed between them. The gun placements were set. The two rows of barrels, linked together with heavy chains, stood on the rim of the steep slopes, ready to thunder down on an approaching enemy.

The day dawned slowly through a gathering overcast. The British guns directed their fire on the works. But it was soon ap-parent to the men crouching behind the fascines that the enemy cannon could not be elevated sufficiently to reach their perch. Washington mounted one of the gun emplacements and spoke to them.

"Remember, it is the fifth of March," he said, "and avenge the death of your brethren."

It was the sixth anniversary of the Boston Massacre of 1770, in which the first Americans had been killed by British regulars.

Massacre Day! The men swung their shovels and rifles over their heads and cheered.

Again the rooftops of Boston and the hills around the city were filled with spectators, waiting for another Bunker Hill spectacle. Eight miles to the southeast, the bombardment rattled the windows of Abigail Adams' house. It had kept her awake all night. She bundled the children against the biting March wind and went to the top of Penn's Hill to watch with her neighbors the distant flashing of cannon fire and listen to "the amazing roar."

"I could see every shell which was thrown," she wrote to John that night. "The sound, I think, is one of the grandest in nature, and is of the true species of the sublime. 'Tis now an incessant roar; but O, the fatal ideas which are connected with the sound! How many of our dear countrymen must fall!"

During the afternoon the wind rose. It howled through the tangled brush of the Dorchester works and sent the surf pounding on the beach below. Heavy rain began to fall. The men on the heights saw that the British transports loaded with troops that had put out from the fort in the harbor were in trouble. Soon they were dropping their anchors.

By dark the wind and rain had reached gale force. The storm lasted through the night and all the next day. Washington, watching the work progressing on the barricades, was as drenched as any of his men. He lost one of his pistols in the mud and posted a two dollar reward for its return.

When, the next day, the weather cleared, both sides resumed their bombardment. A messenger brought a letter to Washington. It was signed by the Tory selectmen of Boston. Howe was planning to evacuate the town, it said, and would do so peaceably if Washington agreed to stop bombarding it. Otherwise, he would

set it afire. Washington answered that, since the offer hadn't
come from Howe himself, he could not honor it. Nevertheless, he
cut down the cannonading.

Among the troops massed in the long perimeter of redoubts
around Boston were volunteers from Rhode Island, Connecticut,
New Hampshire, Virginia, Maryland and Pennsylvania. But the
hard core were still the men of Massachusetts, the former minutemen who had responded to the angry village bells the morning
of Lexington and Concord, almost a year ago. Washington's attempt to drive the British out of Boston meant more to them
than it could to the others. It was their province that had been
the battlefield so far. Their homes and families were closest to
the enemy.

The seventeenth of March started for them as just another
Sunday away from home. It was St. Patrick's Day, a sunny day,
warm for March. The sky was clear. The bombardment that had
died away during the night was not resumed by either side. Suddenly the men on Dorchester Heights saw the ships clustered
around the Boston wharves unfurl their sails. First one, then another pulled away and headed out to sea. Soon the harbor was a
white expanse of sails.

After nearly two years of occupation, the British army was
pulling out of Boston.

The elation of the Americans was matched by the misery of
another group of Massachusetts people—the Tory families of Boston and those from the interior who had taken refuge with them
after Lexington. They were Americans, too, as American as the
men cheering on Dorchester Heights. But they had cast their lot
with Britain.

Among them were the middle-aged Thomas Flucker, royal
secretary of the province, and his wife. At first they had fully
expected that Howe would be able to drive the rebels off Dorchester Heights. But by the time the storm had passed the fortifications had been made too strong to be taken by assault. With
the rebel cannon commanding the city, they realized, it was only
a matter of days until Howe would have to leave.

When the word came, they packed the few possessions they

could carry with them, closed their house and went with the rest aboard the British ships. To add to their bitterness, the man in charge of the rebel artillery across the bay, young Henry Knox, was married to their daughter, Lucy. They wondered if they would ever see her again.

Among the few who were glad to leave was Elizabeth Loring, Howe's pretty blonde mistress. She was sure New York would be much more interesting than Boston. Billy—the general, William Howe—had told her they would go there after a brief stopover in Halifax to drop off the Tory families. Billy might be, as her husband sometimes good-naturedly assured her, a rather fumbling military leader. But he was a lot of fun. He was an excellent card player and an amusing lover.

The man who had forced Howe to take his army out of Boston stayed away from the ramparts where the men were waving their guns and cheering. George Washington spent the morning at his desk at Headquarters. If he was elated he didn't show it. There was work to be done, much work. Although he had no direct word, he felt sure Howe would move his forces to New York. Already Washington had sent off some of the rifle companies to start building defenses there. Now he ordered General Heath to follow them with more troops and part of the artillery.

Looking ahead, he saw that if he was to lead America to victory the road would be long and rugged. Howe's army was still formidable, and his own was unseasoned and untried. What would the outcome be at New York? What was in store after that?

He decided it would be well to set an example for everybody concerned. When the village bell rang the summons to afternoon services, he put on his uniform and walked gravely across the square and into the meetinghouse.

NOTES

PAGE 40.

One of the most discerning historians of the American Revolution, Harold Murdock, suggested that Samuel Adams may well have been the manipulator who contrived the clash on Lexington Green that started the War for Independence. Murdock, who devoted most of his adult life to sifting colonial records and reducing the story of Lexington and Concord to its authentic details, pointed out the folly of sixty to seventy-odd poorly armed volunteers standing up to 700 trained British regulars on an open field. He wondered, was it entirely Captain John Parker's idea to line up the Lexington minutemen, guns primed and loaded, directly in the path of the oncoming mass of redcoats?

Captain Parker, a tall, rangy farmer of 45, the father of seven children, was an experienced soldier. He had been one of the colonists who served under Wolfe when the latter stormed the Plains of Abraham and captured Quebec in 1759. He had been in on the taking of Louisburg. There was evidence that he was one of Rogers' Rangers. Would a man with his battle training be inclined, on his own initiative, to risk the lives of his good friends and neighbors, family men like himself, by lining them up against ten times their number?

General William Heath of the Massachusetts Militia, who was at Lexington later that day, wrote in his *Memoirs*: "This company continuing to stand so near the road, after they had certain notice of the advancing of the British in force, was but a too much braving of danger; for they were sure to meet with insult or injury which they could not repel. Bravery when called to action should always take the strong ground on the basis of reason."

John Adams, who had no illusions about his conniving cousin, Sam, said, in reviewing the Lexington action years afterwards, "I suspect that this was the explosion which had been intentionally wrought up by designing men who knew what they were aiming at, better than the instruments employed."

PAGE 82.

Elbridge Gerry, the future vice president of the United States, and two other Committee of Safety members, Azore Orne and Colonel Lee, were staying overnight at the Black Horse. Awakened by the sound of the approaching troops, they stood at their upstairs window watching them pass. When a patrol started for the tavern, the three ran downstairs. Gerry headed for the front door, but the tavern keeper, Weatherby, got there ahead of him.

"For God's sake, not out this way!" he yelled. "They're coming in here!"

The colonial dignitaries rushed out the kitchen door in their bare feet and nightshirts. Before them lay a boulder-scarred field covered with last year's corn stubble. The only hiding place in sight was a stone wall on the far side. They raced toward it.

Part way across, Gerry fell. He yelled, "Stop! Wait for me!"

The other two looked back. The same idea struck both of them. Gerry, lying in the stubble, looked like just another boulder in the moonlight. They fell down and lay still until the British column passed.

PAGE 88.

It was never determined which side fired the shots that touched off the fatal blast of British musketry on Lexington Green. Although academic now, it was important in 1775, because each side charged the other with being the aggressor. The Americans hurriedly collected depositions from the provincial participants, all of whom swore they were murderously attacked without provocation, "whilst our backs were turned on the troops." The depositions were rushed from the printer to a fast packet which got them to London ten days before General Gage's account of the incident arrived. The British Whig press scored a temporary propaganda victory.

Gage's stilted report to the British ministry, charging the Americans provoked the encounter by firing on the regulars as they arrived on Lexington Green, was not only the loser in the race; it lacked the spirited indignation and fluent details of the provincial depositions.

Soon after the encounter, Ezra Stiles, the staunch patriot president of Yale College, heard at third hand that Major Pitcairn had told a prominent Boston prisoner of war he was convinced the provincials had fired first. Stiles knew Pitcairn as a God-fearing, honest British officer, "a good man in a bad cause."

"He told this with such circumstances as convince me that he was deceived though on the spot," Stiles wrote in his diary. "He does not say that he saw the Colonists fire first. *Had he said it, I would have believed him,* being a man of integrity and honor. He expressly says he did not see who fired first; and yet believes the peasants began. His account is this—that riding up to them he ordered them to disperse; which they not doing instantly, he turned about to order his troops so to draw out as to surround and disarm them. As he turned he saw a gun in a peasant's hand from behind a wall, flash in the pan without going off;

and instantly or very soon two or three guns went off by which he found his horse wounded and also a man near him wounded. These guns he did not see, but believing they could not come from his own people, doubted not and so asserted that they came from our people; and that thus they began the attack. The impetuosity of the King's troops were such that a promiscuous, uncommanded, but general fire took place, which Pitcairn could not prevent; though he struck his staff or sword downwards with all earnestness as a signal to forbear or cease firing."

Until General Gage's personal papers were bought by William L. Clements and made available to historians in 1930, this third-hand account stood as Pitcairn's version of what he had witnessed. But now, in the Gage papers, we have the major's personal report to his general, dated "Boston Camp, 26th April, 1775." Pitcairn wrote:

"When I arrived at the end of the village, I observed drawn up upon the Green near 200 of the rebels; when I came within about one hundred yards of them, they began to file off towards some stone walls on our right flank. The light infantry, observing this, ran after them. I instantly called to the soldiers not to fire, but to surround and disarm them, and after several repetitions of those positive orders to the men, not to fire &c, some of the rebels who had jumped over the wall, fired four or five shots at the soldiers, which wounded a man of the 10th, and my horse was wounded in two places, from one quarter or other, and at the same time several shots were fired from a meeting house on our left. Upon this, without any order or regularity, the light infantry began a scattered fire for some little time, contrary to the repeated orders both of me and the officers that were present."

Ensign Jeremy Lister was in the foremost company as it arrived at the Green. In his personal narrative, written months afterwards, he also asserted that before any of the regulars had discharged their muskets the provincials "gave us a fire, then run off to get behind a wall."

Lieutenant Sutherland, in his reports to Generals Gage and Clinton, wrote, "Three shots were fired at us, which we did not return, and this is sacred truth as I hope for mercy. These three shots were fired from a corner of a large house to the right of the church [Buckman's Tavern was the only large building to the right of the church], when we came up to the main body which appeared to me to exceed 400 in and about the village, who were drawn up in a plain opposite to the church. Several officers called out "Throw down your arms and you shall come to no harm," or words to that effect which they refusing to do, instantaneously the gentlemen who were on horseback rode in among them, of which I was one, at which instant I heard Major Pitcairn's voice call out, "Soldiers, don't fire! Keep your ranks! Form and surround them!" Instantly some of the villains who got over the hedge [British for wall] fired at us, which our men for the first time returned."

Devout Major Pitcairn's reputation for integrity was such that Stiles said he "would have believed him" if he said he saw the colonists fire first. There is no reason to believe that Sutherland and Lister conspired with Pitcairn in writing their accounts, yet they agree that they also saw impetuous provincials begin the action from behind neighboring stone walls.

It raises an interesting probability: did John Buckman's heady flip generate the spark that set off the Revolution? Told to stay within hearing of the drum, some of the provincials went into Buckman's Tavern after Parker disbanded them at 3:30 in the morning. They had been standing in the chill darkness for several hours. The cold had soaked deep into them. Possibly a few warmed themselves with a tankard or two too many of flip. When the British suddenly appeared, an hour later, did some befuddled hotheads among them rush out and take a few quick potshots at the hated redcoats from behind the nearest cover?

PAGE 112.

Martha Moulton felt she had done her village a meritorious favor in saving it from being burned by the British. She sent the Provincial Congress a detailed account of her ordeal. They apparently agreed with her, for she was awarded three pounds, a handsome sum for that time.

PAGE 136.

John Raymond was among the provincials killed that day. His death provided one of the first atrocity stories of the Revolution. Landlord Monroe recalled it for Elias Phinney's HISTORY OF THE BATTLE OF LEXINGTON in 1825.

"On the return of the British troops from Concord," he said, "they stopped at my tavern house in Lexington, and dressed their wounded. I had left my house in the care of a lame man, by the name of Raymond, who supplied them with whatever the house afforded, and afterwards, when he was leaving the house, he was shot by the regulars, and found dead within a few rods of the house."

A generation later, another Lexington historian, Frederick Hudson, supplied further indignant details:

"The officers with Percy resorted to Monroe's Tavern. The occupants of the house left the place in affright, leaving John Raymond, an aged man, who was at the time one of the family. The intruders ordered him to supply them with all the good things the house afforded, which he readily did. But after they had imbibed too freely, they became noisy, and so alarmed Raymond that he sought to escape from the house; but was brutally fired upon and killed in his attempt to flee from danger."

The lame and aged John Raymond was enshrined as one of America's early martyrs, victim of the fiendish brutality of Gage's redcoats. The story sounded off-key and over-orchestrated to the late Harold Murdock, a historian with a detective instinct for separating fact from fancy.

He knew that Percy and his officers could hardly have been carousing at the Monroe Tavern, a mile away, at the same time they were directing the destruction of a stone wall and the burning of houses to protect the troops from snipers in the village center. It was Smith's detachment, sent to the rear to rest and take care of their wounded, who had gathered in the neighborhood of the tavern.

The exhausted troops probably had done some drinking, and Raymond had probably served them. But Percy was setting a fast timetable. He arrived in Lexington at 2:30 in the afternoon, according to Lieutenant Mackenzie, who kept careful tab on the time, and he had the wounded dressed and carriages commandeered and ready to move them back to Boston an hour later. It was quarter to four, by Mackenzie's watch, when the column fell in for the return march.

Murdock took a look at the vital records of Lexington. He found that John Raymond was born September 5, 1731. So he was forty-three years old in April, 1775; hardly "an aged man." He was enrolled in Captain Parker's company of minutemen and should have mustered with the others on the Green in the morning. Since the rolls showed that he hadn't, a temporary lameness may have been the reason. But it could not have been anything permanent or he would not have been one of the minutemen.

Murdock deduced further that if the British had discovered Raymond's military status, which was probable, they would have considered him a prisoner of war. So, if he tried to escape, they had a perfect right to shoot him.

A sentence in Lieutenant Mackenzie's diary adds another possibility. He wrote that "one or two provincials were killed on the march (back to Boston) while prisoners, by the fire of their own people."

"Is it possible," Murdock wondered, "that Raymond was taken from Monroe's Tavern as a prisoner, and killed *by an American bullet* before or as soon as the march began."

PAGE 154.

George Washington wrote of this incident a month later: "If the retreat had not been as precipitate as it was—and God knows it could not well have been more so—the ministerial troops must have surrendered, or been totally cut off. For they had not arrived in Charlestown (under cover of their ships) half an hour, before a powerful body of men from Marblehead and Salem was at their heels, and must, if they had happened to be up one hour sooner, inevitably have intercepted their retreat to Charlestown."

NOTES ON ENGRAVINGS OF THE BATTLES OF
CONCORD, BREED'S HILL, AND LEXINGTON

The Engagement at the North Bridge in Concord. Here, the provincials are on the left side of the bridge, the regulars on the right. An interesting feature of the picture is the three British soldiers in the manse field in the foreground. For years it was assumed that Doolittle had merely placed them there for decoration. Then, in 1927, Lieutenant William Sutherland's reports to Generals Gage and Clinton were brought to light. They revealed that the figures were Sutherland and two of his men. Sutherland was wounded and one of the men, seen falling in the print, was left dying, later to be finished off by a misguided Concord youth with a hatchet.

The Battle of Breed's Hill. This is a contemporary engraving, sketched by Bernard Romans in 1775. Boston is on the right, across the Charles River, and Charlestown afire in the center. The provincials are drawn up in a more regular line on the crest of the hill than the records indicate. The broken British line and a windrow of dead are shown on the slope below them.

The Battle of Lexington was engraved by Amos Doolittle in 1775 from on-the-spot observations. It is interesting that none of the provincials in the picture are shown offering resistance to the British regulars. It is a massacre rather than a battle. Fifty years later, nettled by Concord's claim that "the first forcible resistance" was staged there, the aging Lexington survivors had embellished their remembrances considerably. In 1830, a lithographer named Pendleton revised the picture accordingly. His print copied faithfully the Doolittle setting, but now eight of the provincials were standing up to the enemy and six of them were firing back. By 1868, when Hammatt Billings pictured the scene, the provincials were belligerently standing their ground and a round dozen were returning the British fire. Then, in 1886, Henry Sandham painted his heroic interpretation, which now hangs in Lexington's Cary Memorial Hall. At last the scene has reached full battle pitch. Not a man has turned his back. A blazing exchange of musketry covers Lexington Green with billowing black-powder smoke.

A View of the South Part of Lexington by Amos Doolittle shows the rescue of Colonel Smith's detachment by Lord Percy. Smith's harried regulars are coming into Lexington on the right and on the hill in the background. Lord Percy's column is drawn up on the left center to meet them. Between the two forces are Percy and Smith on horseback. The groups on either side of Percy's column are his flankers. His fieldpiece, which drove off the provincials for a while, is shown on the hill to the right of the two figures on horseback. Provincials are firing on them from behind the stone wall in the foreground.

BIBLIOGRAPHY

BOOKS

ADAMS, JAMES TRUSLOW, The Adams Family, Boston, 1930.
——, The Epic of America, Boston, 1931.
ADAMS, JOSIAH, Address Delivered at Acton on July 21, 1835, Boston, 1835.
ALLAN, HERBERT S., John Hancock, Portrait in Purple, New York, 1948.
ALLEN, ETHAN, A Narrative of Colonel Ethan Allen's Captivity, 1779.

BARKER, JOHN, The British in Boston, Cambridge, 1934.
BELCHER, HENRY, The First American Civil War, London, 1911.
BOWEN, CATHERINE DRINKER, John Adams and the American Revolution, Boston, 1950.

COOPER, SAMUEL, Diary of Samuel Cooper, Lancaster, Pa., 1901.
CUTTER, BENJAMIN AND WILLIAM R., History of the Town of Arlington.

DAWSON, HENRY B., Battles of the United States by Sea and Land, New York, 1858.
DEBERNIÈRE, HENRY, General Gage's Instructions, Boston, 1779.

FORCE, PETER, American Archives, IVth Series.
FOX, EBENEZER, The Adventures of Ebenezer Fox in the Revolutionary War, Boston, 1838.
FRENCH, ALLEN, Historic Concord, Boston, 1942.
——, General Gage's Informers, Ann Arbor, 1932.
——, The First Year of the American Revolution, Boston, 1935.
——, The Day of Concord and Lexington, Boston, 1925.

FORBES, ESTHER, Paul Revere and the World He Lived In, Boston, 1942.

FORBES, HARRIETTE MERRIFIELD, New England Diaries, 1602-1800, Privately Printed, 1923.

FROTHINGHAM, RICHARD, JR., Life and Times of Joseph Warren, Boston, 1865.

———, Rise of the Republic of the United States, Boston, 1872.

———, The Siege of Boston, Boston, 1849.

GIBBS, ROBERT W., Documentary History of the American Revolution, New York, 1853.

GORDON, WILLIAM, The History of the Rise, Progress and Establishment of the Independence of the United States of America, New York, 1788.

GOSS, ELBRIDGE H., The Life of Col. Paul Revere, Boston, 1891.

HEATH, MAJOR GENERAL WILLIAM, Memoirs of the American War, Boston, 1789.

HERSEY, FRANK W. C., Heroes of the Battle Road, Boston, 1930.

HOLLAND, H. W., William Dawes and His Ride with Paul Revere, Privately printed, 1878.

LISTER, ENSIGN JEREMY, Concord Fight, Cambridge, 1931.

LOSSING, BENSON J., Pictorial Field Book of the Revolution, New York, 1851.

MACKENZIE, FREDERICK, A British Fusilier in Revolutionary Boston, Cambridge, 1930.

MARLYN, CHARLES, The Life of Artemus Ward, New York, 1921.

MILLER, JOHN C., Sam Adams, Pioneer in Propaganda, Boston, 1936.

MOORE, FRANK, The Diary of the Revolution, Hartford, 1875.

MURDOCK, HAROLD, The Nineteenth of April, 1775, Boston, 1923.

MUZZEY, A. B., Reminiscences and Memorials of the Men of the Revolution and Their Families, Boston, 1883.

NILES, H., Principles and Acts of the Revolution in America, Baltimore, 1822.

PRICE, LUCIUS ROBINSON, History of Cambridge, Boston, 1877.

PHINNEY, MAJOR ELIAS, History of the Battle of Lexington, Boston, 1825.

POTTER, ISRAEL RALPH, Life and Remarkable Adventures of Israel
  Potter.

RIPLEY, REV. EZRA, A History of the Fight at Concord on the
  19th of April, 1775, Concord, 1827.
ROWE, JOHN, Letters and Diaries, Edited by Anne Howe Cun-
  ningham, Boston, 1905.

SABINE, LORENZO, Loyalists of the American Revolution, Boston,
  1847.
SCHLESINGER, ARTHUR M., The Colonial Merchants and the Amer-
  ican Revolution, New York, 1918.
SEARS, LORENZO, John Hancock, The Picturesque Patriot, Bos-
  ton, 1912.
SEWELL, SAMUEL, The History of Woburn, Boston, 1868.
SHATTUCK, LEMUEL, A History of the Town of Concord, Boston,
  1834.
SMITH, SAMUEL ABBOT, West Cambridge on the 19th of April,
  1775, Boston, 1864.
STEDMAN, CHARLES, The History of the Origin, Progress and Ter-
  mination of the American War, London, 1794.
STARK, JAMES H., Loyalists of Massachusetts, Boston, 1910.
STILES, EZRA, Literary Diary, New York, 1901.
SWAYNE, JOSEPHINE LATHAM, The Story of Concord, Boston, 1939.

THOMAS, WILLIAM S., American Revolutionary Diaries, New
  York, 1923.
TRUMBULL, JOHN, Autobiography, Reminiscences and Letters
  from 1756 to 1841, New Haven, 1953.

WATSON, ELKANAH, Men and Times of the Revolution, New
  York, 1956.

NEWSPAPERS OF THE PERIOD

Boston Gazette.
Essex Gazette, Salem.
Massachusetts Spy, Boston and Worcester.
Rivington's Gazette, New York.

PERIODICALS, BROCHURES AND MANUSCRIPTS

Belknap, Jeremy, Journal of My Tour of the Camp, Massachusetts Historical Society Proceedings, IV, 1858-60.

Gage, William, British Headquarters Paper, William L. Clements Library, Ann Arbor, Mich.

Gordon, Rev. William, An Account of the Commencement of
Hostilities Between Great Britain and America, Force, IVth
Series, Vol. II.

Humphrey, David, An Essay on the Life of the Hon. Major General Israel Putnam, Massachusetts Historical Society Proceedings, 1886-89.

Old South Leaflets, Old South Church, Boston, Paul Revere's
Own Account of His Midnight Ride.

Oliver, Peter, The Origin and Progress of the American Rebellion to the Year 1776, Massachusetts Historical Society, F. L.
Gay Transcripts.

Prescott, William, The Prescott Memorial, Massachusetts Historical Society.

Proceedings of the Lexington Historical Society, 1886-89.

INDEX

251